Advance acclaim for
Multiple Streams of Internet Income

"Robert Allen has done it again! *Multiple Streams of Internet Income* is a *big* winner. I'm pretty savvy about the Internet, being the cofounder of a growing dot-com e-learning company, but I picked up several ideas I could use to make money in every chapter I read. *Wow!* Read it . . . or weep."

Dr. Tony Alessandra
Author of *Charisma* and cofounder of MentorU.com

"This is an extraordinary book! It shows you how to make more money, faster and easier, on the Internet than you ever dreamed possible—even if you've never used a computer before. I began applying these ideas in my business before I finished the first chapter."

Brian Tracy
Speaker, author, consultant

"If you sincerely want to get rich by using the Internet, get a copy of Robert Allen's new book and read it *immediately!* If you don't, you will probably spend endless amounts of time and money fumbling around with a computer like a clueless idiot who doesn't have a prayer of ever making a Web-related dime."

Gary C. Halbart

"If you're ready to make a massive, passive cash flow, read this book."

Mark Victor Hansen
Cocreator, #1 *New York Times* best-selling series
Chicken Soup for the Soul®

"Robert Allen is my favorite prosperity mentor. If you want to make money on the Internet, this book is a must-read! I highly recommend it."

Jack Canfield
Coauthor, *Chicken Soup for the Soul® at Work*

Multiple Streams
of
Internet Income

ROBERT G. ALLEN

John Wiley & Sons, Inc.
New York • Chichester • Weinheim • Brisbane • Singapore • Toronto

Published by John Wiley & Sons, Inc.
Published simultaneously in Canada.

Library of Congress Cataloging-in-Publication Data
Allen, Robert G.
    Multiple streams of internet income : how ordinary people make extraordinary money online / Robert G. Allen
        p.   cm.
    Includes index.
    ISBN 0-471-41014-4 (cloth : alk. paper)
    1. Electronic commerce.   2, Internet.   3. Success in business.
    4. Money.   5. Income.   I. Title.

HF5548.32.A45 2001
658.8'4—dc21

                                                    2001017676

Printed in the United States of America.

10 9 8 7 6 5 4 3 2

CONTENTS

ACKNOWLEDGMENTS   v

INTRODUCTION Online Success: *Money While You Sleep*   1

CHAPTER 1   Show Me the E-Money: *How to Earn $24,000 in
24 Hours*   5

CHAPTER 2   Crossing the Digital Divide: *How to Guarantee
Your Success on the Internet*   13

CHAPTER 3   Internet Marketing 101: *A Few Simple Strategies
Can Make You Rich*   31

CHAPTER 4   Internet Marketing 201: *12 Powerful Principles
for Creating a Feeding Frenzy*   45

CHAPTER 5   Internet Marketing 301: *Going Deep—The Secret
to Online Streams of Income*   57

CHAPTER 6   Netpreneurs, Start Your Search Engines!
Six Powerful Ways to Drive Traffic to Your Site   73

CHAPTER 7   Online Mar-Ka-Ching! *Six Major Ways to
Make Money from Your Site*   99

CHAPTER 8   Beyond Stickiness: *Nine Magnetic Ways to
Keep 'em Coming Back for More*   119

CHAPTER 9   Ready. Set. Launch. *How Fast Can You Go
from Zero to Cash?*   135

CHAPTER 10 Online Stream #1. Joint Ventures: *High-Leverage Ways to Make a Fortune Online*   151

CHAPTER 11 Online Stream #2. Affiliate Programs: *Cash In by Selling Other People's Stuff*   171

CHAPTER 12 Online Stream #3. Selling Information: *Turn Your Ideas into Steady Streams of Cash Flow*   199

CHAPTER 13 Online Stream #4. Eyeballs for Sale: *Making Advertising Pay*   227

CHAPTER 14 Online Stream #5. Picks and Shovels: *Making Money from the Infrastructure of the Net*   239

CHAPTER 15 Online Stream #6. Treasure Hunting: *Turning Junk into Cash with Auctions*   251

CHAPTER 16 Automatic Pilot: *Making Money 24/7/365*   271

INDEX   273

This book is dedicated the many mentors who have coached me over the years. I have been fortunate to have been mentored by dozens of wonderful experts.

First, to my father, John L. Allen, who laid the foundation. His words were few but his example spoke volumes. My mother, Amy Judd Allen, passed away the day I was born. Every breath I take is a tribute to her sacrifice. My father hired a housekeeper, Sally Hippard, when I was but 6 years old, and she became my surrogate mother for the next 12 years. Thanks, "Mom," for all you taught me. James and Margaret Bridge, and "my cousins next door," provided me a place to grow up normal.

In my twenties, David Filmore took me under his wing and taught me how to sell. Paul Jewkes provided me a template for becoming a moral multimillionaire. Paul Brown and Pat Wyman taught me the real estate business. Lowell Christensen showed me how to crunch the numbers. Bob Steele, A. D. Kessler, Jack Miller, and John Schaub taught me creative real estate investing. Dian Thomas taught me how to find a publisher. Peggy Fugal taught me the beginning steps of marketing. David Canaan showed me how to design a project with style. Stan Miller became a constant spiritual friend and business guide and Steve Grow a trusted attorney. Dr. Blaine Lee gave me important guidance at a critical point in my life. Ron Sumner taught me how to dress for success—although I've retrogressed. My brother Richard, an educational genius, taught me how to turn information into systems. My sister Shirley taught me about unconditional love. Roger Larsen and Hollis Norton taught me the seminar business. John Childers taught me how to make money grow. Dr.

Richard Bandler and Don Wolfe taught me how the mind works. Tony Robbins taught me how to turn fear into power. Dr. Denis Waitley taught me the psychology of winning. (I've always said I want to be like Denis when I grow up.) Brian Tracy has been my friend and an incredible example of professionalism and becoming a lifelong student. Arthur Joseph taught me about vocabulary awareness. Dr. Richard Cialdini taught me about influence. Dr. Stephan Cooper taught me how to play the stock market. Jay Abraham and Gary Halbert, the two greatest marketing gurus, taught me about marketing. Collette Larsen taught me and my wife about friendship and residual income. My longtime business partner, Tom Painter, continues to teach me loyalty and marketing prowess. Mark Victor Hansen is teaching me how to think big and then make it happen even bigger. My wife Daryl and my three children, Aimee, Aaron, and Hunter, will be forever teaching me about the importance of family.

To these, my mentors, and my many other unnamed teachers, I offer eternal thanks.

In the writing of this book, I have had to rely on the expertise of many. I hope I have given adequate credit through the pages of this book to the many experts I called upon to help me organize this information. Many thanks.

Over the years, my author friends have shared with me numerous horror stories about their publishers. I simply can't relate because my publisher, John Wiley & Sons, has been absolutely fantastic. My editor, Mike Hamilton, has been wonderful, along with Dean Karrel and Larry Alexander. Class acts, all. Hats off also to Linda Witzling, Laurie Frank, Michelle Patterson, and Kimberley Vaughn. You're the best.

I also offer thanks to the wonderful folks at North Market Street Graphics, especially Chris Furry, for her dedicated efforts to put this material into professional form, and to my incredible assistant, Denise Michaels.

And finally, to the many readers of my books. Without you, none of my multiple streams of income would flow.

Thanks a million to you all.

Robert G. Allen
San Diego, California 2001

Online Success: Money While You Sleep

EVERY DAY
MILLIONS OF INNOCENT PEOPLE
ARE FORCED FROM THEIR HOMES
BY A DISASTER
CALLED "WORK."

Ashleigh Brilliant.com
SANTA BARBARA

© 1990 by Ashleigh Brilliant (www.ashleighbrilliant.com)

Imagine making money while you sleep. Imagine waking up richer every morning than when you went to bed the night before. Imagine receiving streams of money from people all over the world. Imagine a business that operates on automatic pilot—whether you show up or not. Imagine low overhead and high profits. Imagine operating your business from exotic worldwide locations—from a cell phone on the beach in Tahiti or from your laptop in a restaurant atop the Eiffel Tower. If you can imagine these things, you can achieve them using the vehicle of the Internet.

I'm so excited to be sharing this information with you. I know that if you follow the strategies and techniques in this book, you will be well on your way to Internet riches and a lifestyle that will be envied by almost everyone you meet.

If you ask most fledgling entrepreneurs why they want to be in business the usual answer is "to make some money." But when you pin them down with some more probing questions, it will most likely boil down to something like this. . . .

> *After I've taken care of my basic needs, I want to be free . . .*
>
>> To do what I want
>>
>> When I want
>>
>> Where I want
>>
>> With whomever I want
>>
>> For as long as I want
>>
>> Without having to worry about money.

Does that describe you?

If so, then let's make sure that the by-product of your start-up Internet business is *freedom.* It's not to sell a bunch of stuff, or to get 15 gazillion hits a day, or to hire 1,000 employees, or have the coolest graphics, or to have the fastest-growing company in the world, or to have the best products, or to get your name in the paper, or to launch an IPO. Some of these things may even be counterproductive to obtaining freedom. If freedom is your goal, don't lose sight of it.

I mention this because thousands of beginning entrepreneurs launch new businesses each week without asking this all-important question: *Why are we doing this?* If they do ask, they usually come up with the following answer: *"Because we want to break free from our jobs."* Therefore, they escape the low-paying "job prison" for a potentially higher-paying "self-employment prison." Even if you trade golden handcuffs for platinum handcuffs, you're still locked up.

Your Internet Business: A Freedom Machine

With that in mind, let's design a way to make the most money in the least time that will lead to the greatest freedom. Agreed?

In this book I show multiple ways for the average nontechie to earn serious amounts of income from the Internet. This is 24/7/365 money . . . the kind of income that most people only dream about. And it can happen *fast.*

How fast? In testing ideas for this book, I was able to generate almost $100,000 cash in only 24 hours. How did I do it? By using only one of the many powerful methods for making serious money on the Internet that you learn in this book.

I also help you avoid the pitfalls of the Internet. Frankly, too many people jump onto the Net hoping to find fortune. They launch a Web page and expect the money to start pouring in. It doesn't work that way.

When you think of the World Wide Web, it sounds impressive. It's less impressive when you realize that the Web consists of millions of pages of information stored on millions of linked computers. According to *Scientific American,* another million pages of information are being added *every single day.* Swirling in this blizzard of data is your Web site. The more popular the Web becomes, the harder it is for people to find you. Hiring someone to create an eye-popping Web site for you is not the answer. This is not the "field of dreams": If you build it, they *won't* come—not unless you give them a darn good reason.

You need to view the Internet as just another marketing medium, similar to radio or TV with the added advantage of instant interactivity. Once you understand this, then you can use this incredible communication tool to deliver your marketing message faster, cheaper, and more easily to larger and larger numbers of upscale consumers.

Timeless Principles of Marketing Applied to Explosive Growth of the Internet

The success of any business venture boils down to using timeless principles of marketing. According to marketing guru Jay Abraham, a marketer has only three basic goals:

1. To increase the number of customers

2. To increase the amount of the average order

3. To increase the frequency of orders

That's it. There ain't no more. If you can master these three fundamentals, you can grow any business, whether you're on the Internet or not. It doesn't matter whether your product is information or a flyswatter. If you understand marketing, you can make serious income. If you don't understand marketing, your business is going to die.

I understand marketing. In the past 20 years, through trial and error, I have marketed over $250 million worth of information with my name on it. For the first time, I offer in print what I've learned about marketing in my career. I believe that anyone can learn these timeless principles and double their current business in less than a year . . . even without utilizing the Internet. Any current or future entrepreneur will profit from reading this book. But those who wish to profit from the Internet *must* learn these timeless principles of marketing or they will end up in the dot-com graveyard.

The world of technology is changing so rapidly that a book like this can be outdated before the manuscript makes it to press. Because this book is based on timeless principles of marketing, I want you to be able to pick it up 10 years from now and still find relevant strategies for creating endless cash flow.

Finally, I've aimed to make this more than a book about business on the Internet. This is a *business in a book*. This is not just a book that you read. It is a book that you *do*. We don't just talk about making money. When you are finished with the last chapter, I want you to be online and actually earning steady streams of cash—starting from scratch.

Is this possible? Well, I'm famous for my challenges. When I wrote my first book, *Nothing Down,* I threw down the following gauntlet:

> *"Send me to any city. Take away my wallet. Give me $100 for living expenses. And in 72 hours I'll buy an excellent piece of real estate using none of my own money."*

The *Los Angeles Times* challenged me to live up to this claim. They flew me to San Francisco with an *LA Times* reporter by my side. In 57 hours I bought seven properties and returned $20 in change to the reporter.

In these pages, I show you how to launch an Internet business in *hours,* not days or weeks. To prove it, I gave myself another challenge (notice how the word ch*allen*ge has my name embedded in it):

> *"Sit me at the keyboard of any computer in the world with access to the Internet, and in just 24 hours I'll earn at least $24,000 in cash."*

In the next few chapters, I show you how I did it. Then I teach *you* how to do it!

Are you ready? Let's get started. Meet me in Chapter 1.

Show Me the E-Money: How to Earn $24,000 in 24 Hours

"Captain, it looks like we've entered cyberspace."

T his is a book about making money on the Internet.

Rather than spouting obsolete statistics about how many gazillions of people are getting online every minute, about how many trillions of dollars' worth of stuff is being sold on the Internet, or about how the Internet is changing the world—yadda, yadda, yadda—let's just cut to the chase.

Let me show you the money . . . or more precisely, the e-money.

In this chapter, I describe how, using the principles in this book, I earned almost $100,000 cash in only 24 hours using the Internet. Then I will show you how you can do exactly what I have done. Does that get your heart racing?

In my previous three *New York Times* best-sellers, *Nothing Down, Creating Wealth,* and *Multiple Streams of Income,* I've helped thousands of people to achieve financial freedom—even to become millionaires and multimillionaires. Now it's your turn.

Your Next Fortune Is Only a Click Away

Although I've been in business for over 20 years, I was slow to adopt the power of the Internet to market my own seminars and information products. I wasn't alone. Even today, tens of millions of businesses, small and large, still haven't tapped into this power. For me, it took something dramatic to open my eyes.

In the fall of 1998, a friend, David LeDoux, called excitedly to tell me how he had stumbled onto an interesting method of marketing using the Internet.

"Bob," he said, "I made $13,000 in one day!"

I was intrigued. "How did you do it?"

"Rather than *tell* you, let me *show* you."

A few days later, sitting at the keyboard of my home office computer in San Diego, California, David explained how he was attracting visitors to his recently launched Web site. Many of these visitors registered for his free Internet newsletter. After only a few short months, he managed to accumulate about 1,500 subscribers. Every week he sent an e-mail to his growing list of subscribers sharing his latest research. In each e-newsletter (called an *e-zine*), he included advertisements for other products or services. He explained that because the e-mails cost him almost nothing to send, the sales he made were extremely profitable: "Let me show you how it works. Right now, before your very eyes, I'm going to make some money for you."

Yes, he had my attention.

Using my computer, he composed a short e-mail message. It read something like this:

> Hello, again. This is David. At this very moment I am sitting in the home office of best-selling author Robert G. Allen. Through his #1 best-selling books and audio programs, he has helped thousands of people become

millionaires. His hottest-selling audio program, *Multiple Streams of Income*, is marketed for $60 through Nightingale/Conant. I've prevailed upon Mr. Allen to offer you this popular program at a reduced price. For the next 60 minutes *only*, he has agreed to let any of my subscribers purchase his powerful six-tape program for only $29.95. If you're interested, please respond immediately with your name, address, and credit card number with expiration date. Have a nice day. David.

He asked me to verify the exact time. Then he sent the message to his 1,500 subscribers. I had no idea what to expect.

Sixty-one seconds later, the first response arrived. *Ding!* (Does your e-mail make a sound when you receive a message?) This first response included a full address and complete credit card information. Over the next hour, as David was trying to explain to me the benefits of marketing over the Internet, I could hardly pay attention. I just kept listening to the sound of each e-mail response—*Ka-ching! Ka-ching! Ka-ching!* Hundreds of dollars of orders. I was amazed. In front of my eyes, with very little marketing cost and almost no effort, he had generated a tidy profit for me.

But it wasn't the instant profit that excited me. It was the potential for huge streams of cash flow with almost zero marketing costs. Do the math with me.

Suppose you want to market a $100 audio program in the bricks-and-mortar world. You rent a mailing list of 10,000 target prospects, create a direct mail letter, and pay for postage. All told, it will cost in excess of 50 cents per letter just to drop the letters in the mail. In other words, it will cost a minimum of $5,000 to mail 10,000 marketing pieces.

However, the response rate through direct mail is usually less than one-half of 1 percent, which means that these 10,000 letters may generate only 50 paid responses. Fifty customers at $100 apiece is $5,000—just enough to recoup your mailing costs. There's no money left to pay for the tapes, the packaging, and the postage to send the product to the customer via snail mail. You've lost money!

Now, let's assume we do the same mailing using the Internet. This time, however, instead of marketing an audiocassette program, we offer a package of powerful information—digital special reports, digital books, even digital video and audio in a powerful multimedia presentation. Since the information is digital, it can be delivered over the Internet instantly at almost zero cost. Now let's send 10,000 e-mails to a list of targeted e-mail prospects assuming the same one-half of 1 percent response rate.

We generate the same 50 orders at $100 apiece, except this time the marketing costs *and* the product costs are nearly zero. The entire $5,000 in proceeds is almost pure profit!

Did you get that? Let's do a profit and loss statement for our new Internet business:

Marketing costs	0
Product costs	0
Shipping charges	0
Credit card charges	3%
Profit	97%

Now, let's think big. If 10,000 e-mails generate $5,000, then 100,000 e-mails produce $50,000, right? And a million e-mails could generate a $500,000 profit! Talk about a bottom line! What if you did this once a month? Heck, once a week?! Now you can see why I was so excited.

I began immediately to develop my own Web site. After several false starts, we finally launched www.robertallen.com during the first week of August 1999. Using various methods (which I'm going to teach you), during the next nine months we gathered an opt-in list of over 11,500 subscribers to my free Internet newsletter. (Just to set the record straight, I don't believe in sending unauthorized e-mail, or *spam,* and nothing I teach you will resemble anything illegal, immoral, or in violation of the spirit of the Internet.)

People often say that those who ask for free information are not willing to spend money. They're just "looky-loos." This is generally correct. The vast majority of the "free" subscribers to my Web site are not willing to spend a penny on any of my products or services. They are perfectly content to sample my free offerings. However, I also know that if the offer is right, *a small percentage* of any interested audience (free or paying) can

be enticed to open up their wallets or purses. Let's put this theory to the test . . . *for real.*

In the early months of the year 2000 I was approached by representatives of one of the world's leading producers of infomercials, the Guthy/Renker Corporation. They wanted to create a new infomercial marketing an information product based on my best-selling book, *Multiple Streams of Income.* They called the show *Real Streams of Cash.*

In designing the show, the producers encouraged me to come up with a dramatic way to prove that my moneymaking ideas work. I immediately remembered how powerful David's demonstration had been. Using this as a model, I made the following statement:

"Sit me at the keyboard of any computer in the world with access to the Internet, and in just 24 hours I'll earn at least $24,000 in cash."

The producers of the show were skeptical. They wanted me to lower the figure. They reasoned, "A thousand dollars in 24 hours is still a lot of money to the average person." I must admit that I, too, had my doubts, but I just had a gut feeling that, given 24 hours, I could generate at least $24,000. Maybe more.

On May 24, 2000, at a studio in Burbank, California, at exactly 12:38 P.M., in front of live cameras, I sat down at the keyboard of a computer belonging to the producer of the shoot, Packy McFarland. With a simple click of the mouse, I sent a special message to my list of 11,518 subscribers. Would anyone respond with cash? Frankly, I had no idea. This was marketing without a safety net.

The first order was generated in less than four minutes. A man in Houston sent me $2,991. The second order came from my friend, David LeDoux. He had been monitoring my progress and sent me $200. Thereafter, every several minutes another order *ka-chinged* into my e-mail box.

After 6 hours and 11 minutes the total was . . .

$46,684.95!

I slept very peacefully that night. I was convinced that while I slept even more orders would pour in. I was right. The next morning, still dressed in my bathrobe, with live cameras rolling, I checked the total number of orders. It was now up to . . .

$78,827.44!

This was exciting! And I still had about four hours to go.

That afternoon, 24 hours after the challenge had begun, we did a final tally. The total was . . .

$94,532.44

Almost $100,000 in just one day! And the orders kept pouring in. Within just a few days the total had climbed to over $115,000.

Before you get too excited, let me remind you that it had actually taken over nine months to set up this process. I had to launch the Web site. I had to draw traffic to my site. I had to gather the names of people for my Internet newsletter. But what if you could work for a full year with zero income and then, in one day, recoup all of your expenses and walk away with a net profit of $10,000 . . . $30,000 . . . $50,000 . . . maybe even $100,000? Moreover, what if you could repeat this process once a month for the rest of your life?! Would that be worth the effort?

This book takes you step by step through the process that I used to achieve such incredible results. Although the product I was marketing was an information product, these same principles can be used to market any-thing—products, services, even business opportunities.

Behind the Scenes

Now, that you know the results of my live Internet challenge, I'd like to take you behind the scenes and teach you the timeless marketing princi-ples I used to increase the odds of success.

The serious planning began about 60 days before the May 24 shooting date. My first step was to call on my mentors. I can't stress enough the importance of building a powerful mastermind team. Successful people rely heavily on their mentors. Ordinary people don't. It's that simple. My marketing team consisted of Tom Painter, Daren Falter, Bob Gatchel, Saul Klein, Mike Barnett, Ken Kerr, Ken Varga, and Scott Haines, sup-plemented by conversations with at least a dozen others. Here's how I presented the concept to my mentors:

> *"Suppose you have a goal to market a product and earn $24,000 in 24 hours using the Internet. Suppose it's more than a goal—suppose your life is on the line. If you succeed, you get to live. If you fail, you face the firing squad. How would you do it?"*

In other words, what if your life literally depended upon your success? Would you prepare differently? Most people *try* things. I don't. As Yoda taught Luke Skywalker, there is no *try*. There is either *do* or *do not*. When I design a marketing campaign, I assume that it *must* work. I plan for zero failure. It either works or I die.

Of course, I don't *really* expect to die . . . but I put that kind of intensity into the design. I don't expect to fail. I expect to win.

When Spanish explorer Hernán Cortés conquered Mexico in 1519, he faced overwhelming odds . . . tens of thousands of Aztec warriors against his 400 soldiers. When his troops began to mutiny, Cortés ordered all but one of his 11 ships to be scuttled and sunk so there was no avenue of escape. Then he rallied his troops with a stirring speech. Conquer or die. Those were the options.

When I gave this do-or-die scenario to my mentors, it focused their advice to me. They thought about it in a different way. Instead of bouncing around a few nice ideas, I got their best advice: "Well, Bob, if my life were on the line, then here is what I would do."

In the next chapter, I share what they told me. Obviously, it worked.

CHAPTER 2

Crossing the Digital Divide: How to Guarantee Your Success on the Internet

There is a growing digital divide in the world—a chasm between the digital haves and the digital have-nots. Despite the excitement about the advantages of marketing on the Internet, millions of Web site owners have been and will continue to be baffled by the Internet and disappointed with the results of their online experience. There seem to be so many new terms to learn—*autoresponders, list serves, affiliate programs, viral marketing,* and *stickiness.* If you're a veteran of the Internet, these terms are familiar to you. But if you're a beginner, the process can be intimidating.

There is a phrase that I learned early in my career. "A confused mind always says no." In this rapidly changing world, with new technological marvels being introduced daily, it's almost impossible not to be confused and overwhelmed. Precisely because things are moving so quickly, you don't have time to be confused—you must decide to say yes to marketing on the Internet. You do not want to be left behind. There's just too much money at stake.

In my opinion, however, the reason people don't make money on the Net is not because of technophobia. It is because people are confused about the concepts of basic marketing. Look at the millions of dollars that have been burned on ineffective Internet marketing campaigns. It's a crime. Really. People ought to be locked up for squandering so much good money.

I personally made more "Net" profit in one day than Amazon.com made in its first five years. Of course, I'm not a billionaire, either. But I don't count my worth in stock certificates. I count my worth the way ordinary people do—by how much spendable *cash flow* it generates *now.*

Ultimately, this is the way Wall Street also evaluates companies. If a company continues to lose money, it eventually becomes toast. I'm just more impatient than Wall Street. I like to make profit from day one. And so should you.

So, what is the most fundamental principle of all marketing?

Gary Halbert, the marketing guru, poses a famous riddle: Suppose you're given the opportunity to launch a hot dog stand on the beach right next to a competing hot dog stand. If you could choose one marketing advantage over your competitor, what would you choose? Would it be a more favorable location, higher-quality ingredients, the world's best advertising copy, or the most beautiful waitresses? Gary says he would only want one advantage: a starving crowd!

Too often, people launch new products and then go searching for a market. You must reverse the process: Find a hungry market in search of a product. The most important marketing question is, "How can I identify a hungry group of people and then create a feeding frenzy?"

If you can answer this question, you will be miles ahead of those cash-poor, equity-rich Internet start-ups. You will sail across the digital divide on the wings of cash flow while your foolish competitors crash and burn.

Three Important Questions

My mentors reminded me that any marketing campaign—especially on the Net—must answer three questions:

1. Who is your target audience?

2. What do they want?

3. How can you motivate this target audience to act *now?*

Most beginning marketers spend 90 percent of their time creating the perfect product and 10 percent of their time finding a perfect audience. The secret is to reverse the ratio: Spend 90 percent of your time finding the right audience. I call this *finding hungry fish.* I prefer to find a school of fish in a feeding frenzy. If you drop your bait (advertising) into such a school of hungry fish, they will attack that bait (ad)—even if it's written by an amateur.

Where do you find the schools of customers like this?

You have two choices: (1) You can either drop your bait into someone else's lake or (2) create your own lake and spawn your own fish.

If you are fishing in other people's lakes, you have to pay them for the privilege. In other words, you have to pay to advertise in their magazines, newsletters, or on their radio or TV stations. Or you'll have to pay a fee to rent names from their private mailing lists. This is the fastest way to find a group of hungry fish . . . but it is also the most expensive.

A slower method is to create your own lake and spawn your own fish. In this case, you also have control over your marketing project and at a much lower long-term cost. (See Table 2.1.)

TABLE 2.1 **Should You Advertise to a Rented List or Build Your Own List?**

Advertise to Rented List	Build Your Own List
Fast	Slower: You build your list one name at a time
Simple	More complicated
Easy: one phone call	More difficult
Tested results	You don't know if it will work
You know there are fish	You have to spawn your own fish
Expensive	Initially, but much less expensive long term
Limited control	Total control: You can create a perfect environment
You pay rental fees	You earn fees by renting to other fishers
These fish are strangers	You have a bonded relationship with your fish
Poor fit with your offer	Customization: You can fit your offer perfectly
Get only one-time use	You have unlimited lifetime use
Competition with other fishers	No competition

In planning to make $24,000 in 24 hours I could have chosen the fast, simple, easy route by renting or buying one of the many e-mail lists available on the Internet. (In Chapter 6 I will show you how to profitably access such lists.) The disadvantage to this method is that it costs money . . . and if you're like the average entrepreneur, money can be scarce. I decided instead to take the slower route and build my own list. The wiser choice for you will be to test your ideas with inexpensive rented lists and, once your business concept is viable, to build your business with a combination of targeted paid advertising while simultaneously spawning your own list of interested customers.

When I launched my own Web site, one of its major features was a free e-zine called the Streams of Cash E-Letter. I encouraged all visitors to my site to leave their e-mail addresses. Using various methods, over the next several months, the subscriber list to my infrequent newsletter grew. Nine months later, the list had over 11,000 subscribers. These people opted in to an e-mail list . . . they are willing recipients. In other words, when I send an e-mail message to anyone on this list, it is not *spam* (unwanted or unsolicited e-mail). In later chapters, I'll show you how to use this technique and many others.

Although it took many months to build my list, I felt it was the best solution to creating a lifetime cash flow. This is the list I used for my Internet challenge. I had used the list for research, but I had never marketed a single product to the people on the list. The question remained: Would this list of freebie subscribers be willing to open up their wallets or purses and actually buy anything? Would I be willing to bet my life on it? When I agreed to the Internet challenge, there was a lot of doubt about whether this was a realistic goal.

One thing I had going for me was my knowledge of marketing. *Marketing* is the science of encouraging interested people to buy. If you make a powerful offer in the right way to an interested audience, you should be able to motivate that audience to buy.

Exactly 14 days before May 24, I began a series of five messages to those on my e-mail list to prepare them for my Internet challenge. Imagine checking your e-mail and receiving a message with the following summary in the Subject line. Would you open it?

From   Subject

Robert Allen   Making massive amounts of money on the Net

As you read the following message, remember that it was being sent to a group of prequalified readers. Therefore, the message is longer than traditional marketing missives. Read it for yourself and try to detect which principles of marketing I am using to create massive action by my drop-dead date of May 24.

Message #1

May 10, 2000
To: Subscribers to Robert Allen's Streams of Cash E-Letter
From: #1 Best-selling financial author, Robert Allen
Re: Making massive amounts of money on the net

Message 1 of 5

You could win thousands of dollars in CASH as a result of reading this e-mail.

As a subscriber to my free Streams of Cash E-Letter, you will be receiving a series of five extremely important messages from me over the next 14 days. On May 24, the final of the five messages will be sent to you at about noon Pacific standard time. As a reward for reading this fifth and final message, I will randomly select several subscribers to receive CASH awards of $1,000, $500, $250, $100, and $50, respectively, and at least 100 of you will receive free autographed copies of one of my best-selling books, *The Road to Wealth*.

Why am I doing this? I think you'll be very interested in my reason. . . .

But first—some news hot off the presses:

My brand-new book, *Multiple Streams of Income*, just hit #12 on the *Wall Street Journal* business best-seller list as of Friday, April 29. People are raving that it's my best book ever. Check out the rave reviews by clicking on the link to Amazon.com at the end of this message. I want to thank those of you who helped me select the subtitle—*How to Generate a Lifetime of Unlimited Wealth*. It's obviously working. I got word today that Staples just ordered 3,000 copies. If you've already bought the book, make sure you take advantage of the FREE four-week live teleconference with me personally (valued at $250). The number to register for this FREE teleclass is on page vii of the *Multiple Streams of Income* book.

Now for the meat of this e-letter: *How to Make $24,000 Cash in 24 Hours on the Internet.*

I am shooting a new TV infomercial with Guthy/Renker, the folks who produced Tony Robbins's megasuccessful show. Last weekend, the producers flew many of my millionaire success stories to Los Angeles to film their amazing testimonials. I am constantly astonished by how much money my students are making—literally millions. (Who needs Regis?)

As a part of this show, I'm going to do a live INSTANT CASH challenge. On television, with live cameras rolling, I am going to demonstrate how to make INSTANT CASH from the Internet. On May 24, at about noon Pacific standard time, we will film the segment where, with just one click of my mouse, I will activate an avalanche of cash flowing into my e-mail box. The goal is to make a minimum of $24,000 in 24 hours.

Here's the $24,000 question: Is it possible for YOU to make more money in a day than the average person *earns in an entire year?*

Would you like to learn how to do this?

If you're interested in learning how to do this, watch your e-mail over the next 14 days. I will guide you through the process IN ADVANCE. You will be the very first group of people on planet Earth to learn how I plan on doing this.

And DON'T MISS THE FINAL MESSAGE on May 24. Even if you're away from your computer, check your e-mail on that day.

Sincerely,

Robert Allen
Best-selling author, *Nothing Down, Creating Wealth, The Road to Wealth,* and now, *Multiple Streams of Income.*

To read the rave reviews from my latest best-seller, *Multiple Streams of Income,* click on the following link: www.amazon.com.

http://www.amazon.com/exec/obidos/ASIN/0471381802/o/qid=954199042 /sr=2-2/103-4093322-6943858

That was the first message. Let's examine it to learn why it was an effective marketing message.

First of all, the subject is about making massive amounts of money on the Net. If this doesn't interest you, better check your pulse—you might be dead. This is the bait that hooks readers into continuing to read further.

There are several other persuasive hooks throughout this message, but at the risk of belaboring the point, I want to remind you that "making massive amounts of money on the Net" would not have been an effective message if addressed to the wrong audience. Remember, this was *my* lake, and this message was just the kind of bait *my* fish were hungry for.

For your message to be effective, it must hit the hot button of your target audience. Do you know what their hot buttons are? Don't just guess what they want—or give them what *you want* hoping that they also want it. Ask them what they want!!

That is exactly what I did in the very next e-mail message. The second message in the series was sent five days after the first. Once again, it is a very long e-mail—which breaks all the rules of traditional e-mail marketing—but something *hidden* in this e-mail message causes a very large number of people to read every single word! As you read it, see if you can spot any of the principles that make this message effective.

Imagine getting the following message in your e-mail box. Would you open it?

From	Subject
Robert Allen	Free report: How to Make $24,000 Cash in 24 Hours

Message #2

May 15, 2000
To: Subscribers to Robert Allen's Streams of Cash E-Letter
From: #1 Best-selling financial author, Robert Allen
Re: Free report: *How to Make $24,000 Cash in 24 Hours on the Internet*

Message 2 of 5

Important Note: just for reading this message, I want to send you a powerful special report titled, How to Make $24,000 Cash in 24 Hours on the Internet. It is valued at U.S.$100.

Please read on. . . .

On May 24, I will be filming a new TV infomercial with America's most successful infomercial company, Guthy/Renker, which has produced shows with such stars as Tony Robbins and Victoria Principal. The title of my show is *Real Streams of Cash.*

Between noon and 5 P.M. Pacific standard time on May 24, the camera crew will film me sending a special e-mail message to subscribers of my Streams of Cash E-Letter. The goal is to generate a minimum of $24,000 CASH in 24 hours. This experience will be documented in a special report titled: *How to Make $24,000 Cash in 24 Hours on the Internet.*

This detailed report will be part of the infomercial product with a value of $100. (I personally think it's worth at least $24,000.)

I would like to give you a *free copy* of this valuable report just for helping me brainstorm how to generate the most amount of money. Obviously, the more I can generate for the television cameras, the better it will look. For those 24 hours only, I'm willing to make some outrageous offers to my subscribers—literally once-in-a-lifetime deals.

Here is a list of some of the items that I might offer based on your feedback. Simply check the appropriate boxes below and return your feedback, and I will send a copy of the special report to you once it is finished.

Which of the following offers would interest you?

Offer #1. *Exclusive banner ad on the front page of my popular site*

This offer is limited to only 10 people worldwide.

I have never before allowed banner ads on my site. Yet in the next several weeks I will be driving massive traffic to my site with 500,000 pieces of mail, constant PR as I go from city to city promoting my new book, and, of course, over 30 references to my Web site in my best-selling book.

Would access to this traffic be useful to you?

_____Yes, I'm interested.   _____No, I'm not interested.

Here is the price I would be willing to pay for a three-month banner:

_____$995   _____$495   _____$249   _____$99

Offer #2. *Exclusive endorsement in my Streams of Cash E-Letter*

My e-mail letter is sent periodically to a special list of over 11,000 interested "Netpreneurs." Do you have a business or service that would be of special interest to my subscribers? If I feel the product is a good fit, I will write a special Net letter about your business and let my subscribers know about it.

This offer is limited to only 10 people worldwide.

Would this be useful to you?

_____Yes, I'm interested.   _____No, I'm not interested.

Here is the price that I would be willing to pay for this endorsement:

_____$995   _____$495   _____$249   _____$99

Offer #3. A special three-day seminar with Robert Allen and his entire millionaire mentoring team

Over 20,000 people invested $5,000 apiece to participate in my powerful 5-Day Wealth Training. From this class have come hundreds, if not thousands, of millionaires. I have designed a more concentrated three-day version of this training called the Millionaire Retreat. During these three intense days you will learn:

How to earn 100 percent or more in the stock market!
How to make $100,000 a year investing in real estate
How to make $1,000 a day or more on the Internet
How to build inner wealth and unshakable confidence
How to build a financial fortress around your assets

You will be trained by me and my team of millionaire mentors.

These three days are guaranteed to change your life forever and launch you on the fast track to financial freedom. If you can't attend, the entire experience will be professionally recorded. All attendees will also receive a copy of the tapes.

This offer is strictly limited to only 100 people!

You may bring your spouse or partner with you at no extra charge.

Would learning this information be useful to you?

_____Yes, I'm interested.   _____No, I'm not interested.

Here is the price that I would be willing to pay for this training:

_____$1,495 _____$995 _____$795 _____$495 _____$249

Offer #4. Personal, one-on-one coaching with author Robert Allen

I rarely consult individually. It is a much more efficient use of my time to work with groups of 100 or more. When I do private consultation, I bill my time at $1,000 per hour or $10,000 a day. Yet on May 24 I will offer to mentor you and only nine other individuals for two power-packed days at my home in San Diego. There will be time for personalized, private, one-on-one consultation. I guarantee to help you double your income in 12 months or the session is free.

This offer is strictly limited to 10 people!

Would this be useful to you?

_____Yes, I'm interested.   _____No, I'm not interested.

Here is the price that I would be willing to pay for this experience:

_____$5,000 _____$2,500 _____$1,495 _____$995 _____$495

Offer #5. *Eight-week conference call with Robert Allen and his millionaire team*

This unique training will be conducted over the phone in a conference call setting. Each class is two hours long. Each class is recorded if you miss the live class. Your instructors will be

• Robert Allen—#1 best-selling author of *Multiple Streams of Income*
• Dr. Stephan Cooper—stock market expert who earned 400 percent last year
• Darren Falter—Internet guru who consults with me on my site
• Thomas Painter—real estate expert and marketing guru
• Ken Kerr—licensing guru who has launched many successful products
• Ted Thomas—on how to earn 25 percent with tax lien certificate

Your satisfaction is absolutely guaranteed.

This offer is strictly limited to only 100 people!

Would this be useful to you?

_____Yes, I'm interested.   _____No, I'm not interested.

Here is the price that I would be willing to pay for this experience:

_____$995 _____$495 _____$249 _____$195 _____$95

Offer #6. *Robert Allen speaking to your company or private group*

My normal speaking fee is $10,000 per day plus first-class travel. Yet on May 24 I have a huge incentive to dramatically lower my fee. Would your company or special group like to learn from one of North America's most famous millionaire makers? In evaluations after the speech, 80 percent of the attendees must give the experience a rating of "excellent" or the speech is free.

This offer is strictly limited to three groups!

Would having Robert Allen speak to your group be useful to you?

_____Yes, I'm interested.   _____No, I'm not interested.

Here is the price that I would be willing to pay for this experience:

_____$5,000   _____$2,500   _____$1,500   _____$1,000

Offer #7. *A bundle of Robert Allen's books, special reports, and audio programs*

	Value
Autographed copy of his new book, *Multiple Streams of Income*	($25)
Autographed copy of a previous best-seller, *The Road to Wealth*	($20)
Six audiocassettes (or CDs) on *Multiple Streams of Income*	($60)
Six audiocassettes called *Empower Yourself*	($30)
A collection of 10 valuable special reports	($50)

_____Yes, I'm interested.   _____No, I'm not interested.

Here is the price that I would be willing to pay:

_____$100   _____$75   _____$50   _____$35

Offer #8. *Real estate home-study system*

These are live recordings from two of Robert Allen's popular programs on how to make a fortune in real estate. Attendees paid $5,000 for each of these seminars. Now you can learn the information that helped launch thousands of millionaires.

The Wealth Training Experience, 12 audiocassettes	$1,000 value
Fortunes in Foreclosures, 24 audiocassettes	$1,000 value

_____Yes, I'm interested.   _____No, I'm not interested.

This offer is strictly limited to 50 people!

Here is the price that I would be willing to pay for both sets:

_____$500   _____$295   _____$195   _____$149

Offer #9. Robert Allen's exclusive information marketing system

In the past 20 years, over $200 million worth of my books, tapes, videos, and seminars have been marketed throughout the world. I shared the secrets to how this was done in a powerful three-day, $3,000 seminar called *Infopreneuring: How You Can Become an Information Multimillionaire.* You can learn these secrets from one of the world's leading experts in information marketing by listening to the complete seminar, recorded on 24 audiocassettes. Included with this offer is a one-time, one-hour phone consultation with Robert Allen personally about your information product.

_____Yes, I'm interested.   _____No, I'm not interested.

This offer is strictly limited to only 25 people!

Here is the price that I would be willing to pay:

_____$1000   _____$495   _____$295   _____$149   _____$99

Your complete satisfaction is guaranteed.

#####

In conclusion, these are a few of the offers that I am considering. Of course, it does neither of us any good unless I am offering information that you want. What else would you like to know?

Thanks in advance for your feedback.

Sincerely,

Robert Allen
Best-selling author of *Nothing Down, Creating Wealth, The Road to Wealth,* and now, *Multiple Streams of Income.*

P.S. Remember, in addition to sending you the free report, I will randomly select several of you to receive CASH awards of $1,000, $500, $250, $100, and $50, respectively, and at least 100 of you will receive free autographed copies of one of my previous best-selling books, *The Road to Wealth* or my brand-new *Multiple Streams of Income* (www.amazon.com).

© 1982 by Ashleigh Brilliant (www.ashleighbrilliant.com)

This was the second of five messages. It must have taken some people upwards of half an hour to complete it. Still, I asked my subscribers to help me decide what I should offer. In other words, I asked them to vote for what they would like to buy. Of course, their feedback is risk-free. They don't have to buy anything. I even offer to send them a special report as my thanks for their input. They are simply asked to tell me what they might like if the price were right. Then I ask them to name their price.

The power of this strategy is that it offers people a riskless action. Enticing your customers to take baby steps is extremely important. In a later chapter I'll share with you why it's so important, but first I want you to see the results. Guess how many people responded to my survey?

I received almost 2,000 responses in less than 24 hours! That's close to a 20 percent response. I was completely astounded.

Table 2.2 shows the results tabulated by my partner and marketing guru, Tom Painter. See if you can learn anything from these results.

As you study Table 2.2, you might be struck by the same thing that struck me: When given a choice to buy one of my information products at the cheapest price, many people chose *the most expensive price* possible.

For instance, notice offer #4, one-on-one coaching with Bob. About half of the 1,046 people who responded that they would be willing to pay

TABLE 2.2 Results of Survey: How to Make $24,000 in 24 Hours

Offer #1. Would you like to buy a banner ad on my site?		
Banner Yes	1,041	53%
Banner No	915	47%
Total responses	1,956	
Banner 995	61	5%
Banner 495	105	9%
Banner 249	256	23%
Banner 99	701	62%
Total who want to buy	1,123	
Offer #2. Would you like an endorsement in my e-letter?		
Endorsement Yes	1,059	56%
Endorsement No	839	44%
Total responses	1,898	
Endorsement 995	78	7%
Endorsement 495	145	13%
Endorsement 249	250	23%
Endorsement 99	603	56%
Total who want to buy	1,076	
Offer #3. Three-day millionaire retreat?		
Millionaire retreat Yes	1,500	79%
Millionaire retreat No	408	21%
Total responses	1,908	
Millionaire retreat 1,495	18	1%
Millionaire retreat 995	167	12%
Millionaire retreat 795	134	10%
Millionaire retreat 495	333	25%
Millionaire retreat 249	695	52%
Total who want to buy	1,347	
Offer #4. Would you like one-on-one coaching with Bob?		
Coaching Yes	1,046	57%
Coaching No	797	43%
Total responses	1,843	
Coaching 5,000	94	9%
Coaching 2,500	130	13%
Coaching 1,495	121	12%
Coaching 995	169	17%
Coaching 495	487	49%
Total who want to buy	1,001	*(continued)*

TABLE 2.2 *(Continued)*

Offer #5. Eight-week millionaire conference call?			
Teleconference	Yes	1,191	64%
Teleconference	No	662	36%
Total responses		1,853	
Teleconference	995	46	4%
Teleconference	495	102	9%
Teleconference	249	133	11%
Teleconference	195	202	17%
Teleconference	95	678	58%
Total who want to buy		1,161	
Offer #6. Robert to speak to your group?			
Group speaking	Yes	309	17%
Group speaking	No	1,477	83%
Total responses		1,786	
Group speaking	5,000	53	16%
Group speaking	2,500	47	14%
Group speaking	1,500	46	14%
Group speaking	1,000	183	56%
Total who want to buy		329	
Offer #7. Bundle of books and audios?			
Bundle	Yes	1,394	75%
Bundle	No	457	25%
Total responses		1,851	
Bundle	150	120	9%
Bundle	100	239	18%
Bundle	75	263	19%
Bundle	50	740	54%
Total who want to buy		1,362	
Offer #8. Real estate home study?			
Real estate	Yes	1,122	61%
Real estate	No	712	39%
Total responses		1,834	
Real estate	500	84	8%
Real estate	295	137	13%
Real estate	195	177	16%
Real estate	149	680	63%
Total who want to buy		1,078	*(continued)*

TABLE 2.2 *(Continued)*

Offer #9. Infopreneur tapes and consult?		
Information Yes	1,254	68%
Information No	577	32%
Total responses	**1,831**	
Information 1,000	56	4%
Information 495	135	11%
Information 295	176	14%
Information 149	250	20%
Information 99	635	51%
Total who want to buy	**1,252**	
Summary		
Banner Yes	1,041	10.5%
Endorsement Yes	1,059	10.7%
Millionaire retreat Yes	1,500	15.1%
Coaching Yes	1,046	10.5%
Teleconference Yes	1,191	12.0%
Group speaking Yes	309	3.1%
Bundle Yes	1,394	14.1%
Real estate Yes	1,122	11.3%
Information Yes	1,254	12.6%
Combined total	**9,916**	

for private mentoring with me chose the cheapest possible price. But 9 percent chose the most expensive option. When given a choice of paying $495 or $5,000, a significant number of the people voluntarily agreed to pay $5,000 (94 people paying $5,000 is almost a half a million dollars)! The same was true with many of the other options.

Having this information was extremely important in designing the ultimate offer. It let me know that a higher price was possible over the Internet. Gathering this data also let me know which offers I should not include in the final list and which offers I could bundle together.

Now, let's review. The most important marketing advice you can ever receive is as follows:

Find the right audience.

Ask people what they want.

Give it to them.

This advice, more than anything else, will guarantee your success in any marketing venture. Sound too hard? It must be too hard because so few businesses do it. It may take months to find your right audience or to build your own list, name by name . . . but eventually, when you've found them and surveyed them, you're ready to use the powerful marketing secrets that I share with you in the next chapter.

CHAPTER 3

Internet Marketing 101: A Few Simple Strategies Can Make You Rich

I'm a big believer in "simple and easy." Beats "complicated and hard" every time. Rather than bludgeon you with an encyclopedia of marketing, including 1,001 ways to write super headlines, 196 ways to generate new leads, and 67 ways to get people to say yes, let's start with the fundamentals.

Besides, according to the 80/20 principle, 20 percent of your marketing ideas will produce 80 percent of your results. So let's boil marketing down to a few bedrock principles. Do these few things well and you'll likely be successful. Don't do these critical few things and all the other ideas combined still won't save you.

According to marketing guru Jay Abraham, when you boil business down to its basics, a businessperson is trying to master only three major activities:

1. To increase the number of customers

2. To persuade these customers to buy more in their initial orders

3. To encourage these customers to buy more frequently

More customers. Larger orders. More often. Got it? If you're starting a new business, these are the three buttons you push to get your business off the ground. If your existing business is in trouble, these are the three buttons you push to make it healthy again.

Getting more customers is all about generating leads—getting your message in front of the right people and enticing them to take a look at your business. Increasing the average order is about persuasion and bundling—giving people a better deal for a larger order. Increasing the frequency of purchase is about the back end—developing long-term relationships with your customers so they want to buy again and again.

In this book, I'll teach you how to accomplish all three of these major activities. And I'll translate these concepts into simple language because I'm always amazed by how people try to complicate things. Here's a great story to illustrate my point.

Charles Jarvis, the great American humorist, tells the story about the man who goes into the pet store to buy a pet bird. He sees dozens of caged birds with tiny price tags dangling from their little legs. He scans each price tag one by one: $5, $5, $5 . . . $50!

"Hmmm," he wonders. "This $50 bird looks like all of the others. What could be special about this one?"

He asks the store clerk. The clerk replies that this one is very special because it can talk. The shopper is impressed enough that he buys this special talking bird and takes it home. The very next day he returns, disappointed.

"The bird didn't talk."

The clerk asks, "Did he look in his little mirror?"

"Little mirror? I didn't buy a mirror. Does he need a mirror?"

"Of course," replies the clerk. "He looks in his little mirror and sees another bird in there. He thinks he's not alone and starts to sing. Starts to talk. Got to have a mirror."

This sounds reasonable, so the customer buys a mirror and leaves. The next day he is back again, disgruntled.

"The bird looked in his little mirror," he says. "But he still didn't talk."

"Well," ponders the clerk, "Did he run up and down his little ladder?"

"Ladder? Does he need a ladder?"

"Of course," replies the clerk. "Don't you feel better after you exercise? When your little bird runs up and down his little ladder, those endorphins start pumping in his little brain. Makes him want to sing. Makes him want to talk. Got to have a ladder."

"How much is a ladder?"

"It's $12.95."

"Give me a ladder." And off goes the customer. The next day he is back, with a scowl on his face.

"The bird walked up and down his little ladder. He looked in his little mirror. But he still didn't talk!"

The clerk listens to the angry customer and then asks, "Did he swing on his little swing? You see, when the bird swings it makes him think he's back in nature. Makes him want to sing. Makes him want to talk."

"How much is a swing?"

"It's $7.95."

The customer grudgingly buys the swing and leaves. But the very next day he is back again, angrier than ever.

"The bird swung on his little swing. He ran up and down his little ladder. He looked in his little mirror. But he still didn't sing and he still didn't talk!"

"Hmmmm," thinks the clerk. "Did he tinkle his little bell?"

The customer doesn't even wait for an explanation. Determined to see this out to its conclusion, he grabs a little bell, throws some money on the counter and storms off. You guessed it—the next day he is back again.

"The bird's dead!" he exclaims.

"Dead?"

"Yup. Dead. His little feet sticking up in the air. He got up this morning healthy as could be. He looked in his little mirror. He tinkled his little bell. He ran up and down his little ladder. He swung on his little swing. And then, just before he keeled over and died, he looked over at me, a little tear forming in his little eye, and he finally spoke to me. He said, "Didn't they sell birdseed?!"

Let that story sink in for a moment.

The Internet is full of dead and dying businesses that have been distracted by the bells and whistles of technology. They've ignored the lesson of the birdseed!

So, what is the "birdseed" of marketing? We learned a few of the secrets in the last chapter.

1. *Find a school of hungry fish!*

Once you've either found a lake teeming with hungry fish (or developed your own lake), your very next critical task is to

2. *Discover what bait they're biting on.*

Given just these two advantages plus a plain-vanilla Web site, you'll run circles around 10,000 other eye-popping, flash-enhanced, multimedia'd, neato-bonito, techobrilliant, venture-capitalized, overhead-sucking, cash-burning Web sites.

But here's the problem. As more and more fishers discover the Internet, the fish are becoming more discriminating. Not only is the competition becoming more fierce, but the variety of bait these fishers use is staggering.

In his excellent book, *Differentiate or Die,* Jack Trout (fitting name) has this to say:

> In 1987, there were 14,254 new products introduced in the United States, according to the reporting firm of Market Intelligence Service Ltd. By 1998, the number had grown to 25,118. To put that number in context, it means sixty-nine new products surfaced every day of the year.*

Each of these new products has to be introduced and advertised, which means more fishers (competitors) with more bait (marketing messages). Eventually ordinary bait won't do. Your message will get drowned out unless you convert your ordinary bait into—*superbait!*

3. *Convert your bait into superbait!*

The third most important skill of a marketer is to make your bait stand out from all other bait.

The importance of differentiating your marketing message from that of your competitors was first defined in 1960 by an advertising agency chairman named Rosser Reeves. He called it the *unique selling proposition,* or USP for short. He taught that every advertisement must offer the customer a specific, unique benefit—a proposition that differentiates it from all other competitors. For example, look at the list of the following eight major companies and see if you can tell me their USPs. (You'll find the answers at the bottom of the page.)

1. Amazon.com   _____

2. BMW   _____

3. Domino's Pizza   _____

4. Federal Express   _____

5. Mercedes   _____

6. Nordstrom   _____

7. Rolex   _____

8. Volvo   _____

*Jack Trout with Steve Rivkin, *Differentiate or Die* (New York: Wiley, 2000), pp. 20–21.

(1) **Books, fast and cheap;** (2) **ultimate driving machine;** (3) **fresh, hot pizza in 30 minutes;** (4) **overnight delivery;** (5) **engineering;** (6) **unparalleled service;** (7) **watches that winners wear;** (8) **safety.**

Companies spend millions finding, creating, and defending their USPs. What is your USP? Whatever it is, it must set you apart. It must make you different. Even after you've found a school of hungry fish—even after you've discovered what they're biting on—your bait will get lost in the whirlpool of competing messages unless you figure out a way to make it stand out from the rest. Here is another excellent quote from *Differentiate or Die:*

> In 1966, Peter Drucker defined leadership when he wrote: "The foundation of effective leadership is thinking through the organization's mission, defining it and establishing it, clearly and visibly." Well, we're now in a new millennium and an age of killer competition. We would change only one word in that definition to bring it up to date: "The foundation of effective leadership is thinking through the organization's *difference,* defining it and establishing it, clearly and visibly.*

I'm personally aware of the power of USP. It made me three fortunes and cost me another. In 1980, I published my first book, which has a powerful USP title—*Nothing Down: A Proven Program That Shows You How to Buy Real Estate with Little or No Money Down.* The companion to this book was a $495 weekend seminar by the same name. The power of this single discriminating USP leapfrogged my book and seminar past all other real estate books and seminars almost immediately. Although I was the new kid on the block, older and more established seminar outfits could not compete with my USP. They began to copy my *Nothing Down* message to market their own seminars . . . but it was too late. I had overtaken them and they never recovered.

Later in the decade, new competitors (e.g., Carlton Sheets and Dave Del Dotto) usurped the lead from me when they used powerful infomercials to offer the *No Money Down* message on audiocassettes. I was slow to respond—stubbornly maintaining that the best way to learn was in a live seminar. I hadn't been listening to my "fish," who were eagerly snapping up the inexpensive home-study copycats. The allure of an audio program over a live seminar is that not only is it less expensive, it can be listened to over and over again. I had been leapfrogged! I closed down my seminar operations and went off to lick my wounds.

A year later, I returned. Rather than fight the new leaders head-to-head, I set off in the opposite direction. By listening to the fish, I discovered that what people really wanted was not to listen to tapes, but to be taken by the hand and actually shown how to do it. More important, they would pay a significantly higher price for the privilege. Rising like the phoenix from the ashes of my previous business, I started offering indepth $5,000 Wealth Trainings—weeklong events with actual field exer-

*Ibid., p. 212.

cises during which the students would buy real property. It was like playing Monopoly with real buildings. I had no competition. Over the next five years, our company taught over 20,000 graduates—bringing in over $100 million from these trainings.

What was my USP? Hands-on, in-depth training. By focusing fiercely on this USP, we did extremely well for many years.

Lately, I've uncovered and pioneered another USP. And it's hot! This new USP is based on the word *mentoring* and features live teleconferences—where real millionaires and multimillionaires actually mentor you in real time in the comfort of your own home. Every week, in several 90-minute teleconferences and over the Internet, my protégés meet to brainstorm and be trained by myself and my millionaire mentoring team. And they absolutely love it.

Can you see how a USP evolves over time? You must be prepared to evolve your product as well.

How Do You Create a Powerful USP?

Let's learn how to create a USP. The letters actually stand for the words *unique selling proposition,* but let me show you how to supercharge your USP—how to create a USP that not only differentiates but actually *sells* what you have. I'll give you words to use as a hook to help you remember the three most important aspects of creating a powerful USP:

Ultimate advantage

Sensational offer

Powerful promise

Ultimate Advantage

What specific benefit do people get from doing business with you that they could not get from one of your competitors? The very first and most important part of a USP is to give the customer a major advantage or benefit. Try to make each benefit something that none of your competitors offer—differentiate your product or service in at least one major way.

In 1873, a tailor named Jacob Davis in Reno, Nevada, was listening very carefully to his customers—mostly miners participating in the later stages of the gold rush. One frustrated customer found that the pockets of his work pants repeatedly tore out. In a flash of insight, Davis decided to strengthen the pockets and the zippers of his customers' pants with copper rivets. That solved the problem, and soon other customers were demanding the same alteration. Business was booming. But Davis was worried. What if someone copied his idea? Lacking the $68 necessary to file for a U.S. patent he contacted the most likely potential partner, Levi Strauss, the famous clothier who had been outfitting working people for almost 20 years. Strauss, recognizing the power of the idea, immediately joined in the patent application, which was granted on May 20, 1873.

> In 1872, Levi received a letter from Jacob Davis, a Reno, Nevada, tailor. Davis was one of Levi Strauss's regular customers; he purchased bolts of cloth from the company to use for his own business. In his letter, he told the prosperous merchant about the interesting way he made pants for his customers: he placed metal rivets at the points of strain—pocket corners and the base of the button fly. He didn't have the money to patent his process, so he suggested that Levy pay for the paperwork and that they take out the patent together. Levi was enthusiastic about the idea, and the patent was granted to both men on May 20, 1873.
>
> He knew that demand would be great for these riveted "waist overalls" (the old name for jeans), so Levi brought Jacob Davis to San Francisco to oversee the first West Coast manufacturing facility. Initially, Davis supervised the cutting of the blue denim material and its delivery to individual seamstresses who worked out of their homes. But the demand for overalls made it impossible to maintain this system, and factories on Fremont and Market Streets were opened.

Levi's simple copper rivet became not only the ultimate advantage but a legally protected advantage since the patent excluded all other clothing manufacturers from copying this revolutionary process. For the next 35 years, until the patent expired in 1908, Levi Strauss jeans became the standard for toughness in men's work clothing. It symbolized the individuality and strength of the American male for the next 100 years.

Can You Discover the "Copper Rivet" for Your Business?

When designing your business, you need to lie awake nights trying to discover ways to separate yourself from all of your competitors. On the Internet you will be competing with people from all over the world. Why should anyone buy from you? What advantage can you offer that truly separates you from the pack?

In other words, what single benefit do your customers get from you that they won't get from a competitor. Take out a package of 3 × 5 cards. Write on each card the words, "You get . . ." and then write one major differentiating advantage on each card.

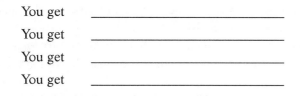

Keep writing until you fill out as many of the 100 cards as possible. You should continually ask yourself this question as your business grows, because people can come along and steal your advantage. They may be able to copy where you've been, but if you keep improving your advantage, you'll always leave them in your dust.

As an example, here are 10 of the advantages that I wrote on my 3×5 cards to describe the benefits enjoyed by those who are enrolled in my current millionaire protégé program.

1. You get to be personally trained by #1 best-selling author Robert Allen.

2. You get to be trained in real time by a team of successful millionaire mentors.

3. You get to do this from the comfort of your own home or from any telephone in the world. (You don't have to travel to be taught.)

4. You get to brainstorm real case studies where you witness real, live, moneymaking success stories *as they happen.*

5. You get to ask interactive questions in an exciting real-time setting.

6. You get to be in the inner circle instead of being out in the cold.

7. You get to be part of a powerful network of millionaires-in-the-making.

8. You get instant connections by having access to the Rolodex of your millionaire mentors.

9. You get to have first access to the moneymaking ideas of your millionaire mentors. For example, your stock market instructor earned 400 percent on his money last year. When he makes a real-time trade, he will send an e-mail telling you what he is doing. You can watch him make money or emulate his winning trades.

10. You get personal transformation. There is a difference between *information* and *transformation.* I don't want to just teach what you need to know, but to transform your ability to *act* upon what you know.

Once your list is complete, try to determine what your *one* major advantage is and then emphasize it in everything you do. Just make sure it is a unique benefit that only you offer. Each one of my 10 advantages is unique from that of my competitors—but one benefit is preeminent, the big kahuna, the major one. This is the one that I emphasize in all of my advertising. Can you guess which one it is?

Over the years, this major advantage has shifted in response to competition. For example, here is how my major advantage has evolved over the years:

1979–1986	*Nothing Down* techniques
1987–1995	Hands-on training
1995–present	Real-time millionaire mentors

In describing my ultimate advantage to my prospective protégés, I use this analogy:

If I've done one thing right in my career, I've always searched out success-ful mentors to guide me. For instance, after graduating with my MBA in 1974, I decided not to go the corporate route and chose instead to work with a multimillionaire real estate mentor at a much-reduced salary. What he taught me in those special six months transformed my life. In the next three years, using what he taught me, I myself was able to become a real estate millionaire. I shudder to think what would have happened to me if I had taken the other route.

Then I decided to write a book about my experiences. I flew to Hawaii with my wife and baby daughter and pounded away on an old typewriter until I had an outline for the book I wanted to write: *Nothing Down: A Proven Program That Shows You How to Buy Real Estate with Little or No Money Down.* Rather than go the traditional publishing route, I approached a very successful best-selling author who happened to go to my church and asked her advice. She agreed to become my mentor and invited me to go with her to the annual booksellers' convention held in Atlanta that year. With her guidance, I had the courage to approach the president of Simon & Schuster, who recognized the value of my book and published it. It went on to become (and still is) the largest-selling real estate book in history.

People ask me why I have been able to accomplish so much, and I tell them that it's all due to the quality of my mentors. Who is your mentor? If you're like most people, your mentors are your best friends. And that's the problem. According to one study, you can determine the income of an indi-vidual by adding up and averaging the incomes of his or her 10 best friends. Did you get that? Your income is the average income of your 10 best friends. If you want to double your income, what do you have to do? Get new friends! You need to add more successful mentors to your life—people who are earning 10, 20, 100 times what you are earning. How else are you going to be able to see beyond your problems except to know someone who has a higher perspective?

For example, when I wanted to learn about the stock market, I put out feelers to find someone who had been able to crack the market and could show me how to play the stock market successfully. When I found this indi-vidual, I said something like this:

"I'm looking for a mentor to show me how to make serious money in the stock market. I don't just want you to tell me—I want you to show me. I'm not interested in reading your books, listening to your tapes, or going to your seminars. I don't want you to sell me a treasure map to the gold mine you've discovered. I've gone that route before. And I've learned that after I've read the book, listened to the tape, been to the seminar, and studied the treasure map, I probably still won't understand how to do it. I'll spend the next three years studying and learning from the school of hard knocks. My three-year education will probably cost me about $20,000, and I still won't be any closer to where I want to be. So, Mr. Mentor, rather than my spending $20,000 and wasting three years of my life, why don't I just give you the $20,000 right now? You say you've discovered a gold mine. Let me go with you. Let's get in your pickup truck. Take me to the mine! Let's go down the mine shaft together. Show me the vein. I want to see it with my own eyes. Let me dig some out with my own hands. Don't tell me about the mine— *take me to the mine!* Now! And I'll make it worth your while."

And that's what he did. We got on the phone and he took me live into the Internet and showed me exactly how to do it. I saw it with my own eyes. I could ask him questions. He gave me immediate answers. He was able to download his lifetime of experience into my brain in a few short weeks. Now I *know* how he does it.

Just as my mentors have taken me into the mine, I want to take you into my mine. Would you like to come?

Can you see how this analogy drives home and highlights my ultimate advantage? What is your ultimate advantage? Take time to figure this out at the beginning of your business and you will be much more successful.

The second letter in the new USP formula is *S*, for *sensational offer.*

Sensational Offer

Do you recognize a good deal when you see it? Suppose you receive an offer to buy a music CD through the mail. The price is $20 but you can have it for only $16. Is that a good deal? Maybe. But in the same batch of mail is an offer to send you eight music CDs for only 1 cent! And if you check a little box on the order form you get another CD absolutely free. Nine CDs for a penny. Is this a better deal? Absolutely! And that is how Columbia House sold millions of music CDs. They hooked you on the front end with a sensational offer and then hoped to make it up on the back end with repeat orders. Such a deal!

How to Create a Sensational Offer

Everyone likes a deal, a bargain, a discount. There are ways to package a deal to make the purchase appear to be a bargain. The other day, while surfing for an airline ticket, I did some comparison shopping at several of the major online travel sites. All of the airfares were within a few dollars of each other, but one site included a 30 percent discount on a future ticket from the same airline. This bonus did two things: It enticed me to buy from this site instead of the others, and it forced me to return to this same site the next time. It locked me up now and in the future. Smart. This little incentive tipped me over the top. The travel company was giving a volume discount: Buy two, get 30 percent off. It's a no-brainer.

Have you ever watched a Ginsu knife salesperson at your local county fair? First, he demonstrates how sharp the primary knife is by cutting leather and a lead pipe. "How much is such a knife?" you're thinking to yourself. "Got to be at least 20 bucks." Then he shows you the fillet knife . . . which he uses to cut the skin off a tomato. Then there's that neat little potato slicer that cuts up a potato like an accordian. Got to have one of those! And then there's a special Orange Juicer. But wait! Have you seen this excellent paring knife? "How much for all of this?" he asks. "Just 20 bucks." Now he's got you. But wait, there's more. "If you buy right now, I'll give you another one of these large Ginsu knives absolutely free . . . so you can give one to a friend." That does it! You're fighting all over each other to hand in your 20 bucks. My wife buys a set of these every year—just for the entertainment value. It's an unbeatable deal. It really is.

You need to lie awake nights figuring out a classy way of offering special bonuses to go along with your main product to make it look like an unbeatable deal.

Here are some examples of things you could offer a first-time buyer:

An extended warranty

A discount coupon

A free special report

A CD-ROM containing a free book or other valuable information

A free banner ad on your site

The goal is to reward your customers for taking action—to make each purchase a surprisingly pleasant experience. But don't stop there. In addition to giving them a bargain on the front end, you should build enough into your price to send them a "surprise" bonus with every purchase—to reward, delight, surprise, and astonish your customer for his or her purchase.

Now, for the final piece of a powerful-selling USP.

Powerful Promise

The thing that clinches a deal is trust, and let's face it, with your first time buyer you don't have any. What is an instant way to gain trust? Offer a clear, unmistakable, no-questions-asked guarantee. But this isn't enough. You need to supercharge your guarantee with a powerful promise.

You see, a guarantee by itself is powerful, but when you attach your guarantee to a powerful promise, you've supercharged it, you've energized it, you've made it real. The promise should heighten your uniqueness.

For example, consider hotel room service. Any hotel can guarantee to deliver your meal quickly. But Marriott goes a step further: "Your meal in 30 minutes or it's free." Now that's a promise with teeth! It heightens and illustrates Marriott's USP of quality service.

In promoting my previous book, *Multiple Streams of Income,* I made a bold promise:

"If you haven't earned an extra $10,000 as a result of reading Multiple Streams of Income *in the next 12 months, call the number in the book and I'll personally refund your money—and you can keep the book as my gift."*

How can I make such a bold promise? Won't thousands of people rip me off and take advantage of my guarantee? Frankly, if a person reads this book and can't make an extra *million* in his or her lifetime, I wouldn't want their money. I'm not worried about the 1 percent of people who *might* take me up on my guarantee. I'm trying to convince the 10 percent who are sitting on the fence to get off and buy now.

An Outrageous Promise

In coming up with a powerful promise, you may need to push the envelope—get outrageous, take a risk. Then work backward to figure out a way to deliver on your outrageous promise.

For example, in planning this book, I started with an outrageous question in my mind: "How quickly could someone launch a cash-generating

WE PROUDLY OFFER A MONEY-BACK GUARANTEE,

CONFIDENT THAT, EVEN IF YOU'RE DISSATISFIED, YOU WON'T TROUBLE TO COMPLAIN.

© 1983 by Ashleigh Brilliant (www.ashleighbrilliant.com)

Internet business from scratch?" Would it take a month? A week? A day? Half a day? None of these numbers seemed outrageous enough. Then I thought, "How about one hour—60 minutes? Hmmm. That sounds outrageous!"

I reworded the promise to make it sound as dramatic as possible. How about this?

Zero to Cash in 60 Minutes!

Yes, that's it! Zero to Cash in 60 Minutes. Now that's a challenge that I could throw my creative juices into! There was only one problem. I had no idea how to do it. I wasn't even sure it was possible. But the more I mulled it over, the more exciting it sounded.

I could see myself on a major radio talk show with a skeptical host. "Well, Mr. Allen. You say you can show our ordinary listeners how to make extraordinary money online. Okay, you've got an hour. Put your money where your mouth is—show us the money!"

Then I imagine taking the host and the listeners through the step-by-step process of setting up a Web site, getting an e-mail address, and marketing a product or idea—and generating at least one cash order in 60 minutes or less.

Would that be dramatic? Absolutely. Would that sell books? Absolutely.

With this vision in my mind, I then proceeded to do the research to make sure that such an outrageous promise is actually deliverable. The result of that research is the book you are now reading.

I'm sure this is the same process that a magician like David Copperfield goes through in trying to create a new illusion to astonish and amaze an audience. He thinks to himself, "I wonder if I could make an elephant disappear? Or a Learjet? No, not dramatic enough. What about the Statue of Liberty? Hmmm. If I could make the Statue of Liberty disappear, that would be memorable!" Then, he works backward to pull off this illusion. What looks like magic to the audience is a carefully prepared illusion. It's not magic when you know the trick.

In your marketing, I'm asking you to go through a similar process. What is your outrageous promise? For example, if your product is about weight loss, what outrageous promise can you make? How much weight could a customer lose safely and permanently . . . in how short a time? Then reengineer your entire company to be able to deliver on that promise.

Let's review. The three powerful bedrock principles of Internet marketing success are as follows:

1. Find a school of hungry fish.
2. Discover the bait that they're biting on.
3. Supercharge your bait with a powerful USP.

The letters USP, an acronym for unique selling proposition, also indicate how to supercharge your USP:

Ultimate advantage

Sensational offer

Powerful promise

If you discover and champion your *ultimate advantage,* if you create a *sensational offer,* and if you then back it up with a *powerful promise,* you will have done more for your business than 99 percent of all businesses in this country.

In the next chapter, I show you how to whip your fish into a feeding frenzy for your product.

CHAPTER 4

Internet Marketing 201: 12 Powerful Principles for Creating a Feeding Frenzy

In this chapter I show you how to get people to beg for your products—how to create a feeding frenzy with your marketing program. But before we go any further, let's make sure we agree on what marketing really is.

Most people equate marketing with sales or advertising. It is much more than that. It starts with identifying the right audience (hungry fish). From your very first connection with a member of this audience, it continues on through every contact—from this person receiving a brochure to visiting your Web site to having a conversation with a live receptionist to the eventual sale and beyond—until your new customer is converted into a raving fan.

Theodore Levitt, the famous Harvard marketing professor, said it this way in 1975: The marketing process consists of . . . "a tightly integrated effort to discover, create, arouse, and satisfy customer needs."*

*Theodore Levitt, "Marketing Myopia," *Harvard Business Review,* September–October 1975.

In his excellent book, *Permission Marketing,** Seth Godin refers to the marketing process as one of converting strangers into friends and friends into customers. I go a step further on both ends of the scale. The marketing process should not start with strangers but with "starving strangers"—people who are predisposed to want what you have. Convert these starving strangers first into friends, then into customers. But don't stop there. Ultimately, you want to convert these customers into partners—loyal allies who profit with you in sharing your business with others. Figure 4.1 shows a visual representation of this process.

As we learned in Chapter 3, first you identify a group of "starving strangers" and dangle your super USP bait in front of them. How can you get them to not only notice your bait but to actually strike it—to chase after it in a feeding frenzy?

As a student of marketing for over 25 years, I have discovered some principles that always work. For more than 10 years, I practiced these principles without knowing that there was a scientific basis for *why* they work. Then someone gave me a copy of Dr. Robert Cialdini's powerful book, *Influence: The Psychology of Persuasion.* The lights went on! Cialdini gives detailed scientific proof explaining why certain marketing principles that have been practiced for millennia always seem to work. With this information, a marketer can design powerful marketing programs to take advantage of innate human tendencies.

When I finished reading Cialdini's book, I was astounded. It reminded me of an old cartoon I saw in an ancient Bennett Cerf joke book in our family library when I was just a kid. Two lone Native Americans from New Mexico are standing next to a fire on a hill trying to send smoke signals when, across the valley, a giant atomic mushroom cloud appears. One Indian turns to the other and says, "Gee, I wish I'd said that!" While you're shopping on the Internet for one of my previous books (*Nothing Down, Creating Wealth,* or *Multiple Streams of Income*), you should also put into your shopping basket a copy of Cialdini's book. It is excellent.

Here are Cialdini's six principles of persuasion:

1. Reciprocation
2. Commitment and consistency
3. Social proof
4. Liking
5. Authority
6. Scarcity

*Seth Godin, *Permission Marketing* (New York: Simon & Schuster, 1999).

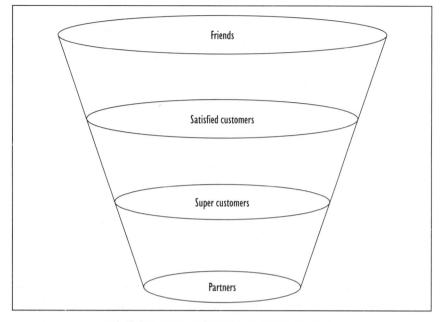

FIGURE 4.1   The marketing funnel: starving strangers.

I used several of them in designing my marketing campaign for the
Internet challenge. In order to demonstrate, let's return to my first two
e-mails sent to my homegrown e-mail list of 11,516 newsletter subscribers.
You might want to flip to page 17 in Chapter 2 and reread the first of these
messages. This is actually a very sophisticated marketing message designed
to create a feeding frenzy starting with the very first words in the subject
line: "Making massive amounts of money on the Net."

One-Step versus Two-Step Process

This is probably a good time to mention that your marketing campaign
can be either a one-step or two-step process. In a one-step process, you
try to go from an ad to a paid order in one step. For example, suppose you
are an attorney trying to attract new business. You run a television ad that
tells about your services and gives your telephone number. You are trying
to go from an ad to an order in one step. This approach attracts only *serious* customers. It's like walking up to a total stranger and proposing marriage. This approach can work—if you talk to enough strangers, you're
bound to find someone who is in the market for a spouse—but be prepared for a lot of rejection.

A two-step ad offers the reader a free taste. Your ad doesn't sell your
attorney services . . . but instead offers to let someone come in for a free

one-hour consultation. You get people to raise their hand and indicate their interest in talking to an attorney. This approach attracts interested people while at the same time giving you a chance to talk to a more qualified group of people. Certainly, in a group of interested people, there must be some serious customers. In the marketing business, this is called *lead generation*, or getting people to *raise their hands*. To use one analogy, it's the dating approach. In our overcommunicated world, the two-step approach takes more time, but it is the best long-term approach.

How do you get people to raise their hands? You have to give them something of value. For years, to market our popular *Nothing Down* weekend seminars, we would offer a 90-minute free preview. Over 2 million people attended these free lectures in the 1980s. I didn't know it at the time, but in offering this free seminar I was actually practicing two powerful persuasion principles explained so eloquently by Dr. Robert Cialdini: (1) reciprocity and (2) commitment and consistency.

In lay terms, *reciprocity* means giving gifts. When you give gifts, people feel a subtle obligation to return the favor (to reciprocate). The entire Internet is based on reciprocity. Almost everything is free. But have you noticed that there are always options to pay for more personalized service?

That is why, in the first of my five messages, I offer the possibility of winning some money. The opportunity to win money is given as a free gift . . . tapping into the power of reciprocity. Giving something for free is always a smart marketing strategy. Why do you think Debbie Fields gives free samples of her famous Mrs. Fields cookies? Everybody wins—the sampler and the marketer. Those who taste and don't like the taste haven't risked anything. Those who taste and want more can pay for the full treatment.

The next of Cialdini's principles is *commitment and consistency.* In lay terms, this means baby steps. To use a bit of Eastern philosophy, "Man who chooses the beginning of the path also chooses the end of it." In his book, Cialdini reports on exhaustive research to prove that these small actions have a powerful effect on influencing a target audience to say yes. Cialdini calls it the *power of commitment and consistency*—if a person will take a baby step or make a small commitment toward a goal, he or she will be much more likely to continue. It's similar to the principle of inertia in physics—an object at rest tends to stay at rest and an object in motion tends to stay in motion. If you can motivate someone to take even a minuscule action, it is much more likely that he or she will continue to move in the same direction.

In the first of my marketing messages, you'll also notice that I mention my new best-selling book. Why? Another important marketing principle is at work here—Cialdini calls it the *power of consensus.* In lay terms, this means popularity. If you see a long line forming outside a theater, you will automatically assume that the movie must be good. In other words, my book *must* be worth buying because so many people are buying it. People always want the hottest thing. If you can provide proof that your product is in demand by a large number of people, it will induce potential buyers to say yes more easily. Review that section of the e-mail and you'll see what I'm trying to convey.

In both of the first messages, I also mention that Guthy/Renker, the famous infomercial company, is shooting an infomercial with me. This builds credibility. People like to deal with experts. It lowers their risk of failure. Cialdini calls this the *authority principle.* In lay terms, this means credibility. You'll notice I use several methods of building credibility.

Another important marketing principle is also at work here. You'll notice that I tell my readers exactly why I'm trying to make $24,000 in 24 hours. I'm not trying to hide or hoodwink. I tell readers that I'm trying to make money to document my infomercial—and I ask for their support. I tell the truth—straightforward and unvarnished. I can't overemphasize the power of telling the truth.

Another very important part of my first e-mail message is using what Cialdini calls the *power of scarcity.* You'll notice that I say there will only be five messages, culminating with the final message on May 24. This highlights the very special, unique, and scarce nature of this promotion. I can't overemphasize the importance of the power of this principle. There is another example of scarcity used in this message. Can you find it?

Again, in the second message (page 19) I return to the power of the principle of reciprocity by promising that each and every person who votes will receive a copy of a valuable ($100) special report. In a sense, I am paying them for the time they spend in filling out my survey.

Other principles are equally as powerful. Here is my expanded checklist of 12 powerful persuaders, translated into simplified language:

Principle 1	Giving gifts
Principle 2	Baby steps
Principle 3	Popularity
Principle 4	Credibility
Principle 5	Scarcity
Principle 6	Honesty
Principle 7	Rapport
Principle 8	Urgency
Principle 9	Greed (pleasure)
Principle 10	Fear of loss (pain)

Principle 11	Belonging
Principle 12	Curiosity

To help you remember the most powerful of these 12 principles, I've boiled them down into the three most important, never-miss ways to supercharge your bait. Once again, the acronym USP appears.

Urgency

Scarcity

Popularity

Question: If a lot of people are competing for a few items with a short deadline, what do you have?

Answer: Feeding frenzy!

Now that you are more aware of these principles in action, let's study the third message, sent a few days later. Notice how the future feeding frenzy is being set up.

Imagine receiving this message in your e-mail. Would you open it?

From: Subject:
Robert Allen   You've Got Cash! Make Streams of Cash Overnight

Message #3

May 18, 2000

To: Subscribers to Robert Allen's Streams of Cash E-Letter
From: #1 Best-selling financial author, Robert Allen
Re: You've got cash! Make streams of cash overnight

Message 3 of 5

Important Note: You can win *$1,000 in cash* just for telling a few of your friends about the Streams of Cash E-Letter.

If you'd like to be $1,000 richer, please read on . . .

Dear Subscribers:

There are three things I'd like to share with you today.

1. First, thanks a million! I'm #8 at New York Times!!

Let me personally thank all of you who recently purchased my new book,

Multiple Streams of Income. Because of you, *Multiple Streams* just hit #8 on the *New York Times* business best-seller list and #11 at *USA Today.* Make sure you call the number on page xiii of the book and let me send you, as my gift, a free copy of my previous best-selling book, *The Road to Wealth.* (FYI: *Multiple Streams* is currently discounted 30 percent at Amazon.com and 40 percent at BarnesandNoble.com.)

2. *I'm overwhelmed by the response to the last letter!!*

At 10:30 P.M. Monday night, I sent the second of five special issues of the Streams of Cash E-Letter asking for your feedback on how to generate huge streams of Internet income for my live TV infomercial shoot on May 24.

Within 12 hours I had received 1,200 responses and counting!!

The power of the Internet constantly amazes me! In addition to voting for your favorite offer, a large number of you included incredible moneymaking suggestions. These ideas alone are priceless. As my thanks to those who voted, I will compile all of these powerful suggestions and share them as part of the special report I promised you: You've Got Cash: How to Generate $24,000 Cash in 24 Hours on the Internet.

If you just joined the Streams of Cash E-Letter and still want to participate in the voting, just go to www.robertallen.com.

3. *Win $1,000 in cash for sharing this message!*

Finally, I'd like to offer you a way to win $1,000, $500, or $250 just for helping me spread the message of the Streams of Cash E-Letter. In these past few issues I've been focusing on generating excitement for my May 24 live TV infomercial shoot.

Obviously, the more people I can invite to participate in this process, the greater probability that I will hit my income target of $24,000 in 24 hours. So I'd like to offer you an incentive for spreading the message.

But first, let me share with you the three major strategies I've used to build awareness for this event:

A. *Cash prizes and other free offers.*

By offering random drawings of cash and other free prizes for those who read the May 24 e-letter, I hope to build anticipation and awareness. Without a doubt, more people will read their e-mails on that day.

In addition, in the next issue of the e-letter, I will be announcing a cash prize for the three people who guess closest to the amount of income that is actually earned. So, watch for the fourth issue of this series. You could win $1,000, $500, or $250 plus one of a dozen other surprise prizes.

B. *Free information.*

All those who responded to the survey in the last issue will be receiving one of the most valuable special reports I have ever created: *How to Make $24,000 in 24 Hours on the Internet.* I know you'll enjoy it.

C. *Cash rewards.*

In this issue, I'm announcing a way to reward those of you who tell others about the Streams of Cash E-Letter. If you send someone to my site who signs up for my free e-letter and happens to win one of the prizes, then you, too, will win an equal prize. For example, suppose you tell your brother about the Streams of Cash E-Letter and he subscribes and wins one of the prizes (let's say $500 in cash) . . . then you, too, will be a winner of $500 in cash . . . just for sending him my way. Both of you win!

Secret Method of Building Traffic

In the next issue of this five-message series, I will reveal the final major method for building traffic. Don't miss the next issue of the Streams of Cash E-Letter.

Prosperity to you and yours,

Robert G. Allen

Best-selling author of *Nothing Down, Creating Wealth, The Road to Wealth,* and NOW, *Multiple Streams of Income.*

P.S. Make sure to check your e-mail on May 24. You could earn a nice chunk of cash.

By now, you're beginning to see a pattern in the advance e-mails. They are building anticipation for the final day—May 24. A powerful motivator is curiosity. People are becoming curious to find out just what the final message is going to look like. I've been told that dozens of people stayed home from work that day, just to make sure that they didn't miss the final e-mail.

Aren't you curious to read the fourth message? Here is a copy of the fourth e-mail sent a few days later.

Message #4

May 22, 2000
To: Subscribers to Robert Allen's Streams of Cash E-Letter
From: #1 Best-selling financial author, Robert Allen
Re: Guess the total and win $1,000, $500, or $250 in CASH

Message 4 of 5

Important Note: You can win *$1,000 in cash* just for guessing how much money the Streams of Cash E-Letter will generate from a special broadcast on May 24. Second prize $250. Third prize $100. Plus dozens of other prizes.

If you'd like to win CASH, please read on . . .

Win $1,000 in cash for guessing the final number!

This is the last message before the big day, May 24. On that day, between noon and 5 P.M. Pacific time, I will send out the fifth and final message. The response will be recorded live for the television cameras and the result will be included in my newest infomercial, *Real Streams of Cash*. (This is my ninth infomercial since 1982.)

I'd like to offer you a way to win $1,000 just for guessing the correct amount of money that the Streams of Cash E-Letter will generate on May 24.

Frankly, I myself have no idea how much money will be generated from my private list of 11,983 subscribers—$24,000 in 24 hours has a nice ring to it, but, honestly, it could be anywhere from $1,000 to $100,000. I will be as surprised as you to see the real result. I'm going to be making some outrageous offers on that day. Don't forget to check your e-mail, because 24 hours later the opportunity will be gone.

What's your best guess?

Click on the link below to enter your answer. You can enter the contest only once. But another way to win is to invite your friends to subscribe to my e-letter. If they enter the contest and win, then you, too, will win a prize equal to theirs.

Give me your best guess about how it will turn out. The winners will be announced the week following May 24. But even if you don't win, I will send you the special report showing you how to duplicate my results.

See you on May 24!

Sincerely,

Robert Allen
Best-selling author, *Nothing Down, Creating Wealth, The Road to Wealth,* and NOW, *Multiple Streams of Income.*

P.S. My publisher just informed me that *Multiple Streams of Income* is the #2 best-selling book this week at the nationwide book chain, Books-a-Million. Its Internet site has a great price on the book also (www. booksamillion.com).

P.P.S. In the third issue of this series, I shared three ways to build traffic and excitement for the launch of an Internet site—like my promotion for May 24. They were (1) cash prizes and other free offers, (2) free information, (3) cash rewards for entering contests.

In this issue, I promised to share the fourth method. Aren't you curious to find out? That's the answer. *Curiosity.* Curiosity is a powerful motivator. Aren't you curious to find out what my e-mail message on May 24 will look like? Aren't you curious to find out who the cash winners will be? Aren't you curious to find out how much money will be generated? Aren't you curious to find out if you will win the $1,000 in cash? Aren't you curious to discover the once-in-a-lifetime deals that will only be available from noon May 24 to noon May 25?

Turn your curiosity into cash. I'll see you on May 24.

This last principle, *curiosity,* is very useful as a bonus motivator. Once you have applied the other principles, adding curiosity acts like salt and pepper—it seasons your offer to give it just the right taste. I don't think a single person on my list felt manipulated or coerced into buying on the final day. There was anticipation—even excitement—in the air. And on my part, there was uncertainty and an element of surprise.

In the next chapter, I'll let you read the fifth message and try to figure out why it worked so well. But before we move on, let's review.

First, I attracted a list of hungry fish. Just like all overnight successes, this one began many months earlier.

Then, using 12 powerful USP persuasion principles, I created an environment in which these people were predisposed to say yes. They wanted to say yes. They were just waiting for the right time.

One marketing expert, Jeff Paul, explains the marketing process eloquently:

"My definition of marketing is setting up automatic, repeatable systems that create the environment where people want to buy from you instead of you having to sell them."

Would you like to learn how to set up these automatic, repeatable systems? Keep reading.

CHAPTER 5

Internet Marketing 301: Going Deep—The Secret to Online Streams of Income

"Fine, Al, and how are you, your charming wife, Joni; your two wonderful children, Charles and Lisa, ages thirteen and fifteen; and your delightful German short-haired pointer, Avondale?"

In my previous book, *Multiple Streams of Income,* I included a general chapter about the Internet called "Your Next Fortune Is Only a Click Away."* I'd like you to study the following chart from that chapter that lists the benefits of marketing online:

---

*Robert Allen, *Multiple Streams of Income* (New York: Wiley, 2000). I've posted a copy of the entire chapter on my Web site (www.robertallen.com) if you'd like to read it. Go to the keyword section and type in Internet Chapter.

Traditional Marketing	Internet Marketing
Snail mail (slow, expensive, unreliable, wasteful)	E-mail (fast, cheap, reliable, efficient)
High mailing costs	Zero mailing costs
Long delivery time	Instantaneous delivery time
Business week/business hours	24/7/365
Local/limited geographic area	Entire world
Limited, shrinking customer base	Unlimited, expanding customer base
High overhead	Almost zero overhead
Real time, real contact	Store-and-forward time (asynchronous)
Average customers	Upscale, wealthy, intelligent customers
Long inquiry time	Instant response time
Dress up/go to the office	Stay home in your T-shirt
Mass marketing	Intimate, one-on-one marketing
Impulse/wait	Impulse/instant gratification
Old, traditional	New, exciting, mysterious
Intrusive marketing (interrupts)	You're in the searching mood (welcome)
One-way marketing	Interactive marketing
One-dimensional marketing	Interactive and multimedia marketing
Ads disappear quickly	Ads are as permanent as you want
High entry costs	Low entry costs/level playing field
High cost of failure	Low cost of failure
Operate from a fixed location	Operate from any computer in the world
Need to be a big player with big money	Can be a nobody with little or no money
High barriers to entry	No barriers
Highly visible/public	Private/anonymous between buyer and seller
You are judged by age, sex, $, looks, race	Judged by the quality of your ideas
Uncool	Cool

© 1976 by Ashleigh Brilliant (www.ashleighbrilliant.com)

That is quite a powerful list of advantages! The most important thing you should take away from reading such a list is the revolutionary nature of these advantages. Internet marketing is turning traditional marketing on its ear.

In Chapter 3 I shared with you Jay Abraham's three major marketing activities: (1) to find more customers who will (2) spend more money (3) more often. The Internet is a perfect vehicle for magnifying these three activities for one major reason: *the free nature of frequency.*

In other words, your marketing message can be delivered over and over again with almost zero cost. In my $24,000-in-24-hours Internet marketing challenge, I was able to deliver five long, powerful marketing messages to the same audience for free. What a marketing luxury! If I had tried to replicate this marketing effort in the bricks-and-mortar world via direct mail, it would have cost me at least $25,000 *up front,* without knowing if I could recoup my costs. Internet marketing is much more forgiving because the cost of failure from a single marketing message is zero. Did you get that?

In the bricks-and-mortar world, the cost of a marketing failure can bankrupt your company! On the Internet, because of the advantage of free frequency, you have the ability to build your message to a powerful crescendo.

Now, let's study the fifth and final message from my Internet marketing challenge. It was sent on May 24 at exactly 12:38 P.M. As I've previously mentioned, the response was overwhelming. Money started to pour into my e-mail box within minutes and gushed to almost $100,000 in just a little over 24 hours. Read it and see if you can tell why.

Message #5

May 24, 2000
To: Subscribers to Robert Allen's Streams of Cash E-Letter
From: Best-selling author Robert Allen
Re: May 24 final offer

!!!FINAL MESSAGE!!!

Over the past 14 days I have sent you four separate messages announcing a special promotion on May 24. THAT'S TODAY! (To read these four messages, click on the link below.)

Today, as I sit at my computer, I want to thank you for participating in this experience. In these past few days, over 2,000 of you have responded to our survey, and hundreds of you have sent friends and associates to register for the free Streams of Cash E-Letter. As a reward for participating in this Internet challenge:

—Three of you will be randomly selected to win *CASH prizes!*
—Three of you could also *win CASH* for referring someone!
—Three of you will win *$500, $250, or $100* for making a guess!
—The *first* 100 guessers will win a signed *million-dollar bill.*
—The *best* 100 guessers will *win a signed book.*
—2,000 of you will receive the powerful special report: *How to Make
   $24,000 Cash in 24 Hours on the Internet.*

And EVERYONE who orders TODAY becomes an INSTANT WINNER because I'm going to make some once-in-a-lifetime deals TODAY ONLY!

Why today?

Because, we are making history TODAY! As I send you this message, live cameras are rolling to document how you can make instant CASH on the Internet. As the responses to this message pour in, our staff will total up the number of orders. I want to make sure that the end result looks impressive.

That's where you come in. Let me ask you . . .

Do you really want to be a millionaire?

In the past few months, Regis Philbin has helped three people become millionaires on the hit show, *Who Wants to Be a Millionaire.* Through my books, seminars, and trainings, I have helped *thousands of people* become millionaires.

And now it's your turn. When would you like to get started?

How about now?!!!

There are three ways I can personally help you become a millionaire:

Package #1. Millionaire Mentoring conference call:

Eight weeks of intense telecoaching with me and my hand-selected Millionaire Mentors.

Package #2. The Millionaire Retreat:

Three powerful days of personal interaction with me and my hand-selected Millionaire Mentors.

Package #3. The Inner Circle:

Two days of intense, personal coaching with me (strictly limited to 10 individuals).

Each of the above methods comes with many valuable bonuses. But first, let me ask you: How would you like to receive your millionaire training?

—By telephone with live Millionaire Mentors?
—At a private Millionaire Retreat, where you can network with other like-minded people?
—With a handful of individuals, where you will receive personal, face-to-face mentoring?

Each way is a different experience that I guarantee you will enjoy and profit from.

Here is what you get with package #1:

The eight-week Millionaire Mentoring conference call

This unique training will be conducted live over the phone in a conference call setting. Each class is two hours long. Each class is recorded in case you miss the live class. Your instructors will be

Robert Allen—#1 best-selling author of *Multiple Streams of Income, Nothing Down,* and *Creating Wealth*

Dr. Stephan Cooper—stock market expert who earned 400 percent last year

Darren Falter—Internet guru who consults on the Robert Allen site

Thomas Painter—real estate expert and marketing guru

Ken Kerr—licensing guru who has launched many successful products, including the California Dancing Raisins, the Smurfs, and many other multimillion-dollar projects.

Ted Thomas—on how to earn 25 percent with tax lien certificates

Plus several millionaire mystery guests. I promise you will be amazed!

As bonuses for this class you will receive:

	Value
1. An autographed copy of my popular book, *Road to Wealth*	($20)
2. Six audiocassettes from my Financial Freedom Library	($30)
3. 10 special reports: The Wealth Collection	($50)
4. Maximum Profits Manual (130 PDF pages)	($197)

Including such tips as . . .

> 58 marketing strategies to increase your profits
> How to double the response from your ads
> How to guarantee 10 to 50 percent more sales with a simple question
> Six marketing principles you must know to make your sales soar
> 11 tested methods to increase the power of your marketing

The cost of this powerful eight-week Millionaire Mentoring program is only $97.

Your satisfaction is absolutely guaranteed. You MUST feel this program is worth 10 times your investment of time and money or your money will be instantly refunded—no questions asked!

Here is what you get with package #2:

The three-day Millionaire Retreat

First, every attendee at the Millionaire Retreat will be allowed to participate in the Millionaire Mentoring conference call (package #1) AT NO CHARGE.

Here is what the Millionaire Retreat consists of.

In the survey, the most popular offer BY FAR was this three-day Millionaire Retreat. Half of those surveyed were willing to pay between $500 and $1,500 per person. Over 100 people were willing to pay $1,495 per person. This is far below my normal price of $3,000 for a three-day session like this—considering that I will be bringing in at least five millionaires to teach the session with me. But since I'm filming this offer for the live television cameras, I want to guarantee a huge response.

Therefore, for 24 hours ONLY I will allow you AND your spouse to attend for an unbelievably low price.

Over 20,000 people invested $5,000 apiece to participate in my powerful 5-Day Wealth Training. From this class have come hundreds, if not thousands, of millionaires. I have designed a more concentrated three-day version of this training called the Millionaire Retreat. During these three intense days you will learn:

How to earn 100 percent or more in the stock market! You will be trained by an expert who himself earned over 400 percent last year in the market.

How to make $100,000 a year investing in real estate. You will be trained by at least three real estate millionaires in addition to myself. Learn the inside secrets to making huge amounts of money in real estate.

How to make $1,000 a day or more on the Internet. The Internet is the ultimate money machine . . . while you eat, while you sleep, money is pouring into your life from all over the world. Let me show you how to really make money on the Internet.

How to build inner wealth and unshakable confidence. Most people want to be successful but lack the inner confidence to break through to new levels of success and achievement. Using powerful new brain technologies you will be able to transform your ability to take action.

How to build a financial fortress around your assets. People ask me if I'm a millionaire, and I say absolutely not. And neither should you. Let me show you how to shield your wealth using strategies that I have never before revealed.

You will be trained by myself and my team of millionaire mentors. These three days are guaranteed to change your life forever and launch you on the fast track to financial freedom. If you can't attend, the entire experience will be professionally recorded. All attendees will also receive a copy of the tapes.

As bonuses, every participant in the Millionaire Retreat will also receive:

1. Everything in package #1 FREE OF CHARGE

2. A FREE ticket for your spouse/partner to attend with you

3. Real estate millions home-study system

Enjoy live recordings from two of Robert Allen's popular programs on how to make a fortune in real estate. Attendees paid $5,000 for each of these seminars. Now you can learn the same information that helped launch thousands of millionaires.

The Wealth Training Experience	12 audios
Fortunes in Foreclosures	24 audios

4. Infopreneuring: Be an information multimillionaire!

In the past 20 years, over $200 million worth of my books, tapes, videos, and seminars have been marketed throughout the world. I shared the secrets to how this was done in a powerful three-day $3,000 seminar called "Infopreneuring: How You Can Become an Information Multimillionaire." You will receive a live audio recording of this exclusive information marketing boot camp with 24 audiocassettes.

5. Special bonus: You will also receive two tickets to the Internet marketing boot camp, June 16–18.

The tuition for this class is $597. I have made an arrangement with my friend, Carl Galetti, who is organizing this conference, to pay your tuition for you. That's right, your tuition to attend is zero. If you can't make these dates, then give the two tickets to someone you know. They will love you forever. I myself will be there. I wouldn't miss it. And neither should you.

If you would like to read about all of the incredible bonuses available to attendees of this conference, just click on the link below. Then you'll see why this bonus alone is worth the entire cost of the Millionaire Retreat.

So, to review, the *Millionaire Retreat* includes three days of powerful training for you and your spouse, plus:

Everything in package #1

A free ticket for your spouse/partner to attend with you

36 audiocassettes on real estate riches

24 audiocassettes on infopreneuring millions

Two tickets to the Internet marketing boot camp

And all of this for three easy payments of $297.

Your satisfaction is absolutely guaranteed. I guarantee that you will learn the ideas, strategies, and techniques to launch yourself to the next level of success.

Here is what you get with package #3:

The Inner Circle—personal, one-on-one coaching with Robert Allen.
This offer is strictly limited to 10 people.

I rarely consult individually. It is a much more efficient use of my time to work with groups of 100 or more. When I do private consultation, I bill my time at $1,000 per hour or $10,000 a day. Yet on May 24, I will offer to mentor you, along with only nine other individuals, for two power-packed days at my home base in San Diego. There will be time for private, personalized, one-on-one consultation.

The tuition for this extremely exclusive private session is only three easy payments of $997. I guarantee to help you double your income in 12 months or the session is free.

You will also receive everything in packages #1 and #2 ABSOLUTELY FREE.

Which of these powerful millionaire training programs would you like to participate in?

Package #1. Millionaire Mentoring conference call $97

Package #2. Millionaire Retreat   3 payments of $297

Package #3. Inner Circle   3 payments of $997

Finally, there is one more package to consider, package #4:

The Professional Internet Marketer option

Strictly limited to 24 people in the world.

Many of you are serious Internet marketers who could benefit from the traffic that I am generating on my site. In the survey, over 1,000 of you indicated that you would like to buy a banner on the Multiple Streams of Income site; 61 people offered $995 for the privilege. Obviously, there is a huge demand and a high value for this very limited space. Therefore, rather than placing a price tag on this scarce resource, I'll let you place your bid for what you feel this would be worth to you and I'll accept the 24 top bids. The 24 winners will receive five specific advantages.

You get a banner ad on the front page of my popular Web site linked to you. I have never before allowed banner ads on my site. Yet in the next several weeks I will be driving massive traffic to my site with 500,000 pieces of mail, constant PR as I go from city to city promoting my new book, and, of course, over 30 references to my Web site in my best-selling book. If you need traffic, here is a perfect vehicle. Choose any four-month period you wish.

You also receive an exclusive positioning for your ads in one of 24 places throughout my site.

1. In addition, you will be able to place 10 classified ads in the soon-to-be-opened Money Classifieds.

2. You will also receive a prominent, endorsed ad in each of four issues of the Streams of Cash E-Letter.

3. And you'll receive professional advertising consultation worth $500.

I'm sure you want your advertising to be as effective as possible. Therefore, I have arranged and paid for a professional marketing expert, Scott Haines, to professionally critique your banner advertising. Scott is my own personal marketing specialist. He normally charges $500 per marketing consultation. However, for this special promotion, I've purchased a block of Scott's time and brainpower for him to supercharge your advertising. Scott is a pro. I myself have hired Scott to help me with several of my marketing campaigns—with great success. I'm impressed with his work, and I know you will be. He will give you powerful suggestions on how to double the response to your advertising. Repeat: This consultation is available at no charge to you. I have already paid the fee for you.

4. You will also receive a four-week Internet action class.

Let my personal Internet guru, Daren Falter, coach you via conference call for four power-packed weeks. He'll show you how to make millions on the Internet.

Bonus: Two tickets to Internet marketing boot camp, June 16–18. Read all about it at the link below. The tuition for this class is $597. I have made an arrangement with my friend, Carl Galetti, to pay your tuition for you. That's right, your cost to attend is zero. If you can't make these dates, then, give the two tickets to someone you know.

If you would like to be one of the 24 people, click on the link below and make your bid. If the results I achieve in the first month don't meet my expectations, I reserve the right to cancel the remaining months of my bid.

Well, there you have it. Four powerful ways I can help you become a millionaire. Click on the link below to choose your package number, fill out your name, address, and credit card number, and send it off immediately.

Robert Allen

Author of the *New York Times* best-sellers *Nothing Down, Creating Wealth,* and *Multiple Streams of Income.*

Now you have had a chance to read all five messages sent over a period of 14 days. Just for fun, which of the four offers I made in the last message attracted you the most? I'd like you to vote, and then I'll show you on the next page how many people voted with their wallets for each option.

Your vote

_____Package #1.	Millionaire Mentoring conference call	$97
_____Package #2.	Millionaire Retreat	3 payments of $297
_____Package #3.	Inner Circle	3 payments of $997
_____Package #4.	Banner advertising	Your bid $____

In all, 173 people either made bids or cash offers for one of the four packages. The following tally includes all additional orders that came in after the 24-hour deadline. This is a response rate of 1.5 percent . . . three times what I expected.

Package #1. 83 people paid $97	$ 8,051
Package #2. 42 people made 3 payments of $297	36,531
Package #3. 17 people made 3 payments of $997	50,847
Package #4. 29 people made bids	19,478
Miscellaneous 3 people ordered individual products	597
Total orders	$115,504

Over the next three months, after cancellations, we were able to deposit over $90,000 in cash orders, with a profit of almost 90 percent.

You're probably asking, *How can I duplicate this?!*

That's what this book will show you. In fact, I want to show you how to do even better, because I learned a lot from this experience. But before I teach you the duplicable systems for consistently creating these kind of cash flows, let me dispel a myth that I'm sure a few of my readers have picked up along the way.

It's the get-rich-quick mentality that pervades business. I, too, am guilty of it. Remember, I'm the guy who promises to show you how to make money in 60 minutes starting from scratch. This gives the impression that I'm only about the quick buck, a thoroughly American pastime. Therefore, I refuse to go any further without clearing up this misunderstanding.

Just as a bee is lured to the nectar of the flower, businesspeople are lured to money. Honeybees accomplish so much in their relentless search for nectar—they pollinate the flowers and bring about glorious growth wherever their industrious bodies carry them. Entrepreneurs are the honeybees of our economy. They are attracted to money and freedom, but along the way they spin off a growing economy with jobs and knowledge and charity. I am proud to be a honeybee in the hive of capitalism. Ultimately, the goal of any entrepreneur is to extend the life of his or her enterprise for a lifetime. In this sense, the short-term goals of making money now collide with the long-term goals of creating an enduring enterprise with endless cash flow.

Therefore, your marketing plan on the front end must emphasize immediate gratification. But the back end of your marketing program must emphasize a deepening relationship with the fish in your hatchery.

Here is where we part company with traditional mass marketers, whose traditional mass-marketing dream is as follows: Send out a million e-mails. Get a 1 percent response on a $100 product. Collect a cool million dollars. Ride off into the sunset.

This is the mass-marketing model—or what I call "going wide." Mass marketers cast a wide net, hoping to get a tiny percentage to respond and make millions. It would seem as though the Internet is perfect for the mass-marketing model. It is. But remember with whom you are competing. The Fortune 1000 companies are spending, on average, a million dollars per Web site to go online. Do you have a million dollars to make your site look snappy and exciting? Don't even go there.

Remember, it's not about the quality of your Web site. In the future, with billions of people online and hundreds of millions of competing businesses from Argentina to Zanzibar, you will never be able to compete on price. People will be able to search the world to shave a penny. Once again, don't go there.

There is only one way you will be able to compete and create lifetime streams of cash flow for yourself: *Go deep.*

What does that mean?

It means that you anoint yourself as the in-depth expert on what your starving crowd wants and create a deepening relationship with them—a lifetime relationship. As the relationship deepens, they will *pull* from you more and more products, services, and information (PSI) at increasingly higher and higher prices—because price will not be the issue. When a stranger in Kathmandu tries to *push* a product that is 10 percent cheaper, your fish will think of the benefits of their relationship with you and quickly reject the stranger's offer.

How do you create this kind of relationship?

It starts with a new attitude about marketing. After you find your hungry school of fish, you must resist the almost universal attitude to focus on selling products. As a businessperson, your ultimate product is a satisfied customer. Over 25 years ago, Theodore Levitt published a powerful article in the *Harvard Business Review* titled "Marketing Myopia." Even though you may not have read it, I'll bet you've heard some of the analogies that he used to make his point.

He clearly showed that the railroad industry declined rapidly from its zenith because its leaders thought they were in the railroad business (product-centered) when they were actually in the transportation business (customer-centered). Because of this myopic view, they didn't even consider the advent of the airplane important. Not only did they miss out on the opportunity, they almost got wiped out by it. The same thing happened to the movie industry when television came on the scene. Why did this happen? Here are a few of Levitt's conclusions:

> In short, if management lets itself drift, it invariably drifts in the direction of thinking of itself as producing goods and services, not customer satisfactions. . . . The historic fate of one growth industry after another has been its suicidal product provincialism.
>
> . . . The entire corporation must be viewed as a customer-creating and customer-satisfying organism. Management must think of itself not as producing products but as providing customer-creating value satisfactions. It

DON'T WORRY —

I'LL STAY
WITH YOU
ALL THE WAY
TO THE END OF
YOUR MONEY.

© 1983 by Ashleigh Brilliant (www.ashleighbrilliant.com)

must push this idea (and everything it means and requires) into every nook and cranny of the organization. . . . In short, the organization must learn to think of itself not as producing goods or services but as *buying customers,* as doing the things that will make people *want* to do business with it.*

In the May 31, 1999, issue of *Business Week,* Jeff Bezos, the CEO of Amazon.com voiced the same sentiment, almost as if he were reading from the same text:

> We want to be the world's most consumer-centric company. . . . We focus incessantly on trying to get the customer experience right. . . . See, we're not a book company. We're not a music company. We're not a video company. We're not an auctions company. We're a customer company.

You might be wondering why I'm delving into theory and philosophy after all this intoxicating talk about making big money in 24 hours or less. The reason I've been able to earn a large amount of money is because of my relationship with my customers. They trust me. I try not to abuse that trust. When I talk, they listen. This trust has taken me 20 years to establish. I am *customer*-centric, not profit-centric. I want my students to win—to succeed.

As you create your business, your most powerful tool is trust. Abuse that trust for a quick buck and you undermine your long-term business. Your customers will tolerate only so much abuse before they swim off to someone else's pond.

*Theodore Levitt, "Marketing Myopia," *Harvard Business Review,* September–October 1975.

Now that you understand the importance of going deep, you might appreciate the framework of techniques and systems that you can put in place to perpetuate your business. Use Jay Abraham's marketing materials as a primary source; I have created a template in Table 5.1 for you to keep

TABLE 5.1 Summary of Jay Abraham's Marketing System

12 Ways to Increase the Number of Leads	9 Ways to Increase Your Closing Ratio	3 Ways to Decrease Attrition/Increase Retention	6 Ways to Increase Size of Your Average Order	6 Ways to Increase the Frequency of Purchase
1. Referrals	1. Increase selling skills of your entire staff	1. Call inactive customers to get feedback	1. Up-sell and cross sell	1. Develop a back end
2. First order at cost	2. Listen to best books and tapes	2. Give extraordinary service	2. Point-of-purchase promotions	2. Continuous communication
3. Guarantee or risk reversal	3. Model your best salespeople	3. Communicate!	3. Bundling/packaging of complementary products together	3. Endorse other people's products to your list
4. Host/beneficiary relationships	4. Get a sales manager		Increase your prices and enhance your margin	Run special/private/closed-door sales
5. Advertising	5. Go out and get sold—model your competitors		Change the profile of your products to be more upscale	Program your customers; educate them into a long-term buying strategy
6. Direct mail	6. Qualify leads up front		Offer larger units of purchase	Use price/purchase inducements like frequent-flyer miles
7. Telemarketing	7. Make ads specific, not general			
8. Special events and seminars	8. Make irresistible offers			
9. Use qualified lists	9. Educate your customers			
10. USP				
11. Client education				
12. Public relations				

in front of you as you make major marketing decisions. It outlines the following:

12 ways to increase the number of leads

Nine ways to increase your closing ratio

Three ways to increase retention and decrease attrition

Six ways to increase the size of your average order

Six ways to increase the frequency of purchase

Jay is a close friend and personal mentor from whom I have learned an enormous amount about marketing. In an extraordinarily generous move, Jay has made his complete marketing manual available for free over the internet. Go to www.freemarketingbook.com and download this powerful 246-page PDF-format book directly to your hard drive. A thousand people paid $1,000 apiece to get advance copies of this material. You can now have it for free. What a bargain. A lifetime of marketing wisdom in minutes. I highly recommend it.

Join me in the next chapter to learn seven powerful ways to drive traffic to your site.

CHAPTER 6

Netpreneurs, Start Your Search Engines! Six Powerful Ways to Drive Traffic to Your Site

"Ladies and gentlemen, start your companies!"

My friend, Bob Gatchel, has a saying about launching a successful online business:

"It's the marketing, stupid!"

Blunt. But true. It's not about having a fancy Web site. It's about the marketing. It does no good to have a Web page if you're the only one who knows it's there. Nobody is going to stumble onto your site by accident. Unless you do something, nobody is coming to check you out.

There are six major ways to attract people to your site. I've already eliminated buying one-minute spots during the Super Bowl. Not because it's expensive but because it's monumentally stupid. It would be like trying to warm the homeless with bonfires of real money.

We're going to do the smart thing and start on a shoestring. If it works, we'll do more of it. If not, we'll have money left over to try something else. In this chapter we learn six major ways to attract traffic to your lonely site:

1. Building your Web presence
2. Search engines
3. Free and paid ads in the online world
4. Free PR in the online and offline worlds
5. Paid advertising offline
6. Word of mouse

Some of these ways are high-leverage. Some are low-leverage. By *leverage* I mean the ability of your marketing efforts to produce multiple, massive, and residual exposure. If possible, you want the effects of your marketing to reach huge numbers of people, multiple times, over a long period of time. By contrast, some of your marketing activities will reach only a few people one time—and then the message is dead.

I always think more clearly when I have a big-picture representation of the overall task I'm trying to accomplish. Figure 6.1 shows an illustration of the six major lakes of potential customers. Starting with this map, we're going to tap into each of these six lakes of potential prospects to drive traffic to your site.

On the high end of the leverage scale is the use of search engines, because one well-structured placement can be seen by millions of surfers over and over again. On the low end of the leverage scale is handing out your business card to a single person, who might just throw it away.

We'll start with the lowest-leverage option because this is where most people start.

The Importance of Building Your Web Presence

If you're going to play online, then act like your life depended on it. Tell everyone you know about it. Embed your Web address and e-mail address in your offline brochures, on your business cards, in every marketing message, and in every advertisement you place. Put it on a bumper sticker, in greeting cards, and in wedding gifts. Put it on your answering machine message. I mean *everywhere*.

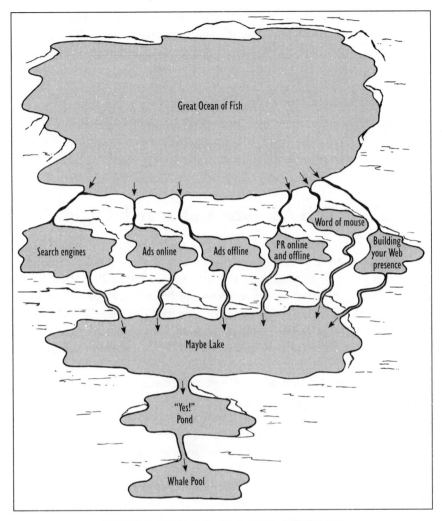

FIGURE 6.1   The six major lakes of highly qualified leads.

Create a signature file to attach to every e-mail that you send. In fact, if you haven't done it already, open up your favorite Web browser and add a marketing message to your e-mail messages right now. Your message should be a short marketing message that directs people to your Web site. Every click counts.

I'm using the Internet Explorer browser, so here is how I add a signature file to my e-mails: Click on Tools, then Options, then Signatures. Compose a message to be added to the end of every e-mail you send.

In addition to these obvious ways of getting your message out, here are five more ways to make your Web presence known.

1. Go to www.usenet.com and join any newsgroups related to your subject. Post messages in appropriate places.

2. Become an opinionated expert at epinions.com

3. Lurk in chat rooms.

4. Participate in bulletin board discussions.

5. Register your freebies at a "free stuff" site. Look around the Net for sites that promote free stuff. Contact these sites and offer some of your own promotional goodies.

Taking Full Advantage of Search Engines

Here is a cardinal rule of marketing: Inbound marketing is much easier than outbound marketing. In other words, it is much easier to make sales when customers are calling you than when you are calling them. Cold calling is hard because you are interrupting people when they are not in the state of mind to buy—they're probably in the state of mind to have dinner. But when customers call you looking for a solution to their problem, they are in the state of mind to buy. They are interrupting you. (Don't you love to be interrupted by a hungry prospect?) It's the difference between reading an ad in a newspaper versus one in the Yellow Pages.

If you're looking in the Yellow Pages, it's most likely because you are actually searching for a solution to your problem. The sale is already made in your mind. You're just shopping for the right price, availability, and relationship.

Which kind of prospect would you like? An angry, interrupted customer or an anxiously seeking customer? Give me the Yellow Pages kind of customer all day long—except for one problem. It costs money and requires a long-term commitment.

Now let's go online. Although there is an actual Yellow Pages online, the traditional form of online searching is through search engines such as Excite and/or directories such as Yahoo!—big companies with big computers will help you search for exactly what you want. The best part is that the vast majority of these searches are free for both parties—the advertiser and the searcher. What a deal!

Suppose you wanted to use the Net to research ways to create traffic to your Web site. Where would you start? First let's research a list of the top search engines. Go to www.goto.com and enter the words "top ten search engines." Scanning down the list of search results, you find a listing similar to the following:

The Major Search Engines and Directories

Summary of the major search engines summarized, with historical background and reasons why each is important to Webmasters or users.

www.searchenginewatch.com

You click on the underlined link and after a few minutes of perusing you find a current list of top search engines and directories in alphabetical order.

AOL Search (for those on AOL)

AltaVista.com

AskJeeves.com

DirectHit.com

Excite.com

FASTSearch.com

Go/Infoseek.com

Google.com

GoTo.com

HotBot.com

IWon.com

LookSmart.com

Lycos.com

NorthernLight.com

RagingSearch.com

RealNames.com

Yahoo.com

WebTop.com

You go down the list and click on the link to Excite.com (because you like the sound of it) and enter the word *traffic* in the search box.

Once again a gargantuan computer scans the entire world and brings back a list of . . . well, as of this writing . . . 2.93 million references to the word *traffic* . . . almost all of them referring to automobile traffic. Nope. That doesn't do us much good. So you refine your search and include the words "Increasing Internet traffic," hoping to narrow the search down a bit. Now there are 9.53 million references!

Here is what happens when you search at some other top search engines:

	Traffic	**Search Words** **Increasing Internet Traffic**
Lycos	10,832,107	163,047
AltaVista	7,554,731	77,603
Northern Light	5,151,479	204,897

Are you beginning to see the problem with search engines? How can you search through a million pages? You can't. So you settle for the first 20 on the list. That leaves millions of other pages out in the dark. If you can figure out a way to be among the top 20 listings, you might attract a traffic jam to your site. If not, it's like finding a needle in the biggest haystack on planet Earth. Impossible.

Still, most research shows that the vast majority of people online begin their searches using one of the top search engines. (See Figure 6.2.)

Here are the facts:

Fact: Over 80 percent of Internet users use search engines to find information.

Fact: A typical search can often generate thousands, if not millions of results.

Fact: Only those Web sites listed in the top 100 will ever see any significant traffic.

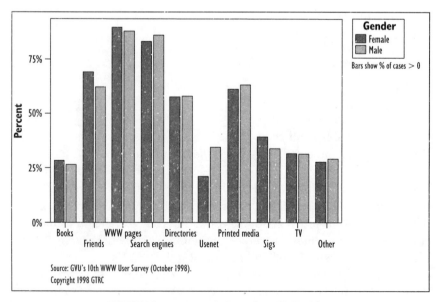

Source: GVU's 10th WWW User Survey (October 1998).
Copyright 1998 GTRC

FIGURE 6.2   How users find out about WWW pages.

Fact: Each day, millions of online businesses are competing for those top 100 spots.

Fact: The odds of little ol' you and me being listed in the top 100 are slim.

Still, there are ways to improve your odds. So you must try . . . if only to understand what the fuss is all about. And who knows, maybe your product, service, or information is unique enough to give you a very rare search engine word that cuts competition to a small number.

Therefore, you have three choices: (1) Do it yourself; (2) hire someone to do it for you; (3) pay for traffic search engines.

Do It Yourself

Surf to the site of every major search engine, read the submission guidelines, and manually submit your Web page and cross your fingers. Before you get started, however, you would do well to check out these three Web sites for tips on how to increase the chances of your success:

www.searchenginewatch.com

www.searchengines.com

www.bruceclay.com

For the do-it-yourselfer, there's an excellent book on the subject by Ken Evoy. It costs about $20. You have to download it from his site at www.sitesell.com. It's exhaustively detailed, and I guarantee that you will learn things you never knew.

If you'd like some software that will help you with your manual submissions, go to www.searchenginecommando.com.

And here's another service to help you track your position on the major search engines: www.wpgold.com.

Frankly, the do-it-yourself approach, although time-consuming, is certainly less expensive and will give you a nuts-and-bolts feel for the inner workings of the Internet.

Hire Someone to Do It for You

If you want to search out a never-ending list of companies that will help you submit your Web page to every search engine and directory in the known universe, just go to any search engine and type in *free search engine submission.* Excite.com lists 1,865 references. You should find plenty of sharp companies in the top 20 to help you. After all, if they have been able to get themselves listed in the top 20 while competing with almost 2,000 companies, they must know something about what they're doing.

Here are three listings that look good to me—but I can't vouch for their effectiveness:

www.submitit.com

www.getsubmitted.com

www.trafficboost.com

Pay-per-Click Search Engines

An excellent alternative to the traditional search engine model is the pay-per-click search engine. The following are top paid search engines:

www.goto.com

www.searchhound.com

In these sites you can bid for the right to be placed in the top 100 keyword positions on a search engine. This puts you much more in control of the listing process. At least you know who your competitors are and can decide to bid up the price of targeted traffic if you think it's worth it.

Go to www.goto.com right now and you'll see what I mean. Type in *free search engine submission* and see the list of the first 40 results. Notice that there is an amount listed in dollars and/or cents to let you know how much the advertisers are paying for you to click on their links and be transported to their sites. If a prospect clicks through and is not impressed, the advertiser is still out the click-through amount, but at least he or she has a more qualified "eyeball" in those who stay. Here are more GoTo listings:

1. Submit a URL to 900+ Search Engines

Search engine registration plans from $19. Let us prepare your site for optimum placement, submit it to 900+ search engines and provide online reporting that allows you to monitor progress.

www.website-submission.com (Cost to advertiser: $0.22)

2. Search Engine Listing Tips

Learn the search engine tricks that will help put you on top! Hints, tips and submission software all in one!

www.homeworkers.org (Cost to advertiser: $0.14)

3. Free Search Engine Submission

Site add makes it free and easy to add your site to the top search engines.

www.siteadd.com (Cost to advertiser: $0.13)

4. Submit Express-Search Engine Submission

URL submission to 40 major search engines in less than two minutes for free!

Also, free analysis of your site to improve rankings when you order our 2500+ submission.

www.submitexpress.com (Cost to advertiser: $0.11)

5. Free Global Spider Download

Free to try before you buy. Submit your site to hundreds of search engines, directories, FFA's and classifieds.

www.globalspider.net (Cost to advertiser: $0.10)

Advertiser-supported searching is definitely a wave that is here to stay. I've asked my friend, Shawn Casey (www.shawncasey.com), to give you a brief description of how the pay-per-click search engines work.

Paying for Traffic

Hi, my name is Shawn Casey and I'd like to show you around the world of pay-for-traffic search engines. In addition to the free search engines like Yahoo!, several search engines allow you to actively bid for positions under search terms. When someone searches for a specific term, the listings show up in the order of highest bidder first, second highest bidder second, and so on. If two companies bid the same amount, the first bid gets priority for the listing and will be listed first.

You pay only when someone clicks on your listing and is delivered to your Web site. The most prominent of these search engines is GoTo.com. Others include Kanoodle.com and RocketLinks.com.

For explanation purposes, I'm going to focus on GoTo because it's the largest and best-developed pay-per-hit search engine. Similar sites have less traffic, but you often pay less because not everyone uses them like GoTo.

GoTo's motto: "It's targeted, cost-per-click advertising and you set the cost per click!"

Two basic concepts apply to using these types of search engines to your best advantage:

1. While you obviously want to pay the least possible amount for each hit you get, you're going to have to bid more if you want a higher listing and, therefore, more traffic. You have to carefully track the traffic you get from the search engine so you know the value of that traffic. If you don't know the value, you could be paying too much for your traffic or missing great opportunities to generate more traffic for a higher price. In other words, let's assume you're selling an item with a $25 profit margin. If 1 percent of visitors to your site buy the product, then each visitor is worth 25 cents to you. If you can draw traffic for less than that, you're making money on each sale.

2. The other concept involves bidding for several hundred keywords at low prices (e.g., a penny apiece). This way you are listed all over the search engine. Each keyword by itself won't bring much traffic, but the total may be 100 or more hits per day. If you're only paying a couple of pennies per hit for this traffic, then it should be profitable for you.

If you search popular words like *business,* you'll find that the cost of being number one is quite high and the position is usually held by larger enterprises such as *Inc.* or *Entrepreneur* magazines. Large companies are often willing to invest millions of dollars in building their brands, so they'll pay more for traffic than it would normally be worth. I strongly suggest you don't compete with them unless you are absolutely sure your business model will justify it.

Often, you'll be able to find a top-10 ranking for a third or less of the price of being number one. Since you're limited to buying only traffic that's profitable for you, this position will probably suit you better. Even if you end up far lower in the rankings, your investment must stay within an appropriately profitable range. You'll probably get less traffic than the number one ranking, but it will be traffic you can make money on. That's far more important.

Here's how to use GoTo. The other search engines will work in a similar fashion.

1. *Create an account with GoTo.*

To start your account, you must register with GoTo and post a balance of $25 or more. Without this account, you can't submit bids. When someone clicks on one of your listings, GoTo will charge the expense against your deposit. When your balance gets low, you simply deposit more money. Since this is a prepaid plan, you have complete control over how and when you spend your money. There's no risk that GoTo will be sending you a large invoice at the end of the month. You spend only as much as you want on advertising.

2. *Determine the value of a visitor to your Web site.*

You can do this for Web site visitors in general or for specific sales promotions in particular. The value may vary by keyword. The simple formula goes like this: Divide the average number of new customers each month (a period long enough to be statistically significant) by the average number of monthly visitors to get the percentage of visitors who actually become customers. If you multiply this percentage times your average profit margin on sales to new customers, you get a good idea of how much a visitor is worth to you on the first visit.

For example: If I average 10,000 visitors per month to my Web site and sell a product with a $20 profit margin to 150 customers, then I can easily calculate the percentage (150/10,000) to be 1.5 percent. Multiplying 1.5 percent by $20 yields $0.30, which is the value of each visitor.

It's interesting to look at the bigger picture of this example as well. While making $0.30 per visitor doesn't seem like much, the dollars grow quickly when you multiply pennies by thousands of visitors. My profits for the month with 150 sales would be $3,000 less advertising costs. If I can generate visitors at $0.10 each, for a total cost of $1,000, then I have a profit of $2,000.

Since, in our example, $0.30 is the maximum value of a customer to the Web site, we'll use $0.30 as the maximum we would bid for any search term. Why would we give up all the profit to get a customer? Presumably, your business plan includes the sales of additional products and services to your newly acquired customers. Even if you break even on the acquisition of these new customers, you should be able to make a profit on additional sales to them. This is why it's important to understand the lifetime value of your customers.

3. *Develop an extended list of keywords for your site.*

Keywords are any terms related to the content of your Web site. You'll want to make this list as extensive as possible. If you are selling computer software, you'd have a list like this:

Computer	Software
Microsoft	Html
Quicken	Games
Corel	C+
Intuit	C++
Spreadsheet	Clip art
Word processor	Excel
Front page	Lotus

Your list will contain a lot of words only marginally related to your site and, often, not high-volume search terms. You want these terms because the bidding for them is usually much lower than for a comparable position under *software.* You'll get less traffic from terms other than *software,* but that traffic can be very profitable for you.

You don't have to pluralize your search terms. The search engines will automatically do this for you when a visitor is searching the terms.

To maximize your success, you'll want to eventually develop a list of at least 1,000 keywords. You don't have to use that many to get started. In fact, you'll probably want to start with 15 or 20 until you get used to the system. To derive the most traffic, however, you need to use as many search terms as possible. If you're wondering how you're going to manage such a huge list, read on for the relatively simple solution.

In fact, this is also how you'll get the least expensive traffic. You'll bid only a penny or two for 90+ percent of your extended list. If you bid a penny on 900 terms and average one hit per term per day, you get 90 hits per day for $0.90. Since you only have to set up the bids once, you can continue to generate traffic like this for quite a while after investing the initial time and effort.

GoTo offers a tool that provides suggested search terms. For instance, if you are checking out *travel*, the system delivers 100 or so related search terms you might want to add to your list.

4. *Develop a title and a description to be used with your keywords.*

When the search engine users get the result of a search, they'll see the highlighted titles for each listing followed by a short description. You should think of this as a classified ad with a headline and short copy.

The keys to your success here are as follows:

- Use an attention-getting headline to get as many people as possible to read the description. You want to be sure to use important, proven, and successful terms like *free* and *you*.

- Write a description that succinctly tells the reader why he or she would be a fool not to click on your link. For most keywords, this is the best plan because you're paying only a penny or two for the click-through. But, you'll want to be more selective about the copy for the more expensive bids. If you're going to pay a quarter for each click-through, then you may want to have higher-quality traffic. You don't want just anyone to click through. You want people who are likely to buy. How do you limit traffic to the higher-quality people? Your description for the expensive bids must provide sufficient information for the reader to determine whether your site/offering/product/service will really be of interest. For example, you wouldn't want to use a teasing phrase (e.g., "learn how to get free software products") when you're paying a lot of money for prospects.

- You can direct each keyword to a separate page on your Web site (although you probably won't want to target 1,000 entry pages), so you'll probably want a separate description for each entry page.

- You should have the ability to track each entry page so you can determine the success ratios of click-throughs to sales. I like to do this for high-priced keywords even though GoTo will allow you to use its own system to track click-throughs. It's nice to be able to double-check your results.

- Test, test, test. You'll take your best shot with your first posting. You should always be testing to see if you can improve the response. Remember, this response can be improved in two ways. The first is by the quantity of click-throughs. The second is the quality of the visitor because higher sales ratios mean greater profitability.

5. *Place your bids.*

GoTo's DirecTraffic Center is the account management tool you'll use to add, modify, or delete your listings. Since this is the Internet, you can use the DirecTraffic Center day or night.

After you've set up your account, you can log in to the DirecTraffic Center. You have two choices of ways to enter your listings. The first method is to manually type in each separate entry. The second method is to create an Excel spreadsheet and simply upload the entries all at once.

Assuming you're starting out with just a few entries, you can manually enter those. In the long run, especially with your list of over 1,000 keywords, you'll want to use the spreadsheet option. Using Excel will allow you to work offline as you enter all of your information into the spreadsheet. Then, you just e-mail the file to GoTo. After a review, GoTo will load the information for you.

If you have the Microsoft Office Standard, you have Excel on your computer. You don't have to figure out how to use the program to create a spreadsheet from scratch. GoTo provides a template that you can download and fill out.

All your keywords and descriptions must be reasonably related to the content of your Web site. GoTo's staff reviews every submission and will refuse listings that are not on topic.

When you submit your spreadsheet with hundreds of search terms, you'll have to do a tremendous amount of research to determine how much to bid for each term. As an easier option, just bid one penny for every term to start. In the next step we'll talk about how easy it is to manage your bids so you can adjust the important ones later.

6. *Reevaluate and adjust your bids.*

At the DirecTraffic Center, you can modify your bids on all your search terms on the fly. If you determine that the traffic generated by a specific keyword is more valuable to you than other keywords, you can go online and immediately raise your bid for that term. You'll instantly increase your traffic.

Sophisticated users of GoTo will even track patterns showing which days and times generate the most sales from GoTo traffic. During this prime time, they will raise their bids to increase traffic. As soon as the slot ends, they will lower their bids to the old levels.

Currently, GoTo searches return 40 listings on the first page. If you're on this page, there's a chance that the searcher will see your listing. Accordingly, your goal is be listed in the top 40 whenever possible.

As you refine your GoTo listings, you'll find yourself jockeying for position on certain pages by raising or lowering your bids by a few cents according to what others are doing. For busy search terms like *travel,* a penny might buy a listing only on page 6, number 203. You're unlikely to get much traffic from this position. You might find that it's worth spending 10 cents to move up to number 75, for example. If you could afford to pay the dime, you'd most likely get a lot more traffic.

Here are the links to some pay-for-traffic search engines:

www.GoTo.com

www.RocketLinks.com

www.Kanoodle.com

That's a brief overview of the pay-for-traffic search engines. I want to thank Shawn Casey (*www.shawncasey.com*) for being our tour guide. Now, let's explore how to buy advertising online.

Free and Paid Ads in the Online World

As a marketer, your goal is to create an online business that is scalable. (I thought I'd drop one of those trendy Internet words to impress you.) *Scalable* means the ability to grow from small to large quickly. The essence of scalable is an old-economy word: *control.*

What if you build a huge business that depends entirely on search engine traffic . . . and someone bumps you off the front page. Poof. There goes your traffic and your business. I don't like the sound of that—do you? No, I want a business where I can control the amount of leads that flow in. That means I need ready access to . . . *an expanding source of hot leads from interested customers at a price that is not exorbitant—hopefully free.*

Search engine traffic, although mostly free, is outside your control. Unless you want to hire a full-time employee or two to constantly fight and jockey for top search engine placement, you'll need to find other sources of leads for your business.

Just as in the offline world, you'll need to advertise. And you'll need to pay money. And this is a problem because the models for effective advertising on the Net are still in flux and probably will be for years to come.

We're just learning what works and what doesn't. For several years, banners were the hot thing until click-through rates dropped. What will be the next hot thing? At present it appears to be the pay-for-traffic search engines. On the horizon are several models where you pay people for reading their e-mail. The following are ways to obtain free or paid advertising online, listed in order of least effectiveness.

Free Classifieds

Have you seen ads on the Net that boast of placing your classified ad on 7,000 Web sites for free? The old adage, "you get what you pay for," certainly holds true in this case. Let's say it's worth a shot (which is what people say just before they plunk down some money for a lottery ticket). That doesn't hide the fact that the odds against winning are astronomical. Just in case you're so inclined, here are three links to free classified ads.

www.buysellbid.com   Millions of fresh classifieds every day. Easy to use.

www.freeclassifiedlinks.com   Free reciprocal-links newsletter that features high-quality Web sites that want to exchange links with you!

www.classifiedclub.com   Links to over 7,000 places on the Web where you can place a classified for free; costs you $29.95 to find out; but probably worth it.

Banner Ads

A *banner* is a rectangular box filled with advertising (and often fancy graphics) that you see displayed as a masthead on many Web pages. Go to www.cnn.com and see which banner ad is running right now in the top center of the page . . . then click on various pages at the CNN site and notice how the banners change. Somebody is paying for those banners, just as people pay for full-page ads in magazines or for commercial spots on TV programs.

The hype about banner ads is that people can quickly click on the banner ad and have their questions answered immediately. The reality is that the click-through rate from banner ads is abysmally low. If you're paying good money, make sure there is a very solid tracking mechanism that enables you to determine the exact cost of a click-through and how many click-throughs result in an actual sale—so you can calculate your advertising cost per sale.

If you search the Web, you see many advertisements for banner exchanges. For a fee, and sometimes for free, you can arrange to have a banner that links to your site placed on dozens, hundreds, and maybe thousands of other Web sites worldwide . . . with the hope that somebody, somewhere will see your banner advertising, click on it, and be transported to your site.

Here are three free-banner-exchange sites.

www.bcentral.com

www.bannerexchange.com

www.bitsonthewire.com

Links to Symbiotic Sites

A close cousin to the banner-exchange concept is to exchange links between your site and other sites with complementary (but hopefully not competing) products or services. A site that sells guitars might link to a site that sells guitar sheet music and vice versa. These links could be free or revenue-sharing, whichever works for your win-win negotiation.

Here is one place where you can learn how to set up link exchanges.

www.linkleads.com

E-Zine Ads

A much more targeted and effective strategy is to buy (or exchange) an advertisement in one of the thousands of regular e-zines that are published on the Net. Here your ad is read by a wide audience interested in your subject generally—similar to a full-page ad in one of the national magazines or newsletters. This can be an extremely good method for creating trackable, scalable, reliable traffic to your Web site.

Here are two directories of major e-zines and how to contact them about buying advertising space in their targeted list of periodic communications.

www.lifestylespub.com   Run a complete, targeted ad campaign for as little as $150.

www.freezineweb.com   Tells how to place a free ad in over 200 e-zines.

If you're trying to find an e-zine on a specific topic, go to www.ezinesearch.com. There will be much more on this strategy in later chapters.

E-Mail Rental Lists

Finally, as in the offline world, it is possible to rent names for targeting your e-mail marketing. The advantage, of course, is that you don't have to pay for postage, which is usually the largest cost of any bricks-and-mortar direct marketer.

One of the leaders in renting e-mail names is www.postmasterdirect .com. Using double opt-in standards (i.e., visitors are asked twice whether they wish to subscribe), Postmaster Direct maintains millions of names and rents them out to various businesses at anywhere from 10 to 30 cents per name. The company handles all of the e-mails, the merge/purge, and the details of the mailing. And you get the result.

Here are a few more choices:

www.bulletmail.com Targeted e-mail campaigns that charge from 15 to 20 cents per e-mail.

www.yesmail.com Major e-mail campaigns that cost 25 cents or more per name.

Free PR in the Online and Offline Worlds

Public relations. PR. Getting your word out to the public. I must credit my ability to generate positive PR to all three of my *New York Times* best-sellers. Getting the word out about a new book starts with a publicity tour—being available to talk to TV, radio, and newspaper representatives. I've appeared on hundreds of shows over the past 20 years. But my most successful PR stunt happened in the early 1980s with my famous challenge to the *Los Angeles Times*. I flew with a reporter to San Francisco, whereupon the reporter took away my wallet, gave me $100 for living expenses, and then proceeded to chronicle how I was able to buy seven properties in the next 57 hours—all with no money down. I guess you could say that I'm sort of the Houdini of the financial world—willing to go to outrageous lengths to prove not only that my ideas work, but that anyone can start with nothing and become financially free. I've been on *Larry King, Good Morning America,* and Regis Philbin's show. Getting word out in front of the public has worked wonders for my book sales.

What is there about you or your business that is newsworthy? Every day, thousands of newspapers, magazines, and radio and TV talk shows must fill up their dead space with content. You need to come up with a newsworthy angle that can put your message out in front of the public. Without question, this is the most powerful and credible way to get your message out there. It is 100 times more effective than any form of advertising—but much more difficult to generate.

Anybody can pick up a telephone, pull out a credit card, and buy a classified ad. But not everyone is willing to jump through the hoops necessary to get noticed by the traditional media. But it's worth it.

Yes, it's hard to get on *Oprah* (I'm still waiting for my first shot), but you'd have to admit that just once is all you need. You might try www.imediafax.com if you want your press release faxed directly to editors and newspeople. Or try the following sources for online PR help:

BY DOING
JUST A LITTLE
EVERY DAY,

I CAN
GRADUALLY
LET THE TASK
COMPLETELY
OVERWHELM ME.

© 1977 by Ashleigh Brilliant (www.ashleighbrilliant.com)

www.xpresspress.com

www.internetwire.com

An excellent article about how to write a press release may be found at the following Web site. There is a copy of it at the end of this chapter.

www.searchengines.com/marketing_cost_press_release.html

Luckily, online publicity is a little easier to get than mainline publicity . . . although the jury is still out about how effective it is. But there is one form of online PR that can be extremely effective. And the price is right, too.

Submit an article to hundreds of online e-zines. In an earlier segment, I introduced you to the power of buying ads in one of the thousands of Internet newsletters called e-zines. Rather than buying an ad, an even more effective strategy is to write an article and offer it for publication. If your article is content-rich and targeted to the right e-zine, it has an excellent chance of being accepted for publication. Of course, you list your contact information at the end of your article so people have a way of contacting you if your information strikes a chord with them. The advantage of this kind of publicity is that it lends enormous credibility to your message. You're not just a paid advertiser. You are a respected expert. The difference can be profound.

In later chapters, I'll show you exactly how to submit your articles for publication in various e-zines.

Paid Advertising in the Bricks-and-Mortar World

Of course, if you own a business that operates offline, it's only natural to want to move your business online. Over 99 percent of the Fortune 1,000 companies have already established an online presence. It would be foolish not to. But what if you own an exclusively online business? Is it smart for a small but growing online business to invest some of its marketing dollars in offline advertising? I'm not referring to buying expensive image-building television ads. The question is, are there ways to effectively advertise your Internet business offline? If you have a fixed budget, should you risk some of that budget in the offline world to drive traffic to your site?

Your answer is determined by two factors: the quality of your message and the potential for finding hungry fish offline.

The Quality of Your Marketing Message

In other words, does your online advertising work? These new dot-com start-ups, flush with IPO cash, blow unconscionable amounts of money on cute, hip promotions that don't attract real customers. When you're starting on a shoestring, you don't have the option of luxurious advertising. Every dollar must produce an increased return on your investment or you're out of business! Experts have often said that one of the greatest causes of small-business failure is running out of money. I disagree. I think that often the cause of small-business failure is too much money— and wasting that money on ineffective marketing. I like marketing that *must* make a profit. It forces you to get real about what you say.

Let me put it this way: Suppose you were down to your last $1,000 and had to buy advertising that would not only return your $1,000, but would produce an extra $1,000 in sales so you could continue to advertise. Suppose the life of your business depended on placing the right kind of ad in the right place—if you succeed, you stay in business; if your ad is a bust, you close the doors. It would focus your thinking, wouldn't it?

Before you make your final decision, don't you think you should do a little free testing first? Place 20 or 30 free classified ads with various headlines to see which one seemed to pull the most leads? Before you rolled the dice, wouldn't you try to refine your offer, add some bonuses, give a great guarantee—and then bounce that message off several thousand people to see if they would be willing to vote with their wallets? Or would you place your last $1,000 and the future of your business in the hands of some kid who just graduated from college with a degree in advertising? Sounds silly, doesn't it? Yet that is what happens every day in millions of businesses.

Before you go spending a dime *anywhere,* you'd better test whether your message works. Start small and ramp up to larger and larger advertising expenditures online as your ads consistently produce a profit.

Maybe *then* you might start the entire process over again in the offline world . . . with paid classifieds in appropriate publications, small ads at first, and then some targeted direct mail. If your advertising money produces a profit, then invest more money. And I emphasize the word *invest.* I'm railing against small-business people who rush into advertising to build market share, worried about other competitors moving in. Face it, you're not Amazon.com. Your company will look a lot better come IPO time if it has real cash flow, real profits, and real business. As my partner, Tom Painter, says,

Keep it small and keep it all.

Finding a School of Hungry Fish in the Offline World

The cardinal rule we learned in Chapter 2 was to start with a hungry school of fish and feed them the bait they are biting on. Where do you find such hungry fish? Start with the Standard Rate & Data Service (SRDS), which offers a multivolume publication (found at most larger libraries) of information about how to advertise in almost every possible advertising medium. I recommend using the library version because getting your own subscription costs hundreds of dollars per year. If you're so inclined, there's a wealth of information at www.srds.com.

Before you spend a dime in advertising, take time to ask yourself some serious questions about your target fish:

What kinds of magazines do they read?

What organizations do they belong to?

What kinds of neighborhoods do they live in?

What newsletters do they subscribe to?

What radio stations do you think they listen to?

Where do they play?

Where do they go to church?

Try to picture your ideal customers. Wander through their houses in your mind and notice what kinds of problems they are grappling with. What kinds of cars do they drive? Where do they shop? What kinds of credit cards do they carry? How would they like to hear about your message? What message would they like to hear? What solution are you providing to improve their lot in life?

Then you can scan through the SRDS volumes and track down the newsletters, the magazines, and the media outlets that might cater to your customers. Get a copy of the newsletters (if they allow advertising); buy a copy of the magazines and look at the ads that compete with your product. Notice the kinds of words they use, the kinds of offers they make, the kinds of hot buttons they push.

Start small. Craft your message as if your life depended on it. Place a small ad and track the results like a wolf tracks a herd of caribou. If your ad produces results, you can increase your budget until you are running full-page ads in every magazine in the country.

Before you reach that stage, you would do well to contact reputable list brokers from the Yellow Pages in your city to find out whether they have lists of prospective customers to whom you could send a targeted mailing for your product or service.

Do the numbers to see whether, after deducting the costs of mailing and assuming a response rate of ½ to 1 percent, you would have a chance of breaking even. Your list broker can help you determine the realistic costs of a direct mail campaign. If the numbers seem reasonable, you'll have to either write a direct mail letter or hire someone to do it for you. An excellent software product that will help you write both online and offline marketing letters is found at www.instantsalesletters.com.

To repeat, start small. Test a few lists. Measure the results and, if warranted, roll out your direct mail campaign to larger and larger numbers.

The Power of Word of Mouse

There are two final concepts in creating massive traffic:

1. Viral marketing

2. Affiliate programs

These concepts are so important to the future of your business that I am going to devote several chapters to them (Chapters 8 and 11). In short, the concept behind word of mouse marketing is to enlist your customers to help you spread your message. In the real world, word of mouth is a potent source of advertising. Online, word of mouse is the most highly leveraged kind of marketing because people can communicate with each other so rapidly. A positive buzz can virtually launch your idea overnight. A negative buzz can kill it instantly. Don't miss the chapters that talk about this subject.

Now, let's review our six strategies for driving traffic to your site.

1. Expanding your Web presence

2. Search engines

3. Online ads

4. Public relations online and offline

5. Offline advertising

6. Word of mouse

Take another look at Figure 6.1. The flow of money starts with the Great Ocean of Fish through six major sources of targeted leads. With your marketing activities you try to attract interested people into your Maybe Lake. Some of these Maybes flow into your Yes Pond by becoming customers. Eventually, a few of these special customers migrate into the Whale Pool and become partners with you in spreading your message.

In the next chapter, we'll focus on six ways to make money from your site.

How to Write a Press Release

A *press release* announces your website to the world. Also known as a *news release*, it should be informative and appealing to reporters and other contacts. State why your company or product or service is beneficial to people. Describe how your site or company was developed. Keep in mind that you are going to send your release to people who have hundreds or thousands of releases to read through. Make your company stand out with a well-written press release.

Your priority is to please the editor/writer. When you write your press release, make sure you consider how your material could catch the editor's eye. Write an untraditional piece; include new angles that make your release stand out from the rest. If possible, find out about the editor or the audience of the magazine or newspaper where they work. Publication is more likely if you appeal to the current interests of the specific publication and the specific editor/writer.

Editors consider the demands of their audience. If your work fails to meet subscriber needs, the story will not be published. Keep your writing timely and be truthful. This will increase your chances of publication.

Going Local: Let's face it, most websites will not get significant attention from large publications on a national or international level. If you have not done anything highly innovative or of interest to the big-time publications . . . you still have a shot at going local. Local and regional publications have a "local boy/girl does good" story and you don't need to be in the realm of rocket science or devising a plan for world peace to get local attention. Personalize your work and, whenever possible, emphasize the local angle, especially for small-town papers. Web, Brick and Mortar: Don't forget to also tell local customers where to find your business off of the Web, whether you have one location or several branches.

Be consistent to gain a good reputation. Mislead your audience and it will backfire. You need to gain trust, so keep your information factual. Once the editor becomes familiar with your company name, he or she will be more inclined to publish your releases in the future. Submit your work on a regular schedule, and if you plan on resubmitting the same story to any another medium, inform the receiving parties. Find out what times are less hectic before you return calls to editors or reporters. Remain in good standing and the rest will take its course.

Let's Do It! How to Write Your Press Release

Lay-out . . .

Press releases should generally be one or two pages in length, double-spaced and typed with 1.5- to 2-inch margins. Use company stationary that includes your logo and slogan, but avoid bright or dark-colored paper. Center the words *News Release* before you begin writing. Under this header, type *Release after:* and the date when you want your information made public. Include an exciting title that reflects the purpose of the release.

At the top of the second page, type *page 2* and follow with your logo and slogan so that the format is similar to the first page. (Leave out the *Release after* and the date that you typed on the first page. Everything else should be the same as your first page.) When your release is completed, type *-30-* or *# # #* (a way of saying *the end*) on the bottom center of the page.

Information to include . . .

Newsworthy information is best presented in the form of an inverted pyramid. This means that the first part of your release should be the key information. Answer the primary questions first, making sure to include any vital *who, what, where, when, why and how* elements. Their order is based on which elements are of greater importance to your particular news release.

Elevator Pitch: Entrepreneurs in Silicon Valley seeking investors talk about the elevator pitch. They imagine being in an elevator with a venture capitalist or angel investor. They have only 5 or 10 floors to explain their business concept and attract the interest of the temporarily captive audience. You can think about the first (and maybe second) paragraphs along the same lines (except you don't have the luxury of a captive editor).

Go straight to the point in the beginning because you hopefully will have time to explain later—that is, you will have time to explain in subsequent paragraphs . . . but only if you pique the interest of the reader in the first paragraph. Begin your release by making the news clear. The main focus of your first section is, "This is what it's all about."

Information that supports or clarifies details in your release comes later, in the second part. Secondary information includes background information or any other details that you need to explain. Because less emphasis is put on this section of the release, get straight to the point and keep it simple. Keep the inverted pyramid format in mind, putting less important information lower in the release.

The last section should include information that closes your release in a smooth but strong way. Don't leave people hanging, but, on the other hand, don't drone on and on. What does your company offer? How might people already be familiar with your company's name? This is the time to establish a connection for people between your website and company name.

What else to include in your press release:

1. Enticing headlines which summarize the material that follows.
2. Follow a problem/solution format in your writing. (Also try comparing and contrasting ideas.)
3. You may want to include photos. Make sure that they are your own or that you have express permission. Make sure that they directly relate to what you are promoting. No stock images! You may also put photos for downloading from your site's press section. Include both black & white and color and a variety of resolution sizes. Magazine and newspapers have varying requirements.

Note: Cover letters aren't necessary unless you want press coverage of a company event.

Where to send your Press Release:

- Appropriate writers @ magazines
- Appropriate writers @ newspapers
- Trade journals in your company's industry
- Print magazines specific to new website announcements
- Online agencies (optional)—they will distribute your release for a cost

Note: If you select an online agency, make sure they are reputable. There are companies that either fail to distribute your release effectively or, even worse, fail to distribute it at all.

Don't assume everyone wants an e-mail. Though it might seem to be the easiest way to send your release, take the time to develop separate contact lists of reporters who prefer e-mail, fax or snail mail (the kind that involves a real stamp and envelope.)

Tips for Your Press Release

- Don't send out mass e-mailings.
- Don't hassle contacts by asking them if they received your release.

- Do the work yourself. Editors won't publish anything sloppy or hard to read.
- Make your news sound like news, not a sales pitch.
- Do research. Send releases only to editors who are likely to be interested.
- Don't be careless. Factual/spelling/grammatical errors make your site and company less credible.
- Only one news release per envelope.
- Mail release by first class if possible.
- Typing your address directly on the envelope is an impressive bonus (versus the use of labels).

Hiring Help for Press Releases

If you choose not to do the writing yourself, you can hire a freelance writer or public relations firm to create your news release. Keep in mind that it's important to thoroughly evaluate whomever you hire. Look in the yellow pages under "Public Relations" to find contacts. Interview candidates and ask to see published samples of their work. Whether or not it's a popular writer or firm, if they aren't getting releases published, they can't help you. See what they can offer you. Look for writers and firms that promise you publication in newspapers or other targeted publications. Not only do they have confidence in their work but they have the connections to get your release to the public.

You have several options when considering a writer. Local reporters not only have the experience of writing for a targeted audience but they can often promise you publication in the newspaper or magazine where they work. Ghostwriters write news releases for you but make it appear as though you wrote it yourself. Other writers will represent your business by being the contact for the media. If you choose the second option, make sure the writer is responsible and familiar with your company.*

*Thanks to the good folks at www.searchengines.com for supplying the previous article on writing press releases. The article can be found at the following Web address: www.searchengines.com/marketing_cost_press_release.html.

CHAPTER 7

Online Mar-Ka-Ching! Six Major Ways to Make Money from Your Site

"Actually, I preferred 'Heaven' too, but then the marketing guys got a hold of it."

Your Web page is the portal through which you will attract multiple streams of income into your life. Some of these streams will be gushers. Some of them will be tiny rivulets—mere trickles of cash flow.

What makes these income streams possible is a steady stream of people. No people, no money. What I said in my previous book about the Internet is truer than ever:

If you want to make money on the Net, having your own Web page is just the beginning. It's like having a billboard in the middle of the Nevada desert . . . if nobody sees it, it's as if it doesn't even exist. It's worthless.

If the three key passwords in real estate are *location, location, location,* then on the Internet, they're *traffic, traffic, traffic.* Your most important task is to drive traffic to your site. If you have no traffic, your site has no value. I repeat: A Web page is nothing. Traffic is everything. By *traffic,* I mean visits by people. The more visits, the more valuable your space.

Think of it this way: Before Las Vegas became the "hot spot" it was nothing but a few lonely buildings in the middle of the desert. Along came gambling and attracted a few people. The casinos needed to attract more people, so they added famous entertainers and glitzy dancing girls. Traffic increased. They offered cheap airfares and inexpensive food. Traffic increased even more. They staged major boxing bouts, and people flew in from all over the world. Traffic increased again. They added a major convention center. Traffic zoomed. Then they added attractions for kids and families. Traffic exploded. With traffic flowing (people circulating) throughout the city, everything else in the city became more valuable . . . the commercial street corners, the office space, the restaurants, the retail stores. Newspaper ads, magazine space, billboards, television and radio spots—all increased in value. However, if the traffic were to stop flowing, the buildings would stand empty, the stores would have no customers, the population would leave. It would become a ghost town.

Your Web site is like an imaginary city in the middle of the desert. If you can attract people to it—traffic—and encourage them to come back again and again and bring their friends, then everything on your site will increase dramatically in value. *You* own all the real estate—the digital property. *You* own the commercial corners, the malls and shopping centers, the residential apartment buildings. *You* own the television stations, the radio stations, the newspapers, and all the billboards on every street corner. Without traffic, all of these assets are worthless. With traffic, *you* can rent out these assets for a fortune! It's all about traffic.*

In Chapter 6 we learned six strategies for building traffic. In this chapter, let me show you how to build an Internet marketing machine—a machine that not only drives traffic to your site but gets people to leave money as they're passing through.

Interested?

Think of your Web page as a convenience store. Joe Customer walks in with the sole purpose of buying a gallon of milk. On his way to the coolers, he grabs a box of donuts. At the cooler, he remembers that he also needs some orange juice. Walking back toward the cash register, he spots

---

*Robert G. Allen, *Multiple Streams of Income* (New York: Wiley, 2000), pp. 253–254.

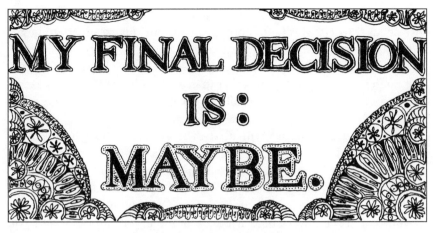

© 1972 by Ashleigh Brilliant (www.ashleighbrilliant.com)

some batteries. At the cash register, he adds some breath mints. He came in to buy one thing and leaves with five items. These impulse buys make up a large percentage of the profit of that store.

Don't forget the main purpose of your site! All of your traffic-generating activities have one purpose in mind—to entice your visitors to sign your guest book and give you permission to contact them again. If you don't accomplish this simple goal, you have failed to build up an asset that will generate your prime source of long-term wealth. I know you want to make money *now,* but before you sign up for a hundred affiliate programs, stop and make sure you have accomplished your most important task. By gathering their e-mail address, you have introduced potential customers into your Maybe Lake—a reservoir of interested-but-not-yet-committed customers.

Once you have obtained permission, you should send an immediate autoresponder e-mail congratulating your prospects on their wise decision and rewarding them with special goodies for reading your first message to them. I call this an *ethical bribe.* You are rewarding them for granting you permission to contact them. In other words, you are paying them for paying attention.

In addition to gathering the e-mail address of every visitor to your site, let's explore the many ways you can induce your Web visitors to leave money. There are at least six main streams of income.

Profit Center 1: The Main Product of Your Site

After you have gleaned permission to continue to communicate with your prospects, the next most important task is to satisfy their primary reason for visiting. Something in your advertisement attracted them. They're interested in your offerings. During this very first visit, you may have only three clicks' worth of time to convince your curious strangers to linger long enough to find something they want.

You should design a first-time buyer's reward—a package of incentives that tip the scales toward a yes rather than a no, as in the Chapter 3 example of discount airline tickets. If all the tickets are priced about the same, I'll go for the one that gives me the extra discount.

What can you come up with that differentiates you from all other options? Could it be a gift certificate for a book or some other valuable premium? Could it be a coupon for a huge discount on a future order? Could it be frequent-flyer miles? Could it be a bundle of free reports? Could it be placing your customer's name in a monthly raffle to win one of your catalog items? Could it be a telephone consultation with you about the customer's area of interest? Could it be free placement of a classified ad in your newsletter or on your Web site?

If possible, try to make the value of your first-time buyer's gift equal to or greater than the value of many of the items in your catalog. Remember, if you treat customers right, they will be back again and again . . . with an increasing volume of purchases. You need to invest in your customers so they'll invest in you.

And that brings us to the second stream of online cash flow from your Web site.

Profit Center 2:
Joining Affiliate Programs

The Web is teeming with affiliate programs, the most famous of which is Amazon.com. The Amazon.com link has been added to hundreds of thousands of Web pages all across the Internet. Each of these links represents a minipartnership between the site owner and Amazon.com. The host site (Amazon.com) agrees to pay the referring site (you) a small fee to provide a link on your site to Amazon.com. If someone clicks on the Amazon.com link on your site and ends up purchasing anything, you will receive a commission for that referral. There are now hundreds of thousands of satellite partners who have an ongoing self-interest in the continuing success of the Amazon.com mother ship.

I start with Amazon.com as an example because this strategy is one of the prime reasons for its incredible growth in gross revenues. The more affiliates the host site has, the better for spreading the message.

Copying this successful strategy are thousands of other businesses marketing a myriad of products, all of which are trying to accomplish the same goal: increased traffic and thus increased business. Eventually, you, too, will want your own affiliate program to market your own products through hundreds or thousands of partnering sites. But before you launch your own affiliate program, you need to experience what it is like to participate in several affiliate programs. In Chapter 11, we will explore how to find and profit from the top affiliate programs on the Net.

Online Affiliate Programs versus Traditional Network Marketing Programs

Similar to affiliate programs are network marketing opportunities. They operate on the same model—a referral fee for steering someone to an existing business. But network marketing has more complicated compensation plans that reward you more extensively for the efforts of people recruited into your organization. Because of this extra layer of complexity and the extra effort required to build and maintain a growing downline, I highly recommend that you participate in only a single, excellent network marketing opportunity.

Both affiliate programs and network marketing companies base their existence on the concept of rewarding people for their positive word-of-mouth advertising.

Have you ever been to a great movie or a great restaurant and told a friend? That's called *word-of-mouth advertising.* Businesses love word-of-mouth advertising because it's more effective than all the money they spend on any other form of advertising, promotion, or marketing. Network marketing is a way for businesses to leverage the power of word-of-mouth advertising.

Let me give you a hypothetical example. Suppose you recommend a great restaurant to your sister. Let's call it Chez Bob. Your sister and her husband make a reservation for dinner, and during the meal, the waiter asks them how they heard about Chez Bob. They mention your name. How would you feel if the owner of the restaurant sent you a thank-you letter and a coupon for a free meal in appreciation for your recommending his restaurant? It would probably make you feel wonderful. The restaurant owner also explains in the letter that because of your recommendation, Chez Bob has gained a new long-term customer. This customer didn't come as a result of a Yellow Pages ad or a radio and newspaper campaign. Therefore, he wants to reward you for this new word-of-mouth customer. Any time your sister visits his restaurant in the future, he will send you a check for 10 percent of the value of the meal as a continuing thank-you.

Sure enough, every several months you receive a small thank-you check. You're so impressed that you encourage others to visit Chez Bob. This generates more free-meal coupons plus more 10 percent word-of-mouth checks. After a year, you are receiving several small checks a month. After several years, you've helped to create dozens of monthly customers that generate hundreds of dollars of extra, no-hassle income to you. That would be nice, wouldn't it?

This is the theory behind *network marketing,* as it is now called. I prefer to call it *relationship marketing* because it is as a result of the relationship that word of mouth derives its power.

Businesses these days spend up to 50 percent of the price of their goods for advertising and marketing expenses. Instead of sending these advertising dollars to wealthy newspapers, magazines, and television stations, several smart businesses have begun to share this money with their best customers. Every time one of their best customers influences someone to buy products, they send this loyal customer a check as a sort of referral fee.

Eventually, these residual income streams flowing from dozens, hundreds, thousands, even tens of thousands of customers can become substantial (as in my personal case). But, as I said earlier, it takes time, dedication, and commitment to build substantial network marketing income streams, so I recommend that you choose only one network marketing opportunity and focus on it until you are successful. While I know of many people who earn income from a variety of associate programs, I know of no one who has successfully built and maintained more than one network marketing business simultaneously. In other words, pick a company and stick with it.

Three Steps to Successful Network Marketing

Step 1. Plant lots of seeds.

It's called the law of the harvest. You reap what you sow. No sow, no reap. Do you want to reap a huge harvest? Then plant huge numbers of seeds. *The more seeds you plant the bigger your harvest.* What are the seeds of your network marketing business? *The prospecting tools of your company.*

Let the tools do the talking. Hand out a tape to people you meet. Send a video to a friend. Give a brochure to a coworker. The prospecting tools will do most of the work for you. But absolutely nothing will happen until you plant the seed.

Try to plant your seeds in fertile soil. Before you hand out any of your company prospecting tools, ask some prequalifying questions.

If you think your prospect is a money person, you simply ask: "Are you interested in making some extra money part-time?"

If your company markets a health product, you simply ask: "How's your health? Would you like to try something that will increase your energy and improve your health in 30 days, guaranteed?"

When prospects say yes to either of these questions, then give them a tape, a video, or a brochure and ask them to read it within 24 hours. Then call them within 24 hours to see what they think.

Step 2. Harvest only fruit that's ripe.

Every person with whom you try to share your message will fall into one of two groups:

Fertile soil   10 percent
Barren soil   90 percent

Nine out of ten people won't be interested in your message. It's not because you are not a good enough salesperson or because your product is not good enough or because the network marketing industry is not good enough. It's simply because they are not interested at this time. Don't be discouraged by their lack of interest. The soil of their life is laced with skepticism and doubt. Spending time with them is generally a waste of your time and theirs. Instead, *seek those who are already sold.*

Here is a powerful quote by Tom "Big Al" Schreiter that I'd like you to memorize.

"Professionals sort. Amateurs convince."

In other words, don't spend time trying to convince skeptical people. (Have you ever met a successful skeptic?) Sort for those who are already interested.

Only a few will be interested immediately. Set an appointment to share your story with them face-to-face. If possible, have your upline there to assist you. If you can't do a face-to-face meeting, arrange to have your upline with you on a three-way call or an online e-mail discussion.

Step 3. Harvest your crops at least seven times.

Suppose you send prospects to your Web site to watch a streaming video about your opportunity. They like what they see and call you to learn more. But after they've heard the complete presentation, some say they're really not interested. What do you do then? Move on? Absolutely not!

Most beginning network marketers have unrealistic expectations. They expect everyone to sign up on the first contact. This rarely happens. Each of us is bombarded with hundreds of advertising messages each day, and advertisers and top sales professionals know that it takes *at least seven contacts* to achieve the maximum harvest. Even the hottest leads today may take several contacts. That's just the nature of the game. So if someone tells you that they are not interested or that they want to think about it, don't take it personally. It's a normal reaction.

Sooner or later, everyone gets interested! **When people tell you they aren't interested, it just means they aren't ripe yet. All it takes is a layoff or a serious illness and they'll go from ice-cold to white-hot in seconds. Remember, your job is to plant the seed and be there to pick the fruit when it's ripe. If prospects say they aren't interested, you need to set the stage for future contacts by saying something like this:**

I realize the timing may not be right for you, but if your job situation is ever in doubt and you need to go into a home-based business fast, this is the ideal home-based business. Little or no start-up capital. Little or no inventory. No long-term leases. No employees. No equipment. You work right from your own home in your underwear if you want. There's nothing like it. And I'll help you every step of the way. So, until that time comes I'll just keep checking with you from time to time.

Or you might say something like this:

None of us appreciates our health until after it's gone. The next time someone close to you has a heart attack or a stroke or is diagnosed with cancer, heart disease or diabetes, ask yourself this question: Am I next? It would be a shame to let your life be cut short by a long, expensive, painful disease that you could easily have prevented! Much better to live a long, vibrant, healthy life with boundless energy. Until you're ready, I'll just keep checking with you from time to time.

A short time later, send another e-mail. Call them on the phone with an exciting new product the company just released. Tell them that the company's stock price just closed at a new high. Just keep contacting them in a friendly way. More than anything, it is your persistent example that convinces people to join you in business. In reality, they are not joining a company . . . they are joining *you*. They are not buying products—they are buying *you*! *You are the product.* If you prove yourself to them by your friendly persistence, they will be impressed enough to take another look. Somewhere between the first look and the seventh look, they'll have no choice but to say yes.

With these three steps in mind, you're ready to start planting and harvesting.

Profit Center 3:
Opening Your Own Bookstore

No matter what your product is, you are ultimately in the education business. Your customers need to be constantly *educated* about the many advantages of doing business with you, *trained* to use your products more effectively, and *taught* how to make never-ending improvement in their lives. Each of your regular e-mail newsletters should be designed to continue the education process. Therefore, each e-zine becomes content that goes into your archives. Each detailed question you answer in your e-mail becomes a template for the Frequently Asked Questions (FAQ) section of your site. Eventually, the content from your FAQs and e-zines will end up as a series of special reports (which can be combined into a full-length book), which you can either sell or offer as a premium bonus in your marketing efforts.

What should you offer in your bookstore? The following four major items:

1. Your own special reports

2. Your own books

3. Resource materials from joint-venture partners

4. Your own selection of traditionally published books

The fastest way to stock your bookstore with books is to become affiliated with a major online bookstore (more on how to do this in Chapter 9). You can display on your site your own private selection of books that pertain to your industry or product line. It stands to reason that if a person is interested in your product line, he or she should also be interested in any related information. Why not profit from this special interest? The disadvantage to this approach is that (1) profits earned from these minor sales will be minimal (3 to 7 percent of the purchase price), and (2) it drives traffic away from your site, perhaps never to return.

A more profitable alternative is to research self-published authors online who have created information content that would be suitable for your visitors and arrange to buy their information products on consignment. The price you can charge for such content is generally higher, with correspondingly higher profit margins, and you don't have to lose the traffic to Amazon.com.

Of course, the highest profit margins are for information products that you create yourself, such as books and special reports. If you plan carefully, a series of special reports can actually be organized into a full-length book.

Dr. Jeffrey Lant, in his impressive book, *How to Make a Whole Lot*

A SMALL PERCENTAGE OF A LARGE POPULATION

CAN STILL BE A LOT OF PEOPLE.

Ashleigh Brilliant

© 1987 by Ashleigh Brilliant (www.ashleighbrilliant.com)

More Than $1,000,000 Writing, Commissioning, Publishing and Selling "How-To" Information, reveals that one of his most powerful profit centers is the creation of five-page special reports. He sells each special report for $6 (three of them for $14). Rarely does anyone order fewer than three at a time. In the back of his book he lists over 100 of these special reports . . . and I defy you to read through the list and not end up wanting a half a dozen for yourself.

What is so incredible about these reports is that they can be created from recycled material such as your FAQs and newsletter articles, thus providing an ongoing cash infusion to your business. Here is what Lant says about profitability.

> Special Reports are very profitable. Because people tend to buy in multiples of three, Special Reports have become a very important profit center for me. No wonder. Consider the cost. Direct costs include the value of my time in creating them (which may mean recycling material from other sources) or getting other specialists to create them for me. . . . Factoring all expenses, including postage, the individual Special Report costs about 45 cents to produce. I sell them for $6 without any problem.*

*Lant, Jeffrey, *How to Make a Whole Lot More than $1,000,000 Writing, Commissioning, Publishing and Selling How-To Information* (Cambridge, MA: JLA Publications, 1993), pp. 184–185.

Of course, Lant's book was written in 1993, before the Internet really exploded. The costs associated with digitally producing and delivering a special report have now been reduced to almost zero!

Lant boasts that he creates 24 to 28 of these five-page special reports per year. (The magic number of five pages keeps the postage down to one first-class stamp.) Each report is personally individualized with the purchaser's name and current date. Another benefit of creating these special reports is the publicity value. To quote Lant again,

> Let me share a secret with you. Special Reports actually have two names. I call them Special Reports when I sell them to individual buyers. And I call them articles when I offer them *without charge* to editors and publishers for immediate publication. Nothing else is different; you need make no changes in the actual title or content for the different markets.

These special reports can become the basis of your PR campaign. Submit them *as is* to newspapers, magazines, and e-zines to help spread your message. Each special report should include a resource box at the end, with details about how to reach you for more information (for a fee, of course). Your special report becomes a sophisticated marketing vehicle.

In time, your resource center can become one of the most profitable profit centers on your entire site.

Now for the next source of site cash.

Profit Center 4: Advertising

In an analogy at the beginning of this chapter, I described how Las Vegas was converted from a desert ghost town into a thriving metropolis because of the traffic flowing through it. Where there is traffic (i.e., *eyeballs*), there is the potential to rent this traffic to other businesses. People want to rent these eyeballs, and other businesses will pay you up front for that privilege. The downside is that these eyeballs may be siphoned off to another part of the online universe, never to return. Of course, your eyeball asset has no value until you have enough eyeballs to make a difference to someone. But with the future in mind, let's explore at least four ways to profit from advertising.

First, let's start with an important policy: Never rent, give, trade, or sell your e-mail names to anyone. Never. Period. And state this in your e-mail acquisition policy. In the offline world, renting a mailing list can be a juicy source of extra revenue. But online, the aversion to spam (unsolicited e-mail) is so intense that you need to make a decision never to violate the goodwill of your "fish in training." This doesn't mean that you can't include a paid ad or two in your periodic newsletter.

Four Ways to Generate Advertising Revenues

1. Selling, renting, or trading banner ads on your Web site.

2. Selling, renting, or trading classified ad space on your Web site.

3. Selling, renting, or trading links from your site to another site.

4. Selling, renting, or trading advertising messages in your periodic e-zines.

We explore exactly how to set up these advertising relationships in Chapter 13.

Profit Center 5:
Selling Picks and Shovels

The fifth major way (there are dozens of minor ways) to earn income from your site is to profit from other people who are coming online. It has been widely reported that the only people who made any lasting money in the California and Alaska gold rushes were the people who supplied the picks and shovels and auxiliary services to the miners themselves. Surviving to this day is one of the most famous "pick-and-shovel coups," Levi's jeans. As an addendum to the Levi Strauss story from earlier in this book, it's instructive to note that Levi's are the only type of clothing created in the nineteenth century that is still being worn today. (I have several pairs hanging in my closet. Don't you?)

Hundreds of millions of new Netpreneurs will join the online gold rush in the next decade. As in previous gold rushes, the majority will be disappointed in their prospecting. Not because there isn't gold in them thar hills but because these prospectors simply don't know how to go about finding it. That's where you come in. You can provide the picks and shovels for them.

What are the picks and shovels of the Internet?

1. Web-hosting services

2. Web site design and consultation

3. Marketing advice

4. Traffic

5. Education and training

6. Advertising services

7. Affiliate programs to help new businesses get started

8. Computer hardware

9. Computer software

10. Credit card services

And many more. Just think of the kind of products, services, and information that it took and continues to take for you to get up to speed in your online business. You can provide the products, services, and answers to hundreds if not thousands of prospective miners. Why not profit from your education in the school of hard knocks? Read more on this in Chapter 14.

Profit Center 6:
Establishing Your Own Auction

Have you ever bought something at an auction? What is there about auctions that is so seductive? Answer: It is a perfect formula for creating a feeding frenzy!

Popularity + scarcity + urgency + curiosity = feeding frenzy

The auction model applied to the Internet is one of those rare business ideas that looks, in retrospect, to be a stroke of pure genius: When millions of people focus on a single item for a limited time frame, those who wouldn't even consider buying such an item in an ordinary department store fight with total strangers to outbid each other over the Internet.

Why shouldn't you participate? Don't you have some stuff in your possession or in your business inventory that would be perfect for an auction? Here are the three major benefits of setting up your own auction:

1. It can generate extra income for you.
2. It's a great way to advertise your Web site and expose more people to your ongoing business.
3. It's the hip thing to do.

We go into more detail on exactly how to set up your own auction in Chapter 15.

Summary

These six ways of creating cash flow will take time, effort, and investment to incorporate into your Web site, but they could become powerful ways of creating multiple streams of income for you. In the following chapters we will explore each in more detail with the goal of not just learning what to do but actually doing it.

An Excellent Example

For an excellent example of a Web site that combines all six sources of continuing cash flow, I point you toward www.datingdating.com. Roam around this site to see if you can spot all six sources of cash flow to the site owners. You may not be in the market for a dating service, but you would do well to emulate much of what you find on this site. In the far bottom right-hand corner of the site you'll see this link:

DATING B2B

When you click on it, you get a page that lists the following information.

Whether you are building or maintaining your own dating service or you are considering making money as an affiliate of a dating service, Dating B2B is here to help you with promotional ideas, additional content suggestions and services to help you add "stickiness" to your dating service web site so you can increase your traffic and make more money!

- ❏ PROMOTIONAL IDEAS
- ❏ EXIT TRAFFIC REVENUE GENERATORS
- ❏ DATING SERVICE AFFILIATE PROGRAMS
- ❏ HTML AND JAVA TIPS
- ❏ BANNER EXCHANGES
- ❏ CLASSIFIED AD SITES
- ❏ WEBMASTERS FORUM

The staff of Dating B2B has personally reviewed more than 1,400 online dating services and found many to be lacking originality, content and traffic. We have a good working relationship with most dating service affiliate program owners and have found that unfortunately they do not offer the resources needed to help their affiliates build traffic and make money. By bringing our suggested tips and techniques to you, and allowing you access to otherwise unknown methods of increasing your traffic, your web site traffic will be able to grow and your revenue to skyrocket using the tips and techniques made available here.

The index on this page lists several links to help subscribers build their businesses. Not only is this a rich source of information, it is an excellent way to help site visitors make money.

INDEX

- ❏ PROMOTIONAL TECHNIQUES
- ❏ CONTENT IDEAS FOR YOUR SERVICE
- ❏ FRIENDLY SERVICES YOU NEED
- ❏ AFFILIATE PROGRAMS TO MAKE $$$

❑ ADD REVENUE STREAMS WITH CONTENT AND BY OFFERING ADVERTISING OPPORTUNITIES

❑ HTML AND JAVA TIPS AND TRICKS

❑ FORUM FOR WEBMASTERS TO DISCUSS ISSUES AND IDEAS

When you click on the Add Revenue Streams link, you get the following page.

Helping Webmasters Everywhere Promote, Add Content, and Build a Better Dating Service!

JOIN AFFILIATE PROGRAMS FOR REVENUE AND ADD MONEYMAKING PROGRAMS WITH CONTENT AND BY OFFERING ADVERTISING OPPORTUNITIES

CONTENT AND ADVERTISING = REVENUE

ACCEPT BANNER ADVERTISING   BOOKS AND VIDEOS   TRIVIA GAMES
ONLINE STORES AND CONTESTS

INTERNET SEARCH ENGINES   FREE GREETING CARDS   CONTESTS

You cannot expect to be the master of everything; your web site will keep you busy enough. Here we will look at ways to increase web site revenue with advertising, content possibilities and "stickiness" for your dating service that will not strain your time or finances. As an added bonus, these ideas will be excellent revenue generators for **EXIT TRAFFIC** areas.

Accept Banner Advertising

This can be as easy as posting a link on your site that says "Advertise Here!" with directions on how to contact you for weekly or monthly advertising periods or as complicated to setting up a **CGI** and **PERL** script that will allow you to post and track banner impressions that you sell on your web site by the 1,000 views (**CPM—Click Per Thousand**). The easiest solution is to outsource the sales of banner advertising using your site traffic to gain membership with one of the larger media clearinghouses that sells space on web sites to advertisers. This will usually guarantee you an income from banner clickthroughs and may offer the possibility of substituting a banner of your own for unsold periods of banner impressions on your web site.

Services

Engage Media (Flycast)

You will need a minimum amount of page views per month to become a member of the Engage Media Advertising Network, at least 30,000 per month. What you get is a high quality of advertising from well-established Internet sites that will make you money for each click your visitors make. Also includes an exclusive Valet Shopping area for extra revenue.

Burst Media

Burst Media works well with a variety of web sites and can work well for you. They have experience with dating services and offer much in the way of flexibility for the banners you show. You can select your advertisers and find great revenue potential here. You must have at least 5,000 page views per month. Look at the Burst!Mail option for your opt-in email newsletters. Another great way to add revenue to your service.

DoubleClick

Featuring a variety of solutions for banner ad revenue for your web site, DoubleClick can provide the resources you need to make this work for you. You do need to have 1,000,000 page views per month to become a publisher with the DoubleClick Network, but less page views will be allowed into the DoubleClick Select network. Visit them and request information on becoming a publisher.

Links to CGI Scripts

SuperScripts—A complete Banner Rotating script is just one of the many CGI scripts available for purchase here. You can allow for advertisers to access their own banner accounts in real time and you have full control over the sales and status of accounts, whether counting banner impressions or banner sales by time period. You get free support with the purchase of a SuperScript membership (includes all scripts!) and learn the ins and outs of CGI scripting whether you are a "newbie" or professional programmer extending your knowledge base.

See the *HTML and JAVA Tips and Tricks Page* for links to these and other resources.

Books and Video

One of the easiest ways to increase your site revenue is to have a select choice of books and videos available for purchase at your site. Whether romance-related or popular-selling items, this can be an excellent area to add content, integrate into polls and forum discussions, and build into a heavily trafficked area that earns you money by finding the impulse buyer in each of us. Works well as an EXIT TRAFFIC area too! When your members click on the "logout" button, send them to your book or video page.

Services
Amazon.com
The World's Largest Bookstore can help you easily earn revenue with their wide assortment of books, videos, toys, computer hardware and software tools. The list goes on.

Barnes & Noble
Books, videos, computer software and hardware, isn't competition great? You can make a great commission on every product you sell and construct the areas that fit in well with your site ideas. This affiliate program is not to be overlooked.

Trivia Games
Everyone knows a little about something. Here is the way you can have your visitors prove it and have fun doing it. It can become a great entry point for forums and chat areas of your web site, as well as a great EXIT TRAFFIC page.

Services
Uproar.com
The biggest is the best here. Join forces with Uproar.com and offer versions of their popular Trivia Blitz games on your web site. Copy and paste a fragment of code and earn revenue every time a new member plays and signs up to win prizes. If only everything could be this easy. This type of service can work well as an EXIT TRAFFIC destination as well as a integral part of your site.

Online Stores and Contest Programs
Build your own store with selected merchants of your choosing and earn commissions with every sale or visitor sent. Begin promoting specific contests that are available and draw traffic to a new revenue generator every day! Some merchants will allow you to place individual products instead of links to their main store. I recommend this type of affiliate merchant program because you can customize it better for your site and visitor needs. This works well as an EXIT TRAFFIC plan as well.

Services
bCentral—Part of the **MSN** Network
   A large collection of pay-per-lead and pay-per-sale affiliate programs.
clickXchange
   Good collection of assorted affiliate programs. Many pay less than programs at larger affiliate program centers, but the best range of pay-per-click advertisers can be found here.
   Commission Junction is one of the largest affiliate program

administrators online. Choose from hundreds of merchants offering a wide variety of pay-per-click, pay-per-lead, and pay-per-sale programs.

A leader in affiliate marketing programs, LinkShare will bring your affiliate program choices to include everything from individual product listings to complete storefronts you can integrate into your web site.

Reporting.net

A great assortment of merchants, many offering individual products and storefronts that you can work into your web site.

WebSponsors

If you are considering offering a freebie page, this is the place to find products and offers for it. Updated regularly, and more important, regular checks mailed out; become an affiliate here.

OnResponse

Mostly working with pay-per-lead advertisers, you will profit more with these programs. Many pay U.S. $1.00 and higher when your visitor signs up for these advertisers' offers, including product samples, free trials, sweepstakes, and a variety of other offers.

Internet Search Engines

Many will offer affiliate programs based on searches performed at your site. This works well with a good EXIT TRAFFIC plan. Revenues from these types of programs can be small unless designed to fit in well with your site and you have lots of traffic.

Services

GoTo.com—Place the search engine form on your site and make money with each search performed. Fixed payment amounts. Search keywords or shopping areas, lots of flexibility here, more than just a search engine form is available here.

7Search.com—Place the search engine form on your web site and make money with each search performed. Commissions variable.

AltaVista.com—Place the search code on your site and earn money with each search performed.

Free Greeting Cards

By offering a Free Greeting Card Service on your web site, you not only provide a great service, you have very little work to accomplish this if you use an affiliate program to provide the service on your site. Of course, you could design and host the service yourself using CGI and PERL scripts to be an original Free Greeting Card Service. The choice is yours.

Services

www.All-Yours.net—Offer free greeting cards by adding links to your web site. Some customization is required; you'll need to create your own Post Office page for sending and picking up the greeting cards. Overall, you get twice the traffic from using greeting cards at your site. One visit by the sender, one by the person receiving the card. This is a great traffic builder.

Contests

Offering easy ways for your visitors to win cash, trips, cars, and other prizes works well. You can include prize details in your newsletters, post it all over your web site and your visitors will come back repeatedly to see what the next contest is that they can play. Rotate contest offers regularly and maybe have just a sweepstakes page that always has changing offers on it. You'll do well with this. Also works well as an **EXIT TRAFFIC** destination page.

Services

Always fresh contests and promotions, you can design great activities around the SpeedyClick program and add a reason for returning to your site day after day.

Links

See the *ONLINE STORES* information above to find contest and sweepstakes affiliate programs to join and promote on your site.

If you discover, in your surfing, a site that best illustrates all six major ways of generating revenue, please e-mail a link to that page to webmaster @robertallen.com. I'll list the winners of the CashFlow Kings award on my site for all to see.

Well, enough theory. It's time to go to the next step. Join me in the next chapter.

CHAPTER 8

Beyond Stickiness:
Nine Magnetic Ways to Keep
'em Coming Back for More

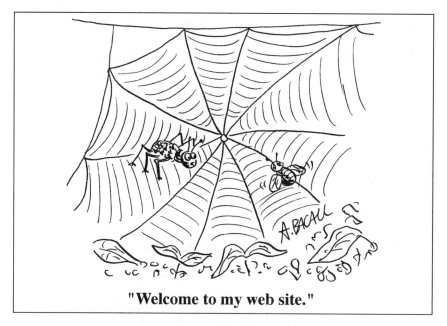

"Welcome to my web site."

You have three seconds. Snap. Snap. Snap. And they're gone. How can you get your visitors to linger longer?

The technical Internet word for enticing surfers to hang around your Web page is *stickiness*. Stickiness is usually associated with three factors:

1. *Duration:* How long do your visitors spend at your site?

2. *Depth:* How deep will they go exploring?

3. *Frequency:* How often do your visitors return?

Big companies spend millions of dollars trying to increase the stickiness of their sites. Every month, Internet tracking company Media Metrics produces fancy statistics to show which sites won the battle of stickiness. The information is free and available at www.mediametrics.com. (Another great site for Internet statistics is www.forrester.com. Especially interesting is its list of the top e-commerce sites called the PowerRankings™.) Study the sample chart shown in Figure 8.1.

In the month shown (August 2000), the average bingo player at bingo.com spent over 500 minutes (that's over eight hours!) playing bingo. The site passed all three tests for stickiness: duration, depth, and frequency. The reason the monster Internet sites like Yahoo!, eBay, and CNN are so interested in stickiness is that their primary model for making money is to sell advertising. They want to show advertisers how many sticky eyeballs are roaming around their site. These advertisers know that the longer those eyeballs ogle the pages, the greater the chance of someone clicking on their banner ads. That's why the monster Web sites are all hot and bothered about increasing their stickiness.

In roaming around one of the stickiest sites, eBay, I stumbled across this quote about stickiness:

> But what exactly makes a site sticky? Doug McFarland, Senior Vice President and General Manager of Media Metrix explains that those mastering stickiness, offer a "mix of the four C's: community, content, communication and commerce." And of the mix, content appears to be the most

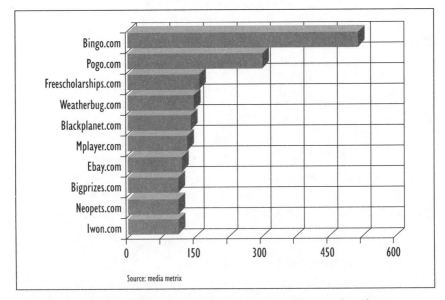

Source: media metrix

FIGURE 8.1   Top 10 stickiest sites in August 2000 total digital media universe—1,167.9 average minutes spent.

important factor. Forrester Research's Media Field Study for January 1999 reveals 75% of users return to their favorite sites for the strong content and a regular churn of information.

This sounds reasonable, but don't get too stuck on all of this talk about stickiness. If you're just launching a Web page, you won't be able to sell advertising space until your Web site has tens of thousands of hits per month. Your primary goal is not advertising. It's to be able to produce immediate (if not sooner) cash flow from the sale of products and services.

You don't have the time or the money to develop a sticky site. Therefore, you're not so concerned with stickiness—how long your visitors stay, how deep they go, and how many times they come back. You are primarily concerned with *quickness*—the speed at which people agree to give you their e-mail addresses. If they'll give you permission to communicate with them, then *you are in control of the stickiness!* You have all the time in the world to educate them via e-mail about the wonders of your site. If you don't get that e-mail address—poof! They're gone.

Stickiness is for big companies. Don't try to be the big guns. Their model is to cast a wide net and invite millions of people to stick to them. Their information is an inch deep and a mile wide. You can't compete with that. You have to do just the opposite: Your information or products should be an inch wide and a mile deep. Become an expert on a very narrow topic. You don't need millions of visitors to make your millions. Of the hundreds of millions of people on the Net, you need to convince only 10,000 highly targeted people to give you permission to develop a relationship with them. Those 10,000 people will make you rich.

Why? Because 70 percent of those who use the Internet do so primarily to access their e-mail, not to surf. If you can get permission to send e-mail messages to them, they may never again need to visit your site. It's not about getting their eyeballs to travel to your site. It's about getting their eyeballs focused on your e-mail messages. Those are the kinds of eyeballs you want!

Ultimate Advantages of the Internet

In reality, the concept of stickiness actually runs counter to the advantages of the Internet. When you think of the Internet, don't you think of speed? What people really want from the Internet is fast solutions to their problems. Do you really want the kind of customer who looks forward to spending several hours a week playing bingo online? (Get a life!) The kind of customers you're looking for don't want a sticky experience. They want fast results, immediate delivery, and instant gratification, mixed with some one-on-one interactivity. Fast. Free. Frequent. Hot tips. If you build your business around these advantages, you'll have all the business that you can handle.

"Quick"-iness versus Stickiness

Eventually, you will seek to add stickiness to your site. But at first you're most concerned with "quick"-iness, the speed at which people agree to give you their e-mail addresses. Here are nine ways to improve the "quick"-iness and the stickiness of your site.

Become an Expert
on Instant Gratification

In all of your marketing you should offer people an ethical bribe (a special report or some other goodie) to persuade them to take a peek at your site. When people hit your site, you only have three to five seconds to get them to stick. So you'd better make sure that the promised "free bonus" is immediately accessible. Spend a few short, enticing sentences reselling them on the value of your free gift. The more they sense the value of the gift you are offering them, the more you tap into the power of reciprocity. They feel they owe you a few extra seconds to repay you for your generosity. Nothing wrong with that. We're all used to it. In fact, most of us sit through commercials to repay the broadcaster for providing such wonderful free TV programming.

Remember, your first and most important task is to entice your visitors to leave their e-mail address and give you permission to contact them again. The more valuable your free gift, the less resistant they will be to leaving their e-mail address.

Designing Your Irresistible Bundle of Goodies

Everything on your site should point toward the bundle of goodies your visitors receive for leaving their e-mail address and their permission to let you contact them again. When these maybes leave their e-mail address, you begin to stock your Maybe Lake. It is critical to the long-term survival of your online business.

In order to entice them to leave their e-mail address you must design a "welcome" basket filled with all kinds of wonderful free goodies. They should feel that they are completely crazy not to take advantage of your generosity. You want to access their greed button. Here are a few things you could offer your visitors for the privilege of giving you permission to prove what a peach of a person you are:

Welcome Basket of Goodies

- Free newsletter
- Free special reports
- Free book
- Free coupons

- Free access to private information vault
- Free checklists
- Free quotes
- Free samples
- Free access to past newsletters
- Free links to other great sites
- Anything else you can think of

Your goal is to instantly gratify your guests. If they sign up for your newsletter, send them an instant e-mail by autoresponder confirming their brilliant decision. Then reward them again! Give them another free gift. If they purchase a product, instantly surprise them with a first-time-customer gift. When they receive their product, reward them again for their wise decision. Keep rewarding them for investing their precious time with you. This generosity will pay huge dividends.

Transform Your Site into a Treasure Trove

Visitors to your site should feel as though they just stumbled onto Ali Baba's cave of treasures. "Open, Sesame," and the cave opens. They are free to pick through the jewels of wisdom that you have assembled there for them. From the first day you launch your site, you should be on the lookout for relevant chunks of information that you can load onto your site for the benefit of your visitors. Most of your visitors are in a Yellow Pages kind of searching mood, so your information will be welcomed. Give your visitors a good reason to add your site to their "favorites" list—and to tell others about their good fortune in finding you. If you are stingy with your free information, your visitors will be stingy with their pocketbooks and their recommendations.

Fresh and Deep

There are two kinds of information that your visitors will seek: (1) fresh, new, hot information—to keep them coming back for more—and (2) in-depth, timeless information. The more you offer of both, the stickier your site will become.

Give Your Visitors a Rich Experience

Once you know that your marketing is working and that you are able to attract a steady stream of visitors and are gradually stocking your Maybe Lake, then you can add some extra features to your site.

Quote of the day. People love quotes. A new quote of the day would be very easy to program into your site. The wisdom of the ages can lend credibility to your offerings.

Joke/cartoon of the day. Everyone loves a good laugh. With a little research you should be able to gather an archive of good, clean humor to fit into the overall theme of your business.

Hall of fame for success stories. People love to see their name in lights. Actively gather success stories of people benefiting from your products and services. It not only builds credibility, it gives your customers an excuse to send other people to your site. Make a big deal of your satisfied customers and they will make a big deal of you.

Useful links to journalistic magazines and news sources. At first these links can be offered as a convenient listing of reputable news and information sources. Eventually, as your traffic grows, these links might even become paid advertising links, as in the following example from *Red Herring* magazine at www.redherring.com:

Sponsored Links

Guru.com	Overworked? Need an expert to help on your project? Get a guru today!
Headhunter.net	Search over 250,000 jobs and 10,000 employers at Headhunter.net.
University of Phoenix	Earn an advanced degree at the University of Phoenix online.
OAG Frequent Flyer Update	The business traveler's secret weapon. It's free!
Hubstorm	Launch your net market in NO time!
Vault.com	Find that killer job! Post your resume and win DVD players or cameras.
DLJdirect	A premier online brokerage firm. Join now and receive 100!
National Discount Brokers	No minimum account balance required! Apply now!
Cruel World	An e-mail-based recruiting service targeting passive job seekers.
Silicon Investor	Lifetime membership ($200 value) for only $49.95.

Provide an Easy Way for Visitors to Recommend Your Site to Others

A growing list of companies on the Internet offer plug-in tools to make it easy for people to instantly recommend your site to their list of friends—while they are actually visiting your site. Your visitors simply click on a convenient button and up pops an instant message box ready to shoot off a recommendation to a friend or an associate.

That's why your site needs the "wow" factor—not fancy flash graphics but fabulous, in-depth, free content. Here are two possibilities for you to check out:

www.recommend-it.com

www.letemknow.com

Recommend-it.com automatically enters the person making the recommendation into a drawing for a $10,000 cash prize. The downside is that it also encourages that person to sign up for one of several opt-in free newsletters. Letemknow.com is a little less intrusive. Check out both these sites for yourself.

Search Engine Plug-In

Several major search engines provide an affiliate program that allows you to include a search engine feature on your site. GoTo.com has an excellent program to add functionality and usefulness to your site. You also earn 0.03 cents for every click-through. The GoTo.com search box is shown in Figure 8.2. It fits nicely on your Web page, ready for your visitors to access.

FIGURE 8.2 GoTo.com search box.

Make Your E-Mail Communications Valuable but Not Too Valuable

As the barrage of e-mail communications (e-zines, tip of the week, etc.) escalates it is absolutely critical that you differentiate your e-mails from all the others cramming your customers' e-mail boxes. It may take several messages before they learn to distinguish your messages from the other e-mail noise. How can you make your brand stand out? Here are some ways to differentiate your messages:

> *Be brief but valuable.* You want to make your message valuable enough to induce people to read it immediately, yet short enough so they don't save it to study later. If they save it they will probably never read it.

> *Reward people for reading your e-mails.* Reward those who take the time to read your message immediately. These rewards could be a coupon for a future discount or a hot tip about some free information that you've uncovered especially for them. You could offer a special surprise from time to time.

> *Add a human touch.* You could also make your e-mail messages valuable by including a humorous segment, a great quote, a useful idea or tip, a super bargain, a moneymaking idea, and something personal to humanize your messages.

Your goal is for your subscribers to anticipate your e-mails . . . to hunger when they haven't heard from you in a while. This subtle reward process will make your e-mails a welcome event rather than an annoyance. You are building your brand awareness in your new subscribers' minds. When they think of you, you want them to be thinking, "Oh, goodie!" instead of "Oh, no, not them again!"

Marketing expert Jeff Paul explains the marketing process eloquently:

> My definition of marketing is setting up automatic, repeatable systems that create the environment where people want to buy from you instead of you having to sell them.
>
> The basic marketing model is lead generation. Get people to raise their hands. Then you've got to repetitively, continuously, never-endingly, unceasingly, dependably, predictably, naggingly, and annoyingly follow up with those people, follow up with those people, and follow up with those people. Unfortunately, most businesspeople just won't do that. They will not follow up with leads and they will not follow up with customers. And the amount of money that they cost themselves is enough to buy a few vacation homes and retire ten years early. The craziest thing is to go out and find new people when you've got all these interested leads that will eventually do business with you.

Get Permission to Gather More Information to Serve Visitors Faster

The sites that are the most valuable to me are the ones that have earned my trust to the degree that I'm willing to give them deeper levels of personal information. For instance, my bank, my Quicken files, and my E*Trade account have all asked me to fill out in-depth personal profiles. Because they are a vital part of my business, I'm happy to do so. Having once invested time in creating a file of personal information, I am extremely hesitant to leave and start all over again with another online service provider. Knowing this, companies like E*Trade are willing to offer people a bribe of up to $75 just to sign up. Once a company has you in its Web, you usually stay there.

Amazon.com has the right idea with their one-click shopping. Why take the extra 60 seconds to buy a book elsewhere when you can buy it from Amazon with one click of your mouse?

Any amount of personalization will make your site stickier.

Design a Frequent-Visitor/Purchaser Program

Who hasn't heard of frequent-flyer miles? They work. They create brand loyalty—or, to use a new-economy word, *stickiness.* By rewarding your most loyal customers with accumulating rewards, you increase the chance that they will come back again and again. They have something to lose if they don't come back.

One online leader in this industry is Netcentives, found at www.netcentives.com. Through its ClickRewards program it has pioneered a way to reward your customers for their loyalty. Here is what its Web site says about the program:

> Online customers want to be rewarded for their loyalty. With so many choices available, who can blame them?
>
> ClickRewards is the only Web loyalty program to reward customers with ClickMiles™, a digital currency redeemable for frequent flyer miles, hotel stays, car rentals and merchandise. Customers simply make purchases or other transactions on a ClickRewards merchant site, and immediately start accumulating ClickMiles.
>
> By creating a powerful promotional network of the Web's top merchants, including E*Trade, barnesandnoble.com and Gap Online, ClickRewards turns curious visitors into buyers and buyers into loyal customers. Member customers make a point of shopping with ClickRewards merchants because they know their patronage is valued.

Merchant implementation is easy. The ClickRewards account team helps market, promote and manage the rewards program, making it the easiest, most cost-effective relationship marketing tool available online.

Your growing business may not yet be large enough to take advantage of such a program, but you should at least model what they're doing. It's obviously working.

Reduce the Distance between Your Visitors and a Live Person

The more and the faster your visitors can interact with real people, the stickier and "quickier" your site will become. This plays to the strengths of the Internet—speed and interactivity. If you can connect with your customers during their feeding frenzy, the more likely you are to make the sale. Unfortunately, this may go against the nature of the ideal hands-off, money-while-you-sleep kind of business that you'd like to create. As you design your business, you'll have to balance these two competing demands. Do you want to make money fast? Or do you want to make money without hassle? I'll bet you answered *both,* didn't you?

Get People Together and They'll Reward You for It

As your site grows, you will attract like-minded people; by default, you can become the central meeting point of a virtual community. Arthur Armstrong, author of *Net Gain,* has this to say:

> Virtual communities are groups of people who share common interests and needs who come together on-line. Most are drawn by the opportunity to share a sense of community with like-minded people—regardless of where they live. But virtual communities are more than just a social phenomena: what starts off being a group drawn together by common interests ends up being a group with a critical mass of purchasing power—based in part on the fact that in communities, members can exchange information with each other on such things as a product's price and quality.*

One of the leaders in creating the software for running virtual communities is InfoPop, found on the Net at www.infopop.com. You can actually download and test a working version of its product for free. It's called the Ultimate Bulletin Board. InfoPop's Web site describes some of the advan-

*Arthur Armstrong, *Net Gain* (Cambridge, MA: Harvard Business School Press).

tages of installing a bulletin board on your site. If done properly, it can be a win-win situation for everyone.

For Consumers

- Introduces others like themselves
- Creates an instantly accessible marketplace
- Fosters an open user forum and knowledge base
- Reinforces purchase decisions
- Concentrates group buying power—auctions, surplus
- Answers service and support questions
- Overcomes buyer objections
- Shares product-usage tips

For Sponsors and Marketers

- Grants insights into buying public
- Concentrates economic focus—auctions, surplus
- Rapidly expands user base through "word-of-mouse"
- Heightens brand awareness
- Generates offer strategies and value propositions
- Pretests new product development
- Assembles an instant focus group
- Generates content
- Builds more meaningful service relationships
- Engenders user-to-user product support

Gateway to the Next Generation of Marketing

- The ultimate realization of target marketing
- Forms in stand market of your affinity group
- Gains more personal information
- Tests ideas and creates a value proposition
- Lets your customers create your advertising
- Relationship marketing, pure and simple
- No postage stamps
- No lost mail
- No spam!

Community—The Key to Web Prosperity

- Message board to attract and retain community
- Visitors free to express themselves
- Collaborative conversations over time
- Greater Web site stickiness (duration of stay)
- An essential forum for user communication

There's a downside to building a virtual community: If your service isn't up to par, there is a forum for your customers to complain to each other and spread the word even faster. Before you build your community you'd better make sure that you build up your customer service.

Now we've come to the final item on our stickiness/quickiness checklist. I've placed it last because its nature is fundamentally different from the others. The first eight points have to do with making your site addictive—creating reasons for people to buy now and in the future, again and again. The final item has to do with making your site contagious—creating a buzz that spreads like wildfire.

Study the Laws of Epidemics and the Principles of Contagiousness

How can you create an explosion of traffic at your site? No amount of advertising can create word-of-mouse power. But you can help it get started. The Internet term for this phenomenon is *viral marketing.*

The term was actually coined by the venture capital firm of Draper Fisher Jurvetson to describe the phenomenon of a company it funded in 1996 called Hotmail. Aside from having a great name, Hotmail was hot because of the way it was marketed. It spread like a virus, going from zero customers to over 40 million in only three years, increasing its subscriber base more rapidly than any company in the history of the world. As *Business Week* reported, the idea for Hotmail came about as almost an afterthought:

> The two principals, Sabeer Bhatia and Jack Smith . . . went to see Draper Fisher Jurvetson, but the investor was unimpressed by their idea for database software for the Net. As they were packing up to leave, [the venture capitalists] asked: "Do you have any other ideas?" Sabeer said they'd noodled over a scheme to offer free, advertising-supported E-mail over the Web. A week and a half later, the venture capitalists ponied up $300,000, and Hotmail was born.*

---

*Andy Reinhardt, "What Matters Is How Smart You Are," *Business Week,* August 25, 1997.

The key to Hotmail's phenomenal growth was the free price tag and the fact that every e-mail contained the following tag line and an implied endorsement by the sender:

Get Your Private, Free Email at http://www.hotmail.com

The more the service was used, the faster the word was spread. In 1998, Hotmail was sold to Microsoft for $400 million! Not a bad return for a free product.

That is the payoff for having the most successful virally marketed business idea in history. Here is a list of a few other hot ideas that spread like wildfire:

Harry Potter	Hugely popular fantasy-novel series
EBay	World's leading online auction site
Who Wants to Be a Millionaire?	Hot ABC game show
Survivor	Hot CBS reality show
Napster	Hot free music site
Surprise.com	Hot gift site
BlueMountain.com	Popular site for electronic greeting cards
ICQ	Instant messaging technology that signed up 12 million people before selling out to AOL for $300 million
Amazon.com	Signed up over 200,000 Netwide affiliates to spread its services
The Blair Witch Project	Popular movie, shot on shoestring, that grossed over $150 million

All of these ideas spread through the population like a virus. How can you launch a virus? All you need is one good idea, right? And you need to understand the theory of a positive virus—how it spreads and what you can do to launch one of your own. There are four excellent books on the subject, all of which you should probably read if you really want to understand viral marketing. Luckily, you can download many excellent parts of them from the Internet for free.

Permission Marketing (Seth Godin)	www.permission.com
The Tipping Point (Malcolm Gladwell)	www.malcolmgladwell.com
Unleasing the IdeaVirus (Seth Godin)	www.ideavirus.com
Anatomy of a Buzz (Emanuel Rosen)	www.emanuel-rosen.com

Start by going online and downloading your own copy of Godin's *IdeaVirus* book at www.ideavirus.com. Then download four free chapters of his first book, *Permission Marketing*. Good stuff.

These books are more theoretical than practical—instructing us on the power of creating a buzz and hyping a product until it catches fire. Studying theory and case studies encourages you to come up with ways to create a positive epidemic of your ideas and products. There is a science to creating a buzz, especially if you know the parameters of the disease.

Steve Jurvetson, the man who coined the term *viral marketing,* said this in a November 1998 article in Business 2.0:

> A good virus will look for prolific hosts (such as students) and tie itself to their high-frequency social interactions. Viral marketing is strongest when it taps into the breadth of its customers' weak connections to others. Tapping a customer's entire address book is more valuable than just reaching his or her best friend.
>
> The typical viral entry strategy is twofold: Minimize the friction of market entry and proliferation, and build in hooks to create barriers to switching.

On his Web site, MalcolmGladwell.com, the author of *The Tipping Point,* says,

> Think, for a moment, about the concept of *contagiousness.* If I say that word to you, you think of colds and the flu or perhaps something very dangerous like HIV or Ebola. We have, in our minds, a very specific, biological, notion of what contagiousness means. But if there can be epidemics of crime

or epidemics of fashion, there must be all kinds of things just as contagious as viruses. . . .

The second of the principles of epidemics—that little changes can somehow have big effects and vice versa—is a also a fairly radical notion. . . . To appreciate the power of epidemics, we have to prepare ourselves for the possibility that sometimes big changes follow from small events, and that sometimes these changes can happen very quickly. . . .

One of the things I'd like to do is to show people how to start "positive" epidemics of their own. The virtue of an epidemic, after all, is that just a little input is enough to get it started, and it can spread very, very quickly. That makes it something of obvious and enormous interest to everyone from educators trying to reach students to businesses trying to spread the word about their product, or for that matter to anyone who's trying to create a change with limited resources. The book has a number of case studies of people who have successfully started epidemics—an advertising agency, for example, and a breast cancer activist. I think they are really fascinating. I also take a pressing social issue, teenage smoking, and break it down and analyze what an epidemic approach to solving that problem would look like. The point is that by the end of the book I think the reader will have a clear idea of what starting an epidemic actually takes. This is not an abstract, academic book. It's very practical. And it's very hopeful. It's brain software.

As I've said, studying these books will give you the theory of how to spread your product like a virus. This gives you the framework to develop a mind-set about making your message contagious. Here is a list of questions (again, thanks to Seth Godin) that you should be asking yourself as your create your marketing plan.

Eight Questions to Use as a Self-Diagnostic Test

1. What can we do to make our product more virusworthy?

2. How likely are powerful sneezers to adopt our virus?

3. Do we know who the sneezers are and how to contact them?

4. Have we figured out what we want our sneezers to say? How are we teaching them to say it?

5. Is it possible to include our viral elements in our product?

6. Have we chosen a hive that we're capable of dominating?

7. How smooth is the transfer of the ideavirus?

8. Have we built in multiple feedback loops so that we can alter the virus as it moves and grows?

To build on the theory of viral marketing, in Chapter 11 I show you a very practical way to create a buzz.

Let's review our list of ways to make your site stickier and quicker. Study this list. Let the concepts roll around in your brain as you contemplate your marketing activities. From this list will come most of your breakthrough ideas.

1. Become an expert on instant gratification.

2. Transform your site into a treasure trove.

3. Give your visitors a rich experience.

4. Make your e-mail communications valuable, but not too valuable.

5. Get permission to gather more information to serve them faster.

6. Design a frequent-visitor and/or frequent-purchaser program.

7. Reduce the distance between your visitors and a live person.

8. Get people together, and they'll reward you for it.

9. Study the laws of epidemics and the principles of contagiousness.

CHAPTER 9

Ready. Set. Launch.
How Fast Can You Go from
Zero to Cash?

"First of all—you need a Web site."

Suppose I drop you in a strange city for a week. I give you a place to sleep, food, and a computer with access to the Internet. Suppose you must start from scratch without relying on any of your own existing Web sites or databases. You have no products to market, no information to sell, no services to pitch. I'm talking about starting from ground zero. Zero to cash. How soon could you be up and making money?

Would you even know where to start?

In previous chapters, we've discussed the marketing principles that form the foundation—the bedrock—upon which the edifice of your cash-flow machine will be constructed. Most businesses fail because they do not build on such a bedrock. Just in case you've forgotten, here they are again:

1. Find a school of hungry fish. (Who is your target audience?)

2. Find out what they're biting on. (What do they really want?)

3. Supercharge your bait. (Use USP and the 12 principles of persuasion.)

4. Build a massive Maybe Lake. (Create a space to turn strangers into friends.)

5. Catch and release. (Create a lifetime relationship with your clients.)

Okay, Bob. Thanks for the refresher course. Time's running out! Now what?

First, the zero-to-cash scenario is obviously not a normal situation. Most people who have time to launch a business will go through all of the steps I've outlined in this book: Research a group of hungry fish, figure out a product to satisfy their needs, create some bait, and start filling up their Maybe Lake. Several weeks or months later, they can start a full-blown marketing program. This, of course, is the prudent course.

But for the sake of argument we're going to shorten the time frame to 72 hours. How fast can we have a Web site up and running? Of the dozens of places on the Net that will host your Web site for free, one company stands out for the depth and breadth of its services. You can be running your own e-business in minutes.

Enough theory. Nobody learns to drive a car by reading about it. You have to get behind the wheel and do it. Let's go online. Right now. Stop reading and go fire up your computer. I'm assuming you have access to the Internet. Go there and get ready. Even if you already have your own Web site, let's go back to square one. I want to take you to a practice site . . . all ready for you to tinker. And the price is right. It's free.

Go to www.vstore.com. This is a very neat site. You can literally design your own Web page from scratch. You don't have to be a genius to do it. And within minutes your store is stocked with as many as *1 million products*—ready to sell, with a credit card merchant account already approved. You can literally be in business *overnight*. No kidding!

The hard part is not setting up the store. It's getting people to visit that store. In this chapter, I show you rapid-fire techniques for filling up your new store with customers. But first, read what the company has to say about it.

About Vstore.com

Vstore.com, a Vcommerce Corporation solution, is a revolutionary new form of e-commerce that empowers anyone to open an online store in just five minutes—for free! The Vstore.com solution eliminates the traditional barriers to e-commerce faced by individuals, online communities, and affinity groups. The Vstore.com store-building wizard allows individuals and small online businesses to select the products they want to sell and to customize the look and feel of their storefront.

Drawing on the Vcommerce infrastructure, Vstore.com provides all hosting, transaction processing, customer service, order fulfillment, merchandising, and marketing programs. Now anyone who has an Internet marketing idea can get the necessary tools and product catalog to create a successful online store quickly and easily. . . . Vcommerce connects its commerce partners to the most extensive supplier network on the Web, incorporating more than 1 million products across thousands of product categories.

Our Vision

Vstore.com has a single vision: to level the playing field in e-commerce by empowering individuals to create their own personally branded, fully stocked, online stores for free.

Vstore.com Mission Statement

Vstore.com has developed a revolutionary new form of e-commerce that empowers anyone to open their own fully stocked, personally branded, online store for free. The Vstore.com solution eliminates the traditional barriers faced by individuals and small Web sites, including hosting, transaction processing, customer service, order fulfillment, merchandising,and e-mail marketing. Liberated from the business details, millions of our store partners can open, market, and profit from their own Internet storefronts while becoming successful online entrepreneurs.

Why Should You Open Your Own Store?

There has never been a better time or smarter way to profit from e-commerce. With Vstore.com, you can open a personally branded, fully stocked, online store in minutes. Vstore.com provides the products, design, marketing tools, and technology for free. All you have to do is customize the store and keep the profits.

Before Vstore.com existed, starting an online business required a big investment in Web site design and technological hardware. Entrepreneurs also had to negotiate with vendors, pay for warehouse and shipping charges, and set up banking relationships to run their business. Now Vstore.com will take care of those details and leave you to enjoy managing and marketing your store.

With Vstore.com, you receive the following benefits completely *free:*

- A customizable store-building system
- High-speed hosting of your store by the Vstore.com system
- Management of all credit card transactions
- A vast selection of brand name products to sell
- Product delivery and service support to satisfy the needs of your customers
- Reports on traffic to your store, sales, and commissions
- Commissions on every single sale in every store you open

Here are only a few of the products that offer high commissions from Vstore.com's wide variety of products:

Product	Price	Commission
Igloo Dome Tent—American Camper	$159.95	$39.99 (25%)
Garment Bag—Bill Blass	$79.99	$12.00 (15%)
Classic Red Tricycle 10″—Radio Flyer	$49.99	$7.50 (15%)
900-MHz Digital Cordless Phone—Toshiba	$69.96	$7.00 (10%)
Augusta Men's Putter—Wilson	$19.95	$2.99 (15%)
InkJet Printer BJC 3000—Canon	$149.96	$7.50 (5%)

Vstore.com is one of dozens of similar options online—and in coming years there will be dozens more to choose from. The barriers to launching yourself in business have been essentially removed. Think of all the excuses that people use for not getting started in their own business:

I don't have the money!

I don't have the time!

I don't have anything to sell!

I don't know how to market!

You can start for free; you have 1 million products in many product categories to choose from; your online merchant accounts are all approved; and Vstore.com will teach you how to sell. There are no more excuses!

Of course, with all of these advantages, there are a few catches. You can't place your own products (at this time) on your storefront—you can only sell the Vstore.com selection. However, you can link your Vstore site to any other site that you own. In essence, you can set it up to act like the Amazon.com affiliate program. If someone clicks on the Vstore link on your main site and purchases a product at your Vstore site, you earn a commission. With the Vstore.com option, you can build, design, and stock your own private store with exactly the kinds of products that fit in with the theme of your site.

What if you don't have another Web site? Let's create one right now! And once again the price is right. It's free. The top Web company for providing a powerful and free Web site is www.bigstep.com.

Go there right now and you'll see that, as with Vstore.com, you can design your own Web page and publish it live on the Web in less than an hour—maybe quicker. I sat down at my computer (and I'm no techie) and launched my own site in minutes. It was amazing. Years from now, when people read these words, I know they'll think this sounds archaic ("Of course you can design your own Web page; kindergartners do it during recess at school"), but in the year 2001, it is rather revolutionary for ordinary people with no technical background whatsoever to launch a professional-looking Web site in minutes. For free! Check out my site at www.zerotocash.bigstep.com.

Here is what the Bigstep.com people have to say:

With an excellent combination of features and control, Bigstep.com makes the transition from a traditional business model to the online world as painless as it can be. Add the fact that basic service is free and you've got a combination that's difficult to beat.

Getting a site started with Bigstep.com is surprisingly simple. A wizard guides you through the initial steps to build a basic site. From there, you move into the back-office management features that let you micromanage every aspect of your storefront. We were able to get quick yet tangible results before moving into the heart of the application.

> One of Bigstep.com's great strengths is its flexibility; you can fine-tune every component of your storefront layout. You can select from a series of site-wide templates, define vertical and horizontal layouts, and apply any color scheme you want. As you build your site, you can control the layout of each page in your catalog with a seemingly inexhaustible range of options.
>
> Bigstep.com goes well beyond mere shopping cart capabilities. You can, for example, create surveys—to collect useful feedback from your customers. And creating and distributing newsletters is also easy. Because Bigstep.com keeps track of information on all customers who have placed orders, content can be personalized to each customer's specific interests.
>
> Bigstep.com clearly understands the needs of small businesses and has put together a solution that is sure to make even the most demanding business owner happy.

Bigstep isn't the only choice on the Net. You can find similar offerings at the following locations:

www.freemerchant.com

www.store.yahoo.com

Now let's return to our original premise: making money in 72 hours. Obviously, the first few hours of our challenge would be occupied with setting up a Web site. The balance of the time would be devoted to the most important part: *marketing.* As I said in earlier chapters, most Web site owners do not understand marketing on the Net. They think that marketing means to list their site with a thousand search engines and hope that people find it (*passive*). This is not marketing; it's wishful thinking. You must go out and find your target audience and entice them to come to your site (*active*). With our 72-hour challenge, we don't have time for passive marketing. We need to use only active marketing strategies that produce immediate results.

Major search engines?	Too slow.	Out!
Traditional PR campaign?	No control.	Out!
Ads offline?	Too expensive.	Out!
Word of mouse?	Too iffy.	Out!
Building a Web presence?	Not enough leverage.	Out!

We don't have time to go out into the big ocean. We need high-quality, surefire, slam-dunk, feeding-frenzy fish—from somebody else's Maybe Lake or Yes Pond. It's probably not going to be free. But at least it should be fast.

We can narrow your marketing options down to a few focused activities.

- Use one of the paid placement search engines and bid for the top spot in your category.
- Place an ad in an online e-zine or a group of e-zines targeted to your audience.
- Rent a list of e-mail names of people who have a specific interest in your subject.

For the past two summers, I have taken my two teenage sons, Aaron and Hunter, on individual, private fishing trips to Kenai, Alaska—home of the greatest king salmon fishing. We only had a few days each time, and I wanted to create some great memories. (In my view, a parent's main job is to create memories. Bottom line: Good parents create good memories. Bad parents create bad memories.) I could have read a few books on Alaskan fishing, rented my own boat, and taken my sons out on the river myself. We might have caught some fish, but I didn't want to leave it to chance. Instead, I hired one of the best outfitters on the river, Kenai River Guides, who fish the river every day. They know what bait to use. They know the highest-probability fishing holes. They know that if the guests catch fish, there will be a great big tip for them at the end of the day. In other words, I hired guides who knew what they were doing and I paid them to take us to the right fishing holes. Did it work? Well, you can see the trophies hanging on my office wall right now—plus a freezer full of fresh king salmon fillets. And some priceless memories.

Moral of the story? If your time is short and results are important, don't spend time searching for fish. Spend your time finding the right guide. Then let them take you to the fish. This is always your surest bet.

Let me introduce you to three guides who are going to take you quickly to the right spots on the Internet. They have years of experience. I'll let them tell you what they would do in their own words.

Our Guide to Fast Results Using Search Engines

Our first guide is Danny Sullivan, editor of the Search Engine Watch Web site at www.searchenginewatch.com and the free Search Engine Report, read by 150,000 people worldwide each week. If it has to do with search engines, he knows about it, so I asked him the following question:

"Danny, suppose you had to generate some sales at a brand-new Web site in 72 hours or less. Is there a search engine that could create leads that fast?"

He responded, "You need to get listed with all the major search engines and take advantage of their express listing options. This will get you added to some of them very quickly. Getting listed doesn't guarantee that you'll come up in the top spot for your particular search words, but it's a start—and you probably will generate some traffic, perhaps substantial traffic. Then use one of the paid placement search engines and bid for the top spot in your category."

Paid placement search engines, such as GoTo.com, Searchhound.com, www.netflip.com or 7search.com, allow businesses to bid for certain keywords. Therefore, you can receive a top search ranking, sometimes within minutes, just by bidding for the highest spot. This top search engine ranking gives you immediate exposure to the thousands of people who are searching, at this very second, for what you have to offer.

Another idea is to go to all the top search engines and, using the keywords that describe your product, find the top three Web sites that fit. They have already won the battle of top search engine placement. Contact the Webmaster of each high-ranking listing and offer to pay for an endorsed mailing to that site's list of satisfied customers. There are dozens of major search engines, so you have dozens of top sites to contact. Someone may take you up on your offer, which could generate some quick sales to beat the deadline.

Our Guide to Getting Quick Results by Buying Paid Ads in E-Zines

Our expert in e-zine ads is Ruth Townsend, owner of Lifestyles Publishers, found at www.lifestylespub.com, which lists a directory of around 1,000 e-zines on the Web. The directory of e-zines displays all the contact information, ad rates, publication schedules, and so forth. Ruth has also become an expert in placing ads in these e-zines—what works and what doesn't. I asked her the following question:

"Ruth, suppose you are a newbie with a brand-new Web page and a product that you are trying to market, but you have no idea how to get your message out to the rest of the world. Suppose your life depended on generating some business quickly— let's say 72 hours from right now—what would you do?"

Now I give the floor to Ruth.

This is exactly the problem I faced when I started my own Internet business three years ago. (See the full story in Chapter 12.) After a lot of trial and error, I finally figured out that the fastest, most effective way to get a message in front of a lot of targeted people is to buy an ad placement in an e-zine. Thousands of e-zines are being sent out every day of the week. You just need to find the right e-zine. For that, turn to my Directory of E-zines, type in the subject matter you're looking for, and up comes a list of all of the e-zines that cover that subject, complete with publication schedules, ad rates, and contact information.

Once you've found your targeted e-zines and decided on an ad budget, contact each e-zine and arrange to have your ad placed—hopefully within your 72-hours deadline. Here are three types of ads you can run in order of effectiveness:

1. Solo blast
2. Sponsorship ad
3. Classified ad

With the solo blast, the e-zine sends your solo advertising message directly to its list of e-zine subscribers. This is the most expensive option, but by far the most effective. The power of a solo blast lies in the fact that there is no competition with other ads. The most effective method is to arrange for an endorsed message from the e-zine owner. The stronger the endorsement, the better your sales are going to be. Of course, the stronger the endorsement, the more profit you have to split—but if my life depended on it, I'd make sure my message was the strongest message possible.

Here is an example of a solo blast to the Big Dog Marketing e-zine. It doesn't include any editorial content but is purely an e-mail ad. In this case, the advertiser is Dell computers who agreed to pay about $1 per click-through. Big Dog e-zine owners received about $1,000 for this promotion.

BIG DOG MARKETING—SPECIAL MESSAGE

~~~~~~
You're receiving Big Dog Marketing because you subscribed to it. Instructions for subscribing or leaving are at the end of this message.
~~~~~~

***DELL COMPUTERS ARE ON SALE For the Next 3 Days Only!

Get the small-business systems you need. For less. $150 off any Dell Inspiron™ notebook!

$100 off any Dell™ Dimension™ desktop. It's your money. Spend wisely. Click now. Offer expires 10/27/00.

http://opt-influence.com/a/d4/

The second option would be to arrange for a sponsorship position for your ad. This usually means that your ad will appear before the content of the e-zine, so your ad is seen first. If your ad is compelling enough, it should generate some traffic to your site. The least effective method, but also the cheapest, is to buy a classified ad in your chosen e-zine. Your ad will be placed in the body of the e-zine message or at the end of the text. Some e-zines will let you place a free classified ad under certain circumstances.

Here are some guidelines for getting the best deal from your e-zine advertising:

1. Subscribe to the e-zine before you buy an ad in it so you can see what you're getting.
2. Make sure that there are no more than five ads in the e-zine. Any more and the effectiveness of your add drops.
3. Look for e-zines that have excellent content.
4. Bigger is not better. A small e-zine sent to 2,000 highly qualified subscribers can sometimes outperform a large e-zine with 50,000 poorly qualified subscribers.
5. Find out how the e-zine builds its subscriber list. Make sure it is 100 percent opt-in.

Here are some of my favorite e-zines that I have tested or used in the past for advertising and that brought me good results. (However, what works for me may or may not work for you.)

DrNunley's Marketing Tips
Kevin Nunley
mailto:kevin@drnunley.com
http://www.drnunley.com

Web Marketing Today
Ralph F. Wilson, Dr.
mailto:rfwilson@wilsonweb.com
http://www.wilsonweb.com/wmt/

BizWeb eGazette
Jim Daniels
mailto:webmaster@bizweb2000.com
http://www.bizweb2000.com

NOBOSS e-Marketing
Dan Schwartz
mailto:emarketing@noboss.com
http://www.noboss.com

The Internet Insider
Thomas Harpointner
mailto:news@aismedia.com
http://www.theinternetinsider.com

The LoveQuote of the Day
Fayez Alameddine
mailto:webmaster@lovequote.com
http://dailyquote.lovequote.com

Your Life Support System
Steve Goodier
mailto:Advertising@LifeSupportSystem.com
http://www.LifeSupportSystem.com

World Wide Recipes—Free Recipes by Email
Joe Barkson
mailto:TheChef@wwrecipes.com
http://www.wwrecipes.com

The DEMC newsletter goes out to about 300,000 business-oriented subscribers each week. A three-line ad costs about $45, and a five-line ad costs $65. Check out the details at www.demc.com.

Another source of e-mail lists where you can buy advertising is www.memail.com, which publishes over 50 e-zines with the MeMail brand on dozens of topics. Here is the explanation from the company Web site:

MeMail.com is your electronic magazine rack on the Internet, offering the widest possible selection of premium and branded content in email deliverable form. Our eMagazines are read by more than 426,000 people in over 120 countries.

MeMail.com offers a large selection of free eMagazines in topic areas such as entertainment (e.g., jokes, horoscopes, quirky news), health and fitness (nutrition, medical breakthroughs, advice, sports scores), science, environment, national and international news. Most of our eMagazines are delivered daily, though some move weekly, twice weekly, or monthly.

The strong relationship that we enjoy with our membership is attractive to the advertisers who sponsor our free email publications. As a trusted gatekeeper facilitating privileged access to the private space of our members' email inboxes, advertisers benefit through association with the MeMail.com brand.

The advertiser's message appears at the top of the email, where it is immediately visible when the reader opens the email. MeMail.com eMagazines also benefit from a high pass-along rate, as subscribers frequently forward the content to friends and colleagues.

Your advertising message in an eMagazine can be up to six lines long and 70 characters wide, including your URL and/or contact email address. CPM rates start as low as $1.00.

Placing ads in targeted ezines will continue to be a highly effective way of generating almost immediate response to your targeted marketing offer.

Our Guide to Renting
E-Mail Mailing Lists

If we want results in 72 hours, we will be able to generate immediate results by renting lists of target e-mail names from such reputable companies as the following:

www.targ-it.com

www.yesmail.com

www.postmasterdirect.com

www.bulletmail.com

www.worldata.com

www.e-Target.com

www.Htmail.com (guarantees at least a 10 percent click-through rate or the mailing is free)

The problem with any list of e-mail names is the possibility of spam—the hated unsolicited e-mail message. If you have been on e-mail for any length of time, you have probably been solicited to buy a CD containing millions of "clean" e-mail addresses for a few hundred dollars. Every expert you talk to will warn you away from such lists. Why? The amount of grief you will receive will far outweigh the potential for profit.

The aforementioned mailing list companies explain that the spam problem has been eliminated because the lists are made up of people who have *opted in* (i.e., agreed to receive e-mail). But now comes a company (among others, to be sure) that promises to deliver hundreds of thousands of totally legitimate, completely happy e-mail recipients who are actually eager to receive your e-mail advertising message. (Talk about eliminating the spam problem!) How do they do it? They pay people to read their e-mails! What would it be like to watch a television show or listen to a radio station and have the advertiser actually pay you to watch the commercials? Interesting concept.

That is the idea behind MintMail.com. Brian Nelson is one of the principals behind MintMail. He'll be our guide to the world of renting e-mail lists. But first, read what the company has to say:

Welcome to the future of email!

Here's how MintMail works:

1. Tell us what kind of email offers you are interested in receiving at our <u>FREE Sign-Up page.</u>
2. We'll start sending you offers from our advertisers and partners. Each time you read an offer we send you, we'll credit your account with 5 cents cash.
3. You can receive this cash monthly. Or, "let it ride" . . . and when your account reaches $25, we'll automatically **DOUBLE** your account balance and send you a $50 gift certificate from your choice of MintMail <u>sponsors</u>!
4. As an added bonus, when you sign up, we'll issue you your own unique "Referral Link" to MintMail.com. Simply refer your friends and associates to your Link. For every one that signs up as a Member, we'll pay you an additional three cents Referral Bonus each time they receive an email from MintMail.com! That's not all! For each Member **THEY** refer, we'll also pay you an additional two cents for each MintMail they receive.

It's simple, fun, easy, and can really add up as the following chart illustrates:

MintMails Received	MintMails Sent To:	YOU EARN WEEKLY: Cash OR Gift Certificates	
5 per week	YOU	$.25	$.50
5 per week	Just 50 of your Referrals	$7.50	$15.00
5 per week	Your Referrals refer an average of just 10 MintMail Members each: Total = 500	$50.00	$100.00
	TOTAL =	$57.75	$115.50

✓ *$231 extra cash a month just for reading 20 emails and telling a few friends about MintMail (Earn even more by telling more friends!)*

✓ *No need to stop with nickels and dimes. You can also mint yourself a DOLLAR each time you refer a Member to MintMail!*

Note! This chart is for example purposes only. Individual results will vary. MintMails must be read and the included link clicked to earn commissions.

Who's paying out all this money?!

Our advertisers! As you no doubt realize, the Internet is a HUGE and rapidly growing marketplace. E-commerce is a revolution that millions of businesses want to tap into. However, they want to do it ethically and that means NO SPAM. **MintMail.com completely eliminates spam from the equation!**

Our advertisers know that our Members WANT to receive their email offers and are paid to read them. Hence, our advertisers are happy to pay us to send their offers to you (enough for both our mailing costs AND to pay you for looking over their offers).

Everyone wins! You get paid to read offers you're interested in. The advertisers get their offers in front of a receptive audience. And MintMail.com earns a small fee for bringing the two of you together.

From a different point of view, here is what MintMail is telling the advertisers:

Email Marketing with MintMail.com

Results 300% to 500% higher than traditional opt-in email

Opt-in email is fast becoming the traffic and lead generation vehicle of choice for online marketers. Unlike banners and other Web-based advertising, email is delivered directly to the consumer, the second they log on to the Web.

People love to receive email (non-spam of course) and the email in-box is as far as many people get when they log on to the Web. *Let MintMail.com put your marketing message in the email box of thousands of prospects who are waiting to hear from you.*

Our Members Have Agreed to Give Your Offer a Shot

Unlike most opt-in email lists, MintMail.com members are truly waiting to hear from you. When an individual joins MintMail.com, they agree to receive commercial email messages from our advertisers and partners, in return for being rewarded if they visit the advertised Website. When your email message is delivered to our members, they know that it's coming from a source they trust—MintMail.com.

Our one-on-one relationship with members and the Member Reward System that we have in place, makes certain that your offer receives the attention it deserves.

Compared to other opt-in email lists, you should receive a 300% to 500% higher click-through rate when presented to our members. That means three to five times more visits to your Website for every dollar you spend.

It's So Easy to Test an Email Campaign

We make it easy and inexpensive to send a test email to our members:

- For as little as $250 you can send an email campaign to 1,000 MintMail.com members.
- Or test 5,000 emails for less than $1,000.

Will this work or not? According to Brian Nelson, it seems to be working extraordinarily well. Here's why:

When you receive an e-mail, should you open it?

From	Subject
Streams of Cash E-Letter	Free report: How to earn lifetime streams of cash online

Only two pieces of information should affect your decision: the sender's name and/or e-mail address and the subject line. Any given e-mail is one click away from deletion. Since people's e-mail boxes can fill up quite quickly, a lot of e-mail that appears to be commercial in nature (even if you requested it) is never opened. Even if it is opened, many people only read a few words into the body of the text before deciding to delete.

According to MintMail, the way to solve this problem—to increase the number of e-mails that are opened *and* read—is to pay people to read their e-mails.

If your life depended on making money fast, you certainly would not go wrong to at least test this source of e-mail names.

Putting It All Together

Using a combination of paid search engines, targeted ads in e-zines, and rented e-mail lists, it is very realistic to be able to drive some highly motivated traffic to your Web site well within the 72-hour self-imposed deadline.

Will your visitors buy when they get there? Well, if your life depended upon your visitors buying something, what would you do?

You'd start right back at the beginning:

1. Find a school of hungry fish. (Who is your target audience?)

2. Find out what they're biting on. (What do they really want?)

3. Supercharge your bait. (Use USP and the 12 principles of persuasion.)

Join me in the next chapter and let's go make some real money.

CHAPTER 10

Online Stream #1.
Joint Ventures:
High-Leverage Ways to Make
a Fortune Online

In an October 1996 issue of *Fast Company,* William C. Taylor interviewed Jeff Bezos, founder and CEO of Amazon.com. At the time of the interview, Amazon.com was barely a year old. I know you've heard the story a thousand times. But read it one more time. And see if you can spot the reason that I want you to read it.

Jeff Bezos was a Wall Street trader and programming star, a top executive at fast-growing D.E. Shaw & Co., when a startling statistic caught his eye: World Wide Web usage was growing at 2,300% per year. He remembers his immediate reaction: "Anything growing that fast is going to be ubiquitous very quickly. It was my wake-up call."

That was the summer of 1994. Bezos, now 32, quit D.E. Shaw and began methodically analyzing the most promising opportunities for Internet commerce. He concluded that online retailing was the next big thing, and that selling books over the Web was the first big retail opportunity. He moved to Seattle, raised several million dollars from private investors, and created the world's largest online bookstore.

Amazon.com opened for business in July 1995. It has since become one of the most admired and talked-about companies on the Web. . . .

"In the summer of 1994, when the Web first caught my attention, I made a list of 20 product categories—books, music, computer hardware and software—and investigated the merits of selling them online. Books were far and away the best category. . . . There are so many of them! There are 1.5 million English-language books in print, 3 million books in all languages worldwide. This volume defined the opportunity. . . . But the largest physical bookstore in the world has only 175,000 titles. We have 1.1 million titles. There's no way you can build a store to handle 1.1 million titles. And you can't offer our selection in a catalog. If you printed the Amazon.com catalog, it would be the size of seven New York City phone books. The only way to build a 1.1 million–title bookstore is on the Web. . . . It sounds counterintuitive, but physical location is very important for the success of a virtual business. We could have started Amazon.com anywhere. We chose Seattle because it met a rigorous set of criteria. It had to be a place with lots of technical talent. It had to be near a place with large numbers of books. It had to be a nice place to live—great people won't work in places they don't want to live. Finally, it had to be in a small state. In the mail-order business, you have to charge sales tax to customers who live in any state where you have a business presence. It made no sense for us to be in California or New York. Obviously Seattle has a great programming culture. And it's close to Roseburg, Oregon, which has one of the biggest book warehouses in the world. We thought about the Bay Area, which is the single best source for technical talent. But it didn't pass the small-state test. I even investigated whether we could set up Amazon.com on an Indian reservation near San Francisco. This way we could have access to talent without all the tax consequences. Unfortunately, the government thought of that first."

Did you get it? If you didn't, go back and read it again.

Jeff Bezos saw an idea, acted on his hunch, quit his job, moved across the country, and did whatever it took to turn his idea into reality. His reward was fame and fortune.

Now I'm going to share with you the highest-probability method for you to do the same thing—perhaps minus the fame. On second thought, who am I to limit your dreams? Go for it. It's probably too late to go head-to-head with the likes of Amazon. Your vein of gold is more likely to come by picking a very narrow sliver of the pie and dominating it.

I'll assume that you have decided on your unique idea, identified your target audience, decided on your USP, and lined up your products. Now what?

In the previous chapters, you've learned at least six major ways to drive traffic to your site so visitors can buy your products. How would you like to learn a powerful, high-speed shortcut to doubling, tripling, even quadrupling your sales online?

Let me introduce you to your online mentor for this chapter. His name is Mike Enlow. Ever heard of him? He shows you how to start with nothing and make a fortune. He shows you how to use a powerful form of leverage available to any beginner.

What is that leverage? It is the power of the existing relationship that other businesses have with their current customers. In other words, you don't have to launch your brand-new business into the cold, cold world. You can gain immediate access to customers through the back door—a sort of Trojan horse strategy. You can go from the back of the line to the front of the line. The velvet rope will no longer keep you out.

I have specifically chosen Mike Enlow to share this strategy with you because, once you hear his story, you realize that you have no excuses. If Mike can make it, so can you.

Mike describes himself as "a Mississippi backwoods country boy, without even a high school diploma." In 1983, while he was working in Louisiana, his life changed forever. Here is Mike's story in his own words.

It was August 28, 1983, 4:50 P.M. I was on my Yamaha 400, burning up the back roads. I was heading home to get ready for a singing engagement when I rounded a curve and met a pickup truck heading straight for me in my lane. We hit head-on.

Then I died.

I was out of my body for a time. I saw the ambulance arrive; I saw the girl who was driving the pickup crying beside my body; and I heard everything the paramedics said as they began to revive me. Just as I was starting to realize I didn't want to return, I was flooded with excruciating pain as I rushed back into my body, which was smashed to pieces. The agony I felt was indescribable. I was barely conscious but I remember telling the girl driving the truck not to cry. I was rushed to the emergency room and my family was notified. Laura, my wife, and I were separated at this time, and she was out of town. I lay there and cried for my mother to bring me some Chap Stick because my lips were dry and burning badly. The pain had escalated from indescribable to unbearable by this time. My brother was there beside me in the ER, and when he asked me what he could do for me, I asked him to let me bite his finger to ease the pain. I had emergency surgery to insert six steel rods in my legs. I had neck and back fractures; my helmet had cracked, and I had a concussion, abrasions, broken ribs, and my arm was crushed.

On the whole, it just wasn't a real good day.

The doctors told me I was in critical condition. No one could tell me whether I'd walk again or be more than minimally functional. I spent weeks in the hospital, fighting the pain and holding on to my will to survive.

I asked one of the doctors if I'd ever be able to play my guitar again. He said no. So I asked a friend to bring my guitar to the hospital. He placed it in my hands, and it hurt like nobody's business, but with a roomful of nurses I played that guitar until they cried. One small victory already. I knew then that I was going to make it out of there. I think they did, too.

In all, I had seven surgeries. I'd suffered compression fractures, and the doctors warned me I might never be able to work again. I finally made it out of the hospital, confined to a wheelchair but determined to survive somehow. When I got home, I had a four-year-old daughter to care for, with no one there to care for me. I had no insurance, no income, no savings—absolutely nothing. Eventually the bank came and took everything. My car, my furniture, everything I had. I was left with nothing and totally helpless. My landlord was sympathetic and let me stay in the house I was living in.

Luckily, two neighbors who lived on either side of me brought my daughter and me food every day. I found out later that these people hated each other, but each brought us food every day, not knowing the other was doing it, too. Strangely enough, they never once showed up at the same time. I survived, and eight months later I moved back to Mississippi.

I began to reestablish my income by selling specialty ads while still in the wheelchair, literally wheeling myself from door to door, often asking strangers on the street to lift me up the stairs. It took me two years to get out of that wheelchair. I'll never forget the day I stood up, pushed the chair back, and walked away from it. I still keep that wheelchair, just to remind me of what I nearly lost, all that I gained, and all that I conquered. If I walked away from that chair, there's nothing I can't do.

Eighteen years later, Mike Enlow has become one of the top marketing gurus in the world. His businesses have grossed millions of dollars, and his programs have helped thousands raise themselves, as their mentor did, from nothing to levels of success only imagined by most people. Mike still suffers chronic pain from his motorcycle accident, but he thanks God for every extra day he's been given to spread his positive message.

I asked Mike to share with you the number one secret of his success. Read very carefully, because these ideas have generated hundreds of millions of dollars' worth of business for Mike and his students. Mike's formula was perfected in the early 1990s, when the Internet was just a gleam in Jeff Bezos's eye. I personally agree with Mike that this secret will be your fastest route to online success in marketing your product. Here is the formula in Mike Enlow's own words.

How to Create Wealth from Others' Overlooked Assets

Few believe me when I tell them of the fortunes they can make starting with nothing. Sometimes I feel as though I'm the only one with macroscopic glasses (to see the big picture) when examining businesses and the many opportunities for creating additional cash flow.

Nearly every business I consult with has no less than 3 (and often 10) different ways to almost immediately create additional cash flow from its existing efforts, clients, and advertisements.

I'm going to share with you one of the simplest of these concepts, which I call *joint venture alliances* or *co-ventures.* I assume you have no knowledge of marketing for the benefit of those of you who are unfamiliar with my marketing techniques.

Let's begin.

Joint Venture Alliances

I've discovered many working marketing concepts and systems. All of them are centered around one word: *leverage!* I want to show you how to use leverage to get greater profits and greater satisfaction out of every dollar spent and every effort expended.

Over the years, I've learned that every business has one need in common—the need to create more cash flow than is spent on overhead. Tens of thousands of businesses do this very successfully. Unfortunately, they overlook many opportunities to gain greater leverage and reap greater rewards from what they do. It takes just as much energy to create an advertisement that produces 100 sales (or leads) as it does to produce 1,000. In the next few pages I'm going to teach you one of the fastest and easiest ways for any business owner to increase his or her profits *by as much as 300 percent* and do so with nobility.

One of the most ridiculous mistakes and oversights in marketing is the failure to recognize the true value of the relationship a business owner has with his or her customers, vendors, and others with whom they deal on a daily basis. Properly utilizing this overlooked asset can mean thousands, and often tens of thousands, of dollars in increased revenue and goodwill.

Let me explain.

People making a purchase prefer to buy from someone they trust and who has treated them fairly in the past. If you were to rent a *cold list* (a list of names of people who know nothing about me, my company, product, service, or offer) you might, with a well-crafted sales letter or presentation, get a 1 to 3 percent response rate on the offer. However, if you go to the owner of that same list and structure a deal where the owner writes or presents the *very same offer* to the *very same people,* you will see a response rate that is so much higher it boggles the mind. I've seen response rates to this type of offer (call it an *endorsed offer*) that skyrocket to as high as 33 percent! This is an *increase* in response rate of between 1,100 to 3,300 percent!

Accordingly, you can literally earn a fortune by showing others how to use this principle to create win-win deals. A good example of using this concept happened a few Christmases ago with a client of mine who is in the pharmacy business. My client had approximately 10,000 customers on file, all of whom loved and trusted him for the excellent service they had received over the years. However, I discovered my client had never ever used this incredible asset of trust in a noble win-win deal.

Like too many businesspeople, my client was myopic (unable to see the big picture) in observing his own business. He failed to realize that although his business is selling pharmaceutical products and supplies, all his customers purchase many other products and services (dry cleaning, groceries, cars, insurance, accounting services, etc.). The relationship with customers provides business owners with the incredible opportunity to use the *endorsed offer.* By doing a *joint venture,* whereby they recommend or refer their customers to another professional and noble company, they could share in a percentage of the profits from the newfound business they create for the company they endorse.

In this particular situation, I learned that my client was friendly with a jeweler in town, and Christmas was rapidly approaching. I saw an instant jackpot. (By the way, these deals can be created without a prior relationship with the vendor you will endorse.)

Here's a brief overview of what can happen with joint ventures, or endorsed offers.

I immediately contacted and interviewed the jeweler to get the "golden nuggets" needed to create a letter for my pharmacy client to share with his customers. I learned that this jeweler regularly flew to New York to purchase diamonds, emeralds, rubies, and other precious stones. More important, by teaming up with another jeweler in New Orleans, this jeweler literally saved a fortune by buying in bulk.

We drafted a sample sales letter something like the following:

Dear Customers and Friends,

Last week my wife and I were browsing through the many Christmas card binders to select a suitable Christmas card to mail to you, our customers, to express our appreciation for your patronage.

Of the many hundreds of Christmas cards available, we couldn't find a single card that expressed our heartfelt feelings and appreciation to our customers. After all, it is customers like you who helped us to send our two children to college and build our business to be one of the most successful pharmacies in the city. Frankly, I decided to say thank-you in a very special way—with actions, not words.

Let me explain.

One of my dearest friends, a local jeweler, has the largest selection of diamonds, rubies, emeralds, watches, and other inventory in the area, but more important, he has developed an incredible method of wholesale purchasing that allows him to save a fortune.

As we were talking, I explained how I wanted to do something very special for my friends and customers this Christmas to express my gratitude for their business. I further explained how I wanted to do something that would benefit and thank them with *actions* rather than just *words* in a Christmas card.

After a bit of arm-twisting, my jeweler friend agreed to offer a 20 percent discount to my customers who show this letter during their holiday shopping! This discount applies to any purchase you make in his store this year. This is my special way of saying thank-you to my valued customers. And my jeweler friend, who offers only the finest-quality jewelry, agreed to participate because he believes you will continue to be his customer for years to come.

So feel free to take this letter to XYZ Jewelers anytime between now and Christmas and you will receive a privileged discount of 20 percent off any purchases—as well as VIP treatment from my friend.

Since almost everyone buys jewelry during the Christmas season, my wife and I feel this is a much better way of saying thank-you than any card we could send.

Enjoy, and Merry Christmas,

Don and Susan Smith, XYZ Pharmacy
 P.S. Oh yes, he did request that I ask you to slide this letter to him inconspicuously so that his other customers won't feel slighted. They aren't getting this VIP discount. Please do me this kind favor when you go in.

This letter of endorsement became the pharmacy's Christmas card for that year. We had prearranged a special deal whereby XYZ Pharmacy would receive half of the profits generated by the letter. Because of that, *we earned an incredible $87,550 mailing Christmas cards* instead of incurring a $5,000 cost to mail the usual Christmas cards to 10,000 people.

The jeweler was delighted after he'd been briefed about how a certain percentage of these newfound customers would become lifelong customers. This marketing education is the key to getting the most from deals like this.

Let me share the approach.

First you have to understand that most people fail to realize the lifetime value of a customer. This is your opportunity to educate the joint venture associate you wish to approach. Few businesspeople realize the residual value of new customers. Not all customers will come back. This will be true even if you give them the best quality, pricing, and service. However, a certain percentage of them will come back. In this case, over 2,780 people took the pharmacist up on his offer. The jeweler gave away the lion's share of the front-end profit, but he will earn much more than most realize. Let's look at a hypothetical example.

Assume only 10 percent of those who took advantage of the offer return the following year and make an average purchase of only $500. The jeweler not only profits from the initial deal, but he earns an additional $70,000 because of the pharmacist's referral. Jewelry is generally "keystone-priced"—meaning it sells at a 100 percent markup. If only 10 percent of the people return and spend an average of $500, that brings in an additional $139,000. At keystone pricing, that's an additional $69,500 profit for the jeweler!

This doesn't even take into account the fact that satisfied customers may return year after year, creating profits that may have been nonexistent without the endorsement of the pharmacist. Are you beginning to see the possibilities? They are astronomical!

POT-SHOTS NO. 2833.

READY ~
AIM ~
SPEND!

Ashleigh
Brilliant
.com

© 1983 by Ashleigh Brilliant (www.ashleighbrilliant.com)

You can make deals like these with car dealers, contractors, dentists, restaurants—almost any kind of business you can imagine. The beauty of it is that *this is a win-win deal for everyone,* and *you* are paid for arranging the deals. In a moment, I'll show you how the endorsed-mailing approach works extremely well on the Internet.

Other Approaches

In the preceding example we used Christmas as a "reason why," but you can create a host of reasons for deals like these:

- "We've just discovered the most incredible . . ."
- "We've learned of a secret method . . ."
- "Since my friend is just getting off the ground . . ."
- "This is the most incredible way for you to . . ."
- "It's only fair to tell you before the rest of the world learns that . . ."
- "We felt we would be remiss if we didn't offer you the first opportunity to try . . ."

The number of approaches is unlimited! I can't think of a single business that couldn't make more money by properly utilizing its customer base to endorse a quality product or service.

How Do You Get These Deals?

One of the most successful ways to get deals like these is to approach your target market with a pitch like this:

"If I show you how to properly utilize an asset you are overlooking and make you look like the knight in shining armor, would you be willing to share 50 percent of the newfound profits with me?"

There are no hard-and-fast rules. You should structure the deal in whatever way you must. The preceding suggestion has proven itself to be a great approach, especially when you guarantee to shoulder the cost to do the deal and take your profits only on the additional income you generate. Most will see the light after a few minutes.

How Do You Ensure You Get Paid?

I use a letter of nondisclosure, stipulating the basic terms of the arrangement, before I share the secret of this incredible concept. Again, the rules are not set in granite. You should be as flexible as you need to be to get the deal. It all depends on the size, volume, and type of deal and your level of involvement. However, you can earn a very respectable income by using this concept to show businesspeople how to redeploy their existing assets.

How Do You Get Started?

Getting started is easy. All you have to do is identify the potential partners. Then write a letter similar to the one that follows. Also, be sure to follow up the letter with a phone call. *Do not* share the intellectual property you have to offer until you have your agreement signed by all parties who will be participating. The following door opener will have your phone ringing off the hook:

Dear Store Owner:

My name is [your name here]. I am a marketing consultant who specializes in creating immediate additional cash flow to you at literally no cost to you.

Over the years I've developed a number of intellectual property concepts that have proven themselves to increase cash flow almost immediately by using little-known, overlooked techniques.

People from almost every business and industry have used the concepts I want to share with you—with extraordinary success. I have already taken the liberty to look over your business and am certain I can create a surprisingly large amount of cash for you. I will do so on a strict contingency basis. In fact, since I have already found the perfect deal for you, I will put my money into the marketing of the concept.

I will call you on Tuesday or Thursday to discuss this in greater detail. All I ask is that you call my voice mail, state your company name, and specify the day that's best for you so we can get together and get the show on the road.

I do these types of deals nationwide, so please call right away so I can fit you into my schedule on the days specified. I guarantee that you will be blown away and quite surprised by how this new concept can add to your bottom line in a matter of weeks. I do all the work, and you reap the benefits.

Since I am very selective in choosing clients with whom to share this incredible concept, I must ask you to sign a simple letter of understanding before I can tell you the details of the deal I have in mind for you.

Sincerely,

Your Name

Marketing Firm Name

P.S. If the dates I've specified are inconvenient for you, go ahead and call just to let me know you are interested. I'll try to arrange a time that is mutually convenient since the deal I have in mind for you is rather significant.

You can be assured that you will receive responses to this letter. Just set up your voice mail and be sure to find the matching product or service before you mail the letter.

How Do I Know Which Products Will Work with Which Clients?

Well, there are no set rules. With a little creative thought, you can come up with dozens of product ideas. Think of the example of the pharmacy and the jewelry store. What made this deal work? The pharmacy had a list of satisfied customers. The jewelry store had the ability to give a great deal. Both businesses won!

As I said earlier, you need to educate one side regarding the lifetime value of gaining new customers in order to get the best deal. You can often get as much as 100 percent of the profit of the sales made by your endorser by simply explaining this misunderstood marketing principle.

How Do I Get the Sweetest Deals?

If I were starting from scratch I would seek out companies with products to sell as opposed to service businesses. These deals are the easiest to get. When you work with attorneys, accountants, and other service businesses, the money trickles in slowly. With product sales, the money comes in over a two- to three-week period.

Look for companies that have an established customer database and, more important, have a good, strong relationship with their customers. The stronger the relationship, the stronger the endorsement. The stronger the endorsement, the greater the profits. Just look for situations in which the endorser has a lot of contact with customers. Preferably, endorsers should be in contact with their customers at least monthly.

The world is a big ocean of products and services. You have to find only one or two products that will yield successful results to your clients. Not only does this provide you with immediate income, it also sets you up to effect similar deals with the same clients in the future.

Here are a few examples of the kind of deals I would put together right away:

Marry car dealers with detail shops that maintain the appearance of cars—and structure the deals so that the detail company offers long-term (one-year) contracts at a savings of X percentage.

Introduce dental patients to companies who sell teeth whitener. Get them on a monthly purchase deal whereby their credit cards are automatically billed and the whitener is automatically shipped for as long as the customer wants the product.

Marry Internet service providers with schools that teach Internet classes. Then bring in software vendors to introduce their products to these students—for an extra profit center—including a percentage of the profits from students who upgrade the software in the long term. This is a trilateral joint venture. As you see, the profit potentials are endless!

Arrange deals whereby software vendors share lists and make offers to one another's customer base. Of course, set it up to take your piece of the pie. . . . This is a very lucrative area, especially if you arrange the deal so that you continue to get a percentage of upgrades.

I hope you are beginning to see the potential. I've used this single concept to earn millions of dollars. If I had to choose *one single way* to make money, this would be it.

I'll never forget how I made this discovery. In the early 1990s, I traveled extensively to study the greatest marketing minds on earth. I met and subsequently became very good friends with Gary Halbert, a highly astute marketing mind and writer of advertising sales copy (space ads, direct-mail sales letters, radio scripts, etc.). Gary taught me a lot about marketing, especially the power of endorsement mailings, the ultimate marketing method!

Become a Deal Maker

There are two major kinds of deals that you can do:

Method 1. You can bring your products and services to noncompeting businesses and arrange for them to make an endorsed mailing to

© 1980 by Ashleigh Brilliant (www.ashleighbrilliant.com)

their existing databases. You agree to pay for the mailing. You split the profits. It's a no-brainer for you and additional income for your new business partner.

Method 2. You can bring two noncompeting businesses together and earn a marketing fee—a percentage of the profit generated from the endorsed mailing. The beauty of this approach is . . . *you don't even have to have a product to do this!*

You become a scout for deals. You find two companies that *should be doing these kinds of endorsement deals.* You introduce them to each other and educate them to the concept. By helping arrange the deal, you take a nice percentage from either or both sides of the arrangement.

I recently did a deal between an attorney who offers credit repair and another gentleman who sells a program on how to eliminate debt. It was a perfect marriage and an opportunity for me to create an ongoing monthly profit center. I should continue receiving checks from this single deal for years to come—all because I helped two parties offer *better service* to their customers.

Nobody loses. Everybody wins. Including you. I've arranged deals like these with Jay Abraham, Gary Halbert, Ted Nicholas, Dan Kennedy, and literally hundreds of others who have introduced their clients and customers to these innovative marketing techniques. These deals are sweet. Your downside is little more than the time it takes to put the deal together, but your effort can yield thousands, tens of thousands, or hundreds of thousands of dollars in immediate sales.

I know, you are asking, "Okay, Mike, well how can I apply this to the Internet?" Here is a step-by-step plan for implementing this system online.

Step 1: Choose Your Product

First and foremost, you have to have something really hot to sell . . . something that offers incredible value, minimal risk—and will make your customers fall in love with you. This is the first and most important step to creating ongoing residual income, which is the real key to great success. Happy customers will buy again and again—as long as they get what you promised the first time.

Maybe you already have an excellent product you are trying to market. If so, follow this formula carefully and read the example at the end of this chapter. For those who don't have an excellent product, I just can't resist saying that I know of no better online product than my own Masters of Marketing Inner Circle Web Site. It's a pass-protected Web site, jam-packed with powerful marketing information—exactly what you need if you really want to be successful on the Internet. And it's so easy to do.

You just give away a free e-book available at www.enlow.com/freebook. Here is what I say on my Web site about the free book:

Turn This E-Book into Your Own Personal Sales Rep

We hear the same complaints, frustrations, and concerns from people who e-mail us every day. They basically boil down to the following:

1. **I can't find a good product to sell!** Either whatever I want costs too much to buy the rights to, or it doesn't have a strong sales letter, or the product itself just isn't that impressive. What can I do?

2. **How can I easily, safely, and responsibly promote a product online?** I don't want to bother people or to risk getting in trouble for spamming. I'm just not a salesperson, and I don't like pushing my offer on people, but I want to make money!

Good news: You're reading the solution right now! You can promote our Masters of Marketing Inner Circle program, and use this e-book as your own personal sales rep. You don't have to sell anything at all. All you have to do is *give away* this free, valuable e-book to those who need it.

Here's why the Masters of Marketing Inner Circle may be the perfect product for you:

- **Top-quality, valuable product worth far more than its selling price.** You'll be proud to stand behind it (very important).
- **It doesn't cost you one penny to sign up and start promoting it.** You can even get this e-book customized so that it actually directs traffic to your associate site. (There's a nominal charge for our staff to do that customization work for you.)
- **We take care of everything** (processing the order, follow-up, customer service, paying you, etc.). All you have to do is pass around the e-book and send us traffic.
- **Proven sales letter and sales process** that is breaking records for hits/sales ratios for high-ticket items online.
- **Pays more in commission than most people earn selling their *own* products.**

To get all the details and find out if this is the opportunity that you have been looking for, just go to www.enlow.com/freebook and follow the links to sign up for our associate program. You'll be glad you did.

Step 2: Use Your Secret Weapon

Go to www.Alexa.com and download Alexa, my secret weapon and my tool of preference. Here you'll find the information you'll need for the next step. Play around with Alexa a while and you'll soon understand how I use it to create incredibly powerful personalized letters. For each site you visit online, Alexa gives you behind-the-scenes information (e.g., the site owner's address and phone number, e-mail addresses, a map and directions). Try it out. It's very useful. And it's free.

Step 3: Rev Your Engine

Using your favorite search engine, search for the following keywords: Internet Marketing, Marketing, Business Success, Advertising, Online Sales, Making Money, MLM, Entrepreneur, E-mail Marketing—and any other keywords that may help you find business owners, e-zine publishers, and the like.

Now that you've done your searches, this next step is literally a paint-by-number process. If you can't make money now, you're beyond hope. I'm serious! If you have read this far and you stop now, you've got no business trying to make money on the Net—it's really that cut-and-dried!

Let's proceed: Once you've done your search and surfed over to the sites you've found, you'll see Alexa doing her magic by providing all of the contact information on the site owner. This is the information you will use to fill in the blanks for the next step.

Step 4: Drum roll, please . . . Fill in the Blanks and Mail This Letter

Take your time to review your prospective joint venture associate's site. Learn a few things about what they are doing/selling so you can write a sentence or two in the first paragraph to get their attention and assure them they *aren't* getting spammed! Let them know they are getting a professional letter for a business proposition. Then send the following letter via e-mail and snail mail:

Dear_____ [If Alexa doesn't list the owner's name, simply put Sir or Ma'am]:

I represent one of the fastest-growing Internet sites for business development on the Net, and since you seem to be doing well (at least I get that impression from your site) [write one or two lines about their site (e.g., "With your promotion of Save-a-Patriot Fellowship)], and since you're obviously stable in business and have been online since _____ with significant success in what you're doing, we want to share an idea with you that we believe will provide you with a nice second stream of revenue while rendering a very noble service to your customers.

We represent a product that is a perfect noncompetitive match with what you offer your current customers. We are prepared to absorb all risk and monetary costs. In the end, everyone wins.

If you'll call me between 9 and 5 one day this week, I'll explain everything in full. It will take only about 10 minutes of your time, but it can mean thousands of dollars to your bottom line.

I think you'll be as excited as I was when I found you on the Net. My number is 888-XXX-XXXX. Just tell whomever answers I'm expecting your call.

Sincerely Yours,

Your name

P.S. By the way, my partner suggested I go directly to http://_____, who seems to be your competitor, but I feel you're better suited. Please do call as soon as you can. We are up against a few deadlines, and I really would like to work with you on this as soon as possible.

[Notice how Alexa will show you a few links to direct competitors for use with this segment of your letter!]

P.P.S. If you prefer, simply reply to this message with your telephone number and the best time to reach you, and I'll call you. Just be sure to include your name in the Subject line so I can quickly identify your e-mail and get right back to you.

You may be thinking, *"Enlow, is it really this simple?"* The answer is an unequivocal *yes, yes, yes!* It's that easy.

All you have to do is commit to work two days a week surfing, finding prospects, and sending out letters. And delegate two days a week, a couple of hours each day to making the calls and arranging the deals. It's that simple . . . and yes, it works. I've made several million dollars myself doing this. Now it's your turn.

Follow this simple step-by-step program and you'll make the phones ring with people who are interested in your proposition. Frankly, you have nothing left to do but sell them on doing an endorsed offer to their list for a share of the profits. Explain how you do all the work and they simply offer their current customers a noncompetitive product. It's that simple, and it works almost every time!

Here is a great success story recently posted by one of my members on our bulletin board.

Formula for success = total desperation + total lack of money + total isolation + a superior product + a couple of moms who wouldn't give up

YES! Our first joint venture deal is truly exciting! And it did make us go out and do it 3 more times at this point, with more being planned. :o)

The way that the whole thing came about is really quite simple. My friend Carol owns and operates Tao Herb Farm. We are both single moms living in the backwoods (literally) of the pristine Kootenay mountains in BC, Canada. For the past year we have been becoming Web-literate out of the simple necessity of having to do things all on our own due to total lack of funds. As Carol put it when I asked her permission to tell everyone, "I'll let you tell about the long sleepless nights, worrying over the stack of bills while the woodpile dwindles, and the sore eyes doing the figures in the dim light to save on kerosene."

About all we had a year ago was a totally superior product, which Carol was sharp enough to get exclusive North American distributorship rights to, and the beginnings of a Web site.

To make a long story a little shorter, we've learned a lot, and Carol can now stay home and work her farm exclusively—entirely due to the software sales. But surviving isn't necessarily good living, and she needs a new roof.

So once again we were in the money crunch. We had been thinking of doing an affiliate program for quite a while, but couldn't afford the software, plus we had the wisdom to realize that a total influx of sales at this point could bring her down.

Also, Carol recognized the need to bring this product into the "real" world. Magazine advertising and brochure mail-outs again cost money, and when you truly don't have any, you need to get creative.

Here is a rundown of how the program is set up. It's amazingly simple once you get the hang of it the first time. Here is a sample of the letter we take IN PERSON to local businesses (it would be personalized).

Dear Retailer,

The Christmas season is fast approaching, and you are probably wondering how you can thank your valued customers for their ongoing support and patronage.

We would like to offer a suggestion whereby you receive a FREE, superb-quality gift to give your customers PLUS earn a generous commission for yourself as well.

Tao Herb Farm has been a licensed business since 1994 and is the sole North American distributor for GrowIt Gold Works. GrowIt Gold is a garden and landscape design software program that is geared to everyone from the true beginner to the most advanced nursery professional. To check out this versatile product, please visit our main Web site at http://www.taoherbfarm.com.

Who would be interested in GrowIt?

GrowIt is attractive to a wide range of clientele, such as landscapers, nurseries, schools, clubs and organizations, as well as the home gardening hobbiest and do-it-yourselfer.

GrowIt's easy-to-use format and low cost, combined with the extensiveness of the six modules offered, makes it an extremely versatile package for any gardening enthusiast.

Here's how the partnering program works.

After joining our program *at no cost whatsoever to you*, you will be given a gift certificate with your merchant name and certificate number on it.

The gift certificate is a $10.00 discount toward the purchase of GrowIt Gold. You can then give the gift certificate to your customers in one or all of the following ways:

- **Hand them to your clients and friends in person**
- **Enclose the gift certificate with your customer's orders and purchases**
- **Add them to Christmas, birthday, and other special-occasion cards and mail-outs**
- **Include them in your catalogs**
- **Via e-mail**
- **As a link on your Web site**

You can even use the gift certificates to generate new business for yourself at trade fairs and other similar venues because your business name is also on the certificates.

When your customers go to purchase the software, they will be instructed to select the Gift Certificate option and then put in your merchant number in order to receive their discount.

For every sale YOU WILL RECEIVE a $15.00 Canadian (U.S.$10.00) commission! This is a win-win situation!

Feel good about being able to offer your customers a wonderful gift at no cost to you now or ever. PLUS obtain the potential to earn extra income for yourself and your business.

Enroll now by visiting our Web site and filling out the registration form.

http://www.taoherbfarm.com/herbs/partnering/partnering.htm

Or telephone us at 250-357-2550.

We will be pleased to help you in any way possible—from providing the actual gift certificates for you to distribute to assisting you with coding for your Web site's links.

With sincere best wishes,

Carol Vickery
Tao Herb Farm
P.O. Box 327
Salmo, BC
http://www.taoherbfarm.com

Enc. Sample Gift Certificate

This now allows people to hand out the gift certificates to clients, family, and friends; enclose them with customer's orders and purchases; add them to Christmas, birthday, and special-occasion cards and mail-outs; make them part of their printed catalog; plus they can send them via e-mail or use them in addition to their Web site.

Retailers can even use them to generate additional sales for themselves at trade fairs and similar venues, because THEIR name is on the gift certificate as well. This way everyone wins. Customer gets a break, retailer gets good PR and a generous commission bonus, Carol gets sales, and we can stay home and let others carry the gift certificates to places we can't cover.

So that is how this joint venture came about. Total desperation, total lack of money, isolation, a superior product, and a couple of moms who won't give up. :o)

Okay, folks. This is Mike Enlow again. I hope this opens your eyes to the possibilities. If I can help you learn more about putting one of these deals together, contact me at my Web site, and don't forget to get your free book: www.enlow.com/freebook.

CHAPTER 11

Online Stream #2.
Affiliate Programs:
Cash In by Selling
Other People's Stuff

In Chapter 7, I hinted at the power of *affiliate programs*. In this chapter, I'm going to show you how. Just for fun, log on to the Internet and check out this site:

www.associate-it.com (directory of Associate programs)

This is one of the top sites tracking the hundreds of affiliate programs on the Net. There is something here for any taste or multiple tastes. But how do you make money from an affiliate program? I've asked my good friend, Bob Gatchel, owner of InternetCheapskate.com and author of *The*

Cheapskate's Guide to Internet Marketing, to share some of his marketing insights. Whether you're a newbie to the Net or an established Internet business, you can learn from his "frugal" wisdom. If they'd listened to Bob, a lot of Internet start-ups would still be up and cranking instead of dead and dying. Bob and his wife Joyce have been instrumental in mentoring me in the exciting field of Internet marketing, so I know you are in good hands. Take it away, Bob.

The Hidden Power of Affiliate Programs

How would you like to start your own proven, online marketing business without having to spend tons of money—even without having a Web site? How would you like a business where you do not have to stock products, handle money, ship products, or deal with customer service issues—but you still make money with that product line? Can that really happen? Can this situation be true? Absolutely, by using the power of the Internet's best-kept secret, the *affiliate program.*

Affiliate programs are probably the fastest, easiest, and most profitable way to make money on the Internet! An affiliate program is nothing more than a joint venture between someone like you, a marketer, and a company that wants to promote a product. Basically, the company with the product provides the product, the Web site, the customer service, the order handling, and the fulfillment. But the company *also* gives you a link so that when you refer clients to purchase its products, *you* earn a nice commission from every sale! The company wins because it has thousands of marketers all over the world recommending its products. You win by being paid to market top-notch products and services. Bottom line, you simply refer people to these sites and you're paid for any resulting sales—period!

Some of the biggest companies in the world are using affiliate programs to expand their markets (Dell Computer, Sprint PCS, Staples, OfficeMax, L.L. Bean, and many, many others). And more companies are jumping onto the e-commerce/affiliate bandwagon every day. There are affiliate programs for food, clothing, software, computers, toys, electronics, long-distance service, and even medicine! You can literally build your own online store with tons of different products and receive commissions for simply referring people to buy from these sites!

The benefits of using affiliate programs to make money on the Internet are quite obvious:

1. *It is easy!* You don't need to create a product or service. You never need to worry about spending the time and money to build and maintain a Web site. You never need to worry about customer service, shipping, or even getting a merchant account to accept credit cards. The company handles every one of those details.

2. *You can make money fast.* Since you need not be concerned with all of the technical details of a Web site and need not build your own company to handle order issues, you can start by simply concentrating on advertising your special link to these sites. You can literally begin making money almost immediately. In some cases, people have been getting their first orders within days . . . hours . . . or even minutes!

3. *You can be sure that the products you are offering will sell!* Suppose you take the time to build your own product, company, and Web site, and your product doesn't go over well. Then you are kind of stuck, since you spent so much time and effort to make a go of it. Being a pioneer and starting a new business can be tough. You end up with a lot of arrows in your back. In an affiliate program, you don't need to reinvent the wheel—the hard work has been done. The market research, product development, and online sales materials have been professionally created. You literally have hundreds of thousands of dollars of marketing and market research done *for you.* And it costs you *nothing* to use it!

4. *You can run more than one program and create multiple streams of affiliate income.* You are never locked into one product. You have as many or as few affiliate programs at your disposal as you wish. I recommend that you try to concentrate on just a few programs and work them well, but if you find that there is a new market to capture and money to be made with a new product, then just sign up for the program and start promoting! Affiliate programs allow you to be an online business change agent.

5. *Free marketing training and tools are provided by the company.* When you sign up for an affiliate program (which is normally *free*), you get not only the ability to represent that company's product line with *no* hassle to you, but many companies provide you, the marketer, with *tons* of great marketing training material. You often get sample advertising copy, sample banners to use on Web sites, and sample sales letters. Again, you are getting some of the best marketing tools and training available to help make YOU and the COMPANY successful—for FREE!

So, where do you find these programs?
Affiliate programs are all over the Internet. If you visit almost any online e-commerce Web site or any site that sells products, you will often see a link to "Join the affiliate program" or "Earn cash" button. As you browse, be sure to look for affiliate opportunities from your favorite online stores.

Several great online databases not only list affiliate programs, but also rate them on how well they pay and how they rank against other affiliate programs. These sites are worth researching:

http://www.refer-it.com

http://www.associateprograms.com

http://www.clickquick.com

http://www.associate-it.com

If you go to any search engine and use the term "Affiliate program," you will find other resources. Remember, the Internet is in a constant state of change, and this list is just a start.

Affiliate Programs: Make Money Now . . . and *More* Money *Later!*

As I have often taught my Internet marketing students, an affiliate program is a *vital* part of any online business venture. Even if you have a well-tested product or service, even if you have a productive and profitable Web site or online marketing presence, an affiliate program is a must to help generate another stream of cash and provide more service to your online customers.

But there is another aspect to an affiliate program that is often overlooked—even by some of the best marketing minds in the world—and that is using affiliate programs to build a huge customer list.

Too often, people think only about the immediate money that can be made from an affiliate program, and that is fine. You can, indeed, with good marketing and advertising, make a great income from an affiliate program. But many times people forget that these customers could actually be *good future customers for other products.*

You see, every direct marketer or mail-order marketer knows the value of having a customer list. If you read any book on marketing, every single one talks about the list you should have. Well, Internet marketing is no different. Internet marketing is a direct extension of offline marketing, and the concepts of direct marketing and mail order apply equally as well here.

Unfortunately, average folks use an affiliate program as follows:

1. They run an ad.
2. The ad contains their special affiliate link.
3. The customer goes to the site . . . and *maybe* buys.
4. The affiliate gets a commission if the sale is made.

Basically, such affiliates are doing what I call *filter-feeder marketing.* They just throw out the link to their affiliate program and hope for the best. Oftentimes, they do get the sales and make money. But this is a huge lack of potential.

You see, many marketing gurus state that the secret to successful marketing is to follow up with prospects and remind them of the offer. In filter-feeder marketing there is no follow-up by the marketer. If they could somehow capture the leads before they send them on to the company affiliate site, then they could keep in touch with these prospects and help them make the decision to purchase.

Therefore, the more advanced marketer will do this:

1. Run the ad.

2. Direct the prospect to contact the marketer (that's *you*).

3. The marketer captures the e-mail and name.

4. The marketer sends the prospect to the affiliate link.

5. The customer may or may not purchase anything.

6. The marketer follows up and continues to pitch the product.

7. More customers will buy.

The fortune is in the follow-up!

This is much better than filter-feeder marketing because it's been shown that the fortune is in the follow-up. From my own experience and the experiences of my students, following up with prospects causes the buy ratio to increase dramatically.

The next problem occurs if you are victim of your own success. If you are getting tons of replies, you need to track when the lead came in, when you sent the first follow-up message, and when to send subsequent follow-ups.

In our systems, we follow up anywhere from 7 to 10 times with a prospect. Could you imagine trying to keep track of which person gets what follow-up message and when? Believe me, if you try to do this manually, you can spend hours and hours each day, and it will drive you crazy. Even though you captured the leads, managing them can be a nightmare.

The Optimal Solution

Since the Internet is all about automation and using technology to make our lives simpler, we recommend a system that uses a specialized Internet marketing tool called a *sequential* or *automatic follow-up autoresponder.* Basically, it's a way to put all of your follow-up on autopilot.

An autoresponder is nothing more than a little online robot that spits out predetermined messages to anyone who contacts it via e-mail. If you send an e-mail to this robot, it will send out your sales message, letter, or pitch 24 hours a day 7 days a week without fail. But these sequential or timed autoresponders go one better. In addition to sending out the first message for you, you can upload all sequential follow-up messages and have them e-mailed automatically to the appropriate prospect at the appropriate time—all without your intervention.

A prospect could get your first sales letter right away, three days later get the next one, a day later get another one, five days later get the next, and so on. You program which message goes out when based on the prospect's initial contact with your little e-mail robot. This follow-up autoresponder literally puts your entire lead capture and follow-up management on autopilot!

Some of these special autoresponders are available free or at a very low cost per month. Here are some that I recommend:

http://www.freeautoresponders.net/

http://www.aweber.com/

http://www.getresponse.com/

http://www.autobots.net/

http://www.autoresponders.com/

http://www.myreply.com/

http://www.mailtrail.com/

http://www.automailer.com/

http://www.fastfacts.net/

The optimal system would work as follows:

1. Run ads.
2. Prospect replies to the autoresponder.
3. Autoresponder sends out sales letter directing prospect to the affiliate link.
4. Autoresponder will follow up for you automatically.
5. Autoresponder *captures* e-mail address and name, which can be downloaded to a database.
6. System can run in your sleep or while you are out—hands off!

Now that we understand how the optimal system should work, let me show you *how I make as much as $3.21 per lead instead of paying for them!*

As stated earlier, there are two ways to think about the use of affiliate programs: (1) as a way to generate cash from the sales of the product or (2) as a way to generate leads for initial and future sales.

Option 2 is the method that is often overlooked. Many folks consider making money from the affiliate sale but *never* consider the value of the folks that replied to the ads or purchased the products.

In my experience, I have found that people who are interested in my initial affiliate product are often interested in other products in that line. By using the autopilot system described earlier, I accumulate a whole cache of names that I can use again and again for further marketing. I believe in teaching by example, so here goes:

1. I joined an affiliate program that sold a $50 product and paid a $30 commission.

2. I purchased some very inexpensive e-zine ads for just a few dollars.

3. I used a follow-up autoresponder that cost me $27 per month.

Here are the results:

Affiliate Program

- $50 cost (no delivery, etc.)
- $30 commission

E-Zine Advertisement

- Targeted to working moms
- Cost $7.50 for 1,000+ circulation

Prospects Respond to Autoresponder—Cost $27/Month

- Send out message directing person to my affiliate link
- Capture e-mail with name and other info
- Follow-ups sent out for two weeks

Responses

- 15 total responses (about 1.5%)
- Three sales

Bottom Line

Gross sales	$90
Expenses:	
Autoresponder	($27)
E-zine advertisement	($7.50)
Net profit	$55.50

As you can see, with no Web site, no product, no merchant account, and no delivery hassles, my investment of $34.50 yielded $55.50 in profit.

But that is not the end of the story. . . . Reinvest and expand! I reinvested $55.50 by running ads in five e-zines at an average cost per ad of approximately $10.00. Average circulation was approximately 9,000.

Same Program, Same Ads, Same System

- Targeted to working moms
- Used autoresponder system
- Followed up for two weeks

Responses

- 42 total responses (about 0.05%)
- Seven sales @ $30 = $210

Bottom Line

Gross Sales $210

Expenses:

   Autoresponder   ($27)

   E-zine advertisement   ($0)

(Remember, I reinvested the $55.50 I made last month, so there was no out-of-pocket advertising cost this month!)

Net profit $183

(with a lower response and conversion)

After two months of this campaign we have generated the following:

Total profits: $183.00

Total *new leads:* 57

This means I got *paid* $3.21 for every lead that I generated.

Now this may not seem like a lot of money. But you can rest assured that I *continued* to reinvest in my system, expanding until I was getting *tons* of leads. Not all of my campaigns were successful; sometimes I actually had a cost per lead. However, overall I have never lost any money on creating my leads list.

> *Read that again: I have never lost money*
> *generating my leads with this system.*

If you are a direct marketer, you fully understand the power of what I just said. In direct mail and mail order, you often have to *spend money on leads*—but using an affiliate program in this manner can act as a "self-funded proposal" and actually pay you money to generate leads.

Even if I broke even and didn't make or lose one penny but generated hundreds of leads in the process, I would still be very successful. Why? Because I now have a *free list* of prospects to market to again and again . . . and again . . . via e-mail.

Do you think I stop promoting products to these leads when I get them? Do you think I just stop after I make a few bucks from this affiliate sale? *No way!*

I found a comparable affiliate program with products and services that would appeal to the targeted list I created. Guess what I did? You are right! I e-mailed my prospects a few weeks later thanking them for their interest in my previous offer and directing them to the other program I was offering. Many did indeed purchase those products, and yes, I made more money from those same leads.

I discovered yet another way to make money with my database—I found other people on the Internet with whom to joint-venture and swap leads. If I had 1,000 leads who showed interest in my products in the past and my new partner had a comparable product, we agreed to an even exchange of leads and marketed our respective affiliate programs to those new people. I also sold my older leads lists to other marketers.

That single $50 sale translated to many, many other streams of income. The moral of the story is, *yes,* use affiliate programs to make money, but the ultimate goal is to use them to create a *targeted e-mail list* that will help you build long-term, back-end, and follow-up sales in the future.

I hope that this introduction gives you a different view on how to use affiliate programs to turbocharge your online marketing ventures. If you would like to reach me to discuss this and other marketing concepts, just visit my site at http://www.internetcheapskate.com. Best of success with your online marketing!*

More Resources to Help You Launch Your Own Affiliate Program

www.cj.com   This company can administer the details of your affiliate program.

www.affiliatezone.com   This company can set you up with the technology to run your affiliate program.

---

*The preceding section on the power of affiliate programs has been provided by Robert Gatchel, owner of InternetCheapskate.com.

Pick Your Niche if You Want to Get "Riche"

One of the most popular affiliate programs on the Web was launched by Dr. Ken Evoy. Ken is president of SiteSell.com, whose 5 Pillar Program is considered by many experts to be the most innovative, partnership-oriented and productive affiliate program on the Net. Here is how he did it.*

Building a Powerful Affiliate Program in 10 Days or Less

Being a great affiliate is not about selling. . . . It's about preselling. The goal of any business, including your affiliate business, is to maximize profits. Profit is simply your income minus your expenses.

As an affiliate, there are exactly two ways to increase your income:

1. Refer more visitors to the merchants you represent.

2. Increase the *conversion rate* (i.e., the percent of your referrals who deliver the response for which your merchant pays, whether it be a sale or a lead).

Simple, right? If you refer 100 visitors per day to a merchant, and 1 percent buy, you are paid for that one purchase. If you send 1,000 visitors per day, and 3 percent buy, you are paid for 30 purchases. Yes, 30 times more! So it's pretty clear how to maximize affiliate income!

Of course, every business has expenses, too. Maximizing profits does not imply that you must minimize expenses. After all, if you spend *no* money or time on a business . . . you have no business! You must get the best possible traffic-building and sales-converting results for every dollar you spend . . . and for every hour you spend on your business.

Let's examine expenses by asking two questions.

Question 1: What does it cost to build traffic to your merchants' sites?

Traffic-building, no matter how you cut it, will cost you in terms of both time and money. Spending dollars is optional, but spending time is not.

There are many ways, both offline and on, to drive traffic to your merchants' sites. Here is the most highly profitable, time- and dollar-effective way to build traffic to your merchants' sites:

Build your own theme-based content site—one that is loaded with high-info-value keyword-focused content pages, that ranks well with the search engines, and that gets the click-throughs to your merchants' sites.

---

*The remainder of this chapter has been contributed by Ken Evoy.

FIRST GOD MADE BUSINESSES,

BUT THE BUSINESS PEOPLE WERE LONELY AND UNHAPPY,

SO THEN GOD CREATED CUSTOMERS.

© 1992 by Ashleigh Brilliant (www.ashleighbrilliant.com)

Let's break that down. For your affiliate Web site to generate traffic to your merchants, it must do the following two things well:

1. Rank well at the search engines so that it pulls in lots of traffic. So far, though, that traffic is still on your site. Therefore, it's not generating income yet. Your visitors are just looking around. So you must . . .

2. Get those visitors to click through to your merchants. (Some affiliate program models can actually place merchant offerings on your Web site. In this case, your traffic does not actually visit your merchant's site. But you still have to get the click to generate income.)

Question 2: What does it cost to maximize conversion rates?

Good news! Maximizing your conversion rate (CR) is simply a question of doing things right. There is no extra dollar or time cost to boosting conversion rates at your merchants' sites. Your goals, and your only goals, are as follows:

1. Maximize traffic to your merchants, spending only dollars and time that maximize profits.

2. Maximize conversion rates. Do things right (no expense).

Don't do just one. Do both. Why? Because your payment is determined by traffic *multiplied by* (not added to) the conversion rate. Your profits grow geometrically when you concentrate on maximizing *both* traffic and conversion rates.

I have spent quite a bit of time reviewing the results of affiliates to my own affiliate program (5 Pillar Program). Here is what I've discovered: The number one reason for low traffic and terrible conversion rates is *banner ads!*

Retinal studies have shown that Web surfers actually avoid banners. Yes, their eyes look away! Click-throughs have plummeted to under one-half of 1 percent. For the few who *do* click, my research shows that banners are *worse* than futile—they are counterproductive. My 5 Pillar Program affiliates who rely on banners have an average conversion rate of 0.5 percent. But those who use *in-context text links* (text links that are part of the content of the Web page) average over 3.5 percent!

How's that for a reason *not* to use banners? Why does this happen?

Banners are cheesy and hurt your credibility because visitors arrive feeling used rather than informed. They arrive in a resistant mind-set rather than with an open, ready-to-buy attitude.

Conclusion? Don't use banners.

Yes, I know, they're so-o-o-o-o easy. It's *always* easy *not* to make money. That's how all those get-rich-quick schemers do so well . . . the allure of easy money. No such thing.

If you simply must use banners, save them for products that you don't really feel great about recommending. (That way, you don't hurt your credibility—after all, it's only advertising.)

Save your in-context text links for super companies with wonderful products that deliver true value to your reader.

Beside the obvious futility of banners, I've spotted another major error: selling instead of *pre*selling.

Picture this: A visitor arrives at an affiliate's site that is really just one, big sales site. Put yourself in these visitors' shoes for a moment. They don't see inspiring, editorial content—they see a sales effort. But they were searching for content!

People resist sales efforts, so your click-through rate actually goes down. Result? Poor conversion rate.

If your site is basically a bunch of sales letters, you have not yet built your credibility and likability with this visitor. Your visitors end up feeling "pitched to." And then they feel "double-pitched" *if* they click through to your merchant's site.

That's why the conversion rate (CR) actually goes down. To make things worse, as they smell a sales pitch, your visitors become less likely to click! So referred traffic drops, too. (As a point of interest, women now represent 50 percent of all surfers, and they control approximately 80 percent of all shopping dollars.)

Let's see. . . . Referred traffic is down. Conversion rate is down. We're going in the wrong direction! Conclusion? Don't sell! Instead, warm up your visitors by *preselling* them with great content that they value and respect. They'll click through with pleasure, arriving at your merchants' sites in an open-to-buy mind-set. It's your *presell* effort that will boost your traffic to merchants and your conversion rate, which in turn maximizes your income.

Put yourself in your customers' shoes. What will they think, how will they feel as visitors to your site? Consider how much higher your CR would be if visitors found you in a bona fide manner (e.g., as a result of using a search engine), then became friends (or trusting admirers if you do a truly awesome job!) because you provided excellent content that eventually led to a context-appropriate recommendation.

Preselling is really all about selling yourself to your customer every step of the way. You reach the right folks in a proper fashion; you deliver valuable, appropriate editorial content; and you recommend visitors to your merchant *after* they have come to respect and like you. Your CR will soar.

Why does preselling work so well? Because a sale via *any* affiliate program is really a two-step process. Your job, as an affiliate, is to presell customers and guide them to your merchant with an open-to-buy mind-set. Let your merchant's site do its job and get the sale. I remember when I used to tell my star baseball pitcher, Joel Leonoff, "Joel . . . you don't have to strike 'em all out. You've got a great team behind you. Let them do their job." Same goes for your merchants. . . . Let them do their job.

In other words, don't *push* your visitors to the click. Make them *want* to click. It makes all the difference if your visitors feel that it's their own idea. Here's a real concrete example.

Earlier, I said that the key to success is to create a theme-based content site that is loaded with keyword-focused, content-rich pages. Now let's come up with a theme to show you how it's done.

Your theme? Let's pull something crazy out of the air. Let's suppose you love concrete. Yes, cement! It's been your hobby, your passion, for years. Concrete statues. Concrete painting. Decorative concrete. Concrete in the garden. Repairing concrete. Various types of concrete. Hand trowels. Things to do with cement blocks. Concrete trade shows. Concrete and swimming pools. Concrete molds. Cleaning concrete. Ready-mixed concrete. Concrete countertops.

Anyway, let's say that you decide to create a *theme-based* site that is all about concrete. Your home page explains how your site is *the* site for everything concrete—from structural to aesthetic.

You also, of course, create high-value, content-jammed, keyword-focused content pages. For example, your page about concrete statues explains how to make striking statues for home and garden. You could even expand it into an entire statue section, with one page on the history of concrete statues, another one about how to market and sell the statues, and so on. The main point, though, is that you create truly excellent, *high-value* content that delivers what your reader sought at the engines.

You also weave *relevant,* in-context text links into the content as appropriate. Links to . . .

- Books about the topic (e.g., concrete statues if that's what the page was about)
- A garden supplier for concrete molds and trowels
- Naturally, a concrete supplier!
- Almost anything concrete-related

See what's happening? By providing great content, you presell your reader, increasing your click-through traffic to your merchants and your conversion rate (sales). And by diversifying your affiliate programs among several related and excellent merchants, you develop multiple streams of income from one site. *This is the way to go.*

Okay, we can summarize what we've learned in a key lesson to take home. I am giving it this title . . .

The Road to Becoming a Master Affiliate

What's the key? *Preselling.* Not selling. You must, must, *must* know how to *presell!* Let's summarize the whole point of preselling with this question: Which would you respond to . . . *a stranger with a sales pitch* or *a knowledgeable friend making a recommendation?*

How to Pick the Right Concept for Your Site

Most people fail in any business because they don't plan adequately. If you pick the wrong concept, if you develop the wrong topics, if you pick the wrong affiliate programs . . . you'll get the wrong results. So let's brainstorm a high-potential idea. Discover the best site concepts for you. Then narrow it down to the one with the most potential. Basically, it boils down to this:

Do what you love. The money will follow.

Everyone, absolutely everyone, has a special interest . . . a passion. Everyone knows something that is of value to others. Passion makes work fun and easy. What is it that you love to talk about? Read about? Do you have a hobby? What do you do for fun and games? What are your natural talents?

Don't forget to look right under your nose. . . . What special body of knowledge have you learned from your job? What do you do day after day without even thinking about it (e.g., child rearing, taking care of sick parents, renovation contractor, customs inspector)?

Think about what you do in a typical day and what you've learned from it. What sections of a bookstore or a magazine shop do you automatically gravitate toward? What kind of TV shows or movies do you like most?

What do you most enjoy about your current occupation? Is it research? Helping customers achieve their goals? Managing other people? Teaching or explaining things to others? Talking/selling on the phone? Organizing things? Making a process easier? Discovering or creating new products or services? Marketing products?

Problems are also a good source of ideas because problems need solutions! What bugs you? What's tedious? What does not work?

We all encounter obstacles, problems, and nasty people in the course of whatever it is that we do every day. What are the three biggest problems in your workplace? What are your biggest pains as a parent, as a stepparent, as a gardener?

Call friends. Ask your kids. Phone your parents, your siblings, or anyone else who can jog your memory. It's so easy to miss what others see.

Your mission, should you decide to accept it (and it is *not* as easy as it sounds) is to find a subject that you really know and like.

Here are a few examples of starting points to get your neurons firing:

Advertising

Aerospace

Agriculture/farming

Antiques and collectibles

Apparel/clothing/fashion

Architecture/buildings

Arts and crafts

Auctions

Automotive

Aviation

Beverages

Books

Business

Chemicals

Children/parenting

Cleaning

Communications/media

Computers

Construction

Consulting

Conventions/trade shows

Design

Disabilities

Education

Electronics

Employment

Energy

Engineering

Entertainment

Environment

Ergonomics

Financial services

Food

Gambling

Games

Government

Health

Hobbies

Home/garden/flowers/plants

Hospitality/entertaining

Information

Jewelry

Law

Manufacturing

Marketing

Minerals

Money

Music

New Age

Office supplies

Publishing

Real estate

Religion/spirituality

Research and development

Retail management

Science

Security

Sex

Software

Sports

Telecommunications

Toys

Trade

Transportation

Travel

Video

Weather

Take your time on this—the final concept will, after all, form the foundation for your affiliate business. Now that you have read this far, review all the preceding brain stimulators with pen and paper (or keyboard) in hand.

Write down concepts as they hit you—make as long a list as you can. Don't censor yourself. Just write down ideas for site concepts as they occur.

Next, pick the three concepts that you love the most and that you think would have some appeal for others—this is your shortlist of site concepts. Remember, if a concept really turns you on, you won't be working. You'll be playing. So focus on topics that you love.

Let's say that you love fashion. You eat, live, and sleep it. You read all the fashion magazines. You head straight to that part of any bookstore. Your friends beg you to "talk about something else for a change!" Fashion is your focus, but can you make any money at it?

Let's do some basic research to find out (1) if there is any demand for this topic and (2) if there are existing sites to fill this demand.

First let's check out the demand for our topic. Is anybody searching the Net using the keyword *fashion?* A great way to find out is to open your browser and start with the following link:

http://www.7search.com/scripts/advertiser/sample_get.asp

This takes you to the Related Keywords tool at the search engine called 7search.com. Enter the word *fashion* and hit Find It! You will be given the 200 most commonly searched keywords that contain the word *fashion.*

The number in the right column is the number of times that each keyword was searched in the preceding month at 7search.com. In a sense, it's an indication of the demand (by *your* potential visitors) for each keyword that contains the word *fashion.*

A similar research tool is available at a more popular search engine, www.goto.com, but you need to be a member to use it. Because GoTo.com is used more frequently, the monthly search numbers are much higher, but using 7search.com at least gives you an idea of the relative popularity (demand) for each keyword or combination of keywords. Table 11.1 shows the first 25 listings along with what people are bidding for each search engine position.

Okay, what do we have so far? We have a good idea of what your potential visitors want. In other words, we know what's in demand— and by how much—for a variety of keywords that contain the word *fashion.*

Now let's check out the *supply* of your *fashion*-containing keywords. In other words, how many sites already provide content for the keywords that we found? Load up the AltaVista search engine at http://www.altavista.com/ and enter each of the keywords (with *fashion* as a root) from your 7search.com research. For example, enter the keywords *fashion modeling.* The AltaVista search returns over 5,000 results. Click on the first 10 to 20 links in your search. As you get into this in-depth research, you'll notice three types of sites:

- *Irrelevant.* For whatever reason (off-topic, geographic, lousy site, etc.), they just don't fit. Skip these.

- *Merchants.* These are possible partners, especially if they have an affiliate program.

- *Content sites.* These sites are your direct competitors. Learn from them. Notice the kinds of ads they display and which affiliate programs they belong to. As you review these content sites, you may get some great ideas for content on your own site. Browse these sites, drilling down into the content. Click on the banner ads and text links and follow them to their destinations to see what kind of merchants that they have chosen as affiliate partners.

TABLE 11.1 Top 25 Listings at 7search.com Search Engine

Related Keyword	Bid to Become #1	Estimated Monthly Searches
1. Fashion	$0.09	3,732
2. Fashion modeling	$0.01	1,883
3. Fashion designers	$0.01	1,051
4. Fashion shows	$0.01	864
5. Fashion show	$0.01	237
6. Mens fashion	$0.03	126
7. Fashion bug	$0.01	91
8. Fashion design	$0.03	83
9. Fashion models	$0.01	73
10. Fashions	$0.01	60
11. Fashion magazines	$0.10	42
12. Fashion apparel companies	$0.02	35
13. Fashion for men	$0.01	28
14. Fashion news resources	$0.02	25
15. Fashion institute of technology	$0.01	25
16. Fashion.com	$0.01	25
17. Fashiontv	$0.01	24
18. Fashion apparel companies Chicago	$0.02	21
19. National institute of fashion technology	$0.01	21
20. Careers in fashion	$0.01	21
21. Fashion designer	$0.03	20
22. Fashion designers Barcelona	$0.01	18
23. Fashion colleges	$0.01	18
24. Fashion trend	$0.01	17
25. Fashion public relations	$0.01	15

Do this for each combination of keywords from the 7search.com list. I know this sounds tedious, but this research will help you pick just the right niche—something that taps into your passion in a profitable way.

Now it's time to pick the keywords with the best potential for profit. These will be the keywords with highest demand (i.e., tons of searches according to the 7search.com list) and low supply (i.e., not too many sites found at AltaVista).

For example, notice that *fashion colleges* was searched only 18 times in the previous month at 7search.com. Your AltaVista search returned 864 matches. Not a bad ratio. If, however, AltaVista had returned 10,000 matches, then it would have been too competitive a field to enter.

When you're ready to create your site, start with the keywords that have the best combination of high demand and low supply. This is a fairly subjective process, but spending a few hours in this kind of exercise can help you brainstorm the kind of affiliate programs you want to focus on.

I have created a software tool called Site Build It!, which takes the guesswork out of this process and helps you discover the best keywords with the greatest probability for profit. If you'd like more information, go to http://buildit.sitesell.com/ken.html.

How to Grow, Prune, and Group the Best Affiliate Programs

All this research should have helped you come up with a site concept that you are passionate about. As you fill your site with excellent content, those people who share your passion will be delighted to browse through your offerings. Embedded in the text of the information at your site will be links to the various affiliate programs you have selected for your site. Let's find three strong affiliate programs to add to your site.

You are going to grow a list of good merchants with affiliate programs that have complementary product lines. Then you'll choose the best ones and group them according to high-profitability keywords.

How do you do this? Go to AltaVista.com and enter one of your keywords plus the word *affiliate,* like this:

+fashion +affiliate

The plus sign (+) means that both words must appear on the Web page returned by the search. This should yield either fashion merchants *with* affiliate programs or content sites that *are* affiliates. Visit the top 10 sites (20 if you're feeling ambitious).

Repeat the process for each keyword in your master keyword list (e.g., replace *fashion* with another keyword like *fashion models:*

+"fashion models" +affiliate

In your searching, you will stumble across several companies that sell products/services through affiliate programs that will be a perfect match for your content site. Now it's just a matter of selecting the right fit. But before you do, there is another way to find affiliate programs that may fit well with your site.

Some terrific folks out there have already compiled exhaustive lists of merchants with affiliate programs. They've even organized them into categories for you. I have listed the 10 most important affiliate directories in approximate order of popularity on the Net.

The Top 10 Most Popular Affiliate Directories on the Net

1. AssociatePrograms.com (10,802 visits). Allan Gardyne has one of the best directories going—it screens out the riffraff. It has an active forum, too. Not to be missed.

   http://www.associateprograms.com/

2. Refer-It.com (10,010 visits). One of the granddaddies, this site has a comprehensive directory and an excellent Webmasters Lounge.

   http://www.refer-it.com/

3. CashPile.com (9,131 visits). Extensive directory, good tools.

   http://www.cashpile.com/

4. Associate-It.com (7,267 visits). Excellent overall resource.

   http://www.associate-it.com/

5. ClickQuick.com (4,885 visits). Useful, in-depth program reviews.

   http://www.clickquick.com/

6. Revenews.com (3,542 visits). Useful forum, top-notch articles.

   http://www.revenews.com/

7. AffiliateWorld.com (2,106 visits)

   http://www.affiliateworld.com/

8. AffiliateMatch.com (1,986 visits)

   http://www.AffiliateMatch.com/

9. 2-Tier Affiliate Program Directory (1,558 visits)

   http://www.2-tier.com/

10. AffiliatesDirectory.com (1,543 visits)

    http://www.affiliatesdirectory.com/

Here's how to use these directories. Drill down through the relevant major categories of the directory until you find good-fit subcategories with your chosen keywords. You'll find one or more merchants in each subcategory that should fit well with your site concept.

Use the forums. Most of the preceding directories have a forum where you can ask questions. Review them for comments about programs that interest you. Don't be shy—ask people if there are any problems that you should be aware of before proceeding.

All this research should yield as many as 10 potential affiliate partners for your content Web site. How many should you select? Is there an optimum number of affiliate programs to attach to your site? Here's an important point to remember:

Reduce risk by diversifying.

One of the major attractions of becoming an affiliate is the small amount of risk involved. Affiliates have little or no . . .

- Product development expenses
- Advertising costs
- Inventory to maintain
- Overhead expenses (salaries, physical location, etc.)

In other words, affiliates do not have millions at stake. But you do have one *big* risk: If a merchant, back-end provider, or affiliate intermediary goes out of business, they take you with them. Let's talk briefly about how to minimize this risk.

How to Know Which Affiliate Programs Are Solid

You can't know, really. Yes, you can weed out the dogs by doing basic research. But most of us just don't have the ability or time to thoroughly analyze a company, its financials, and its business model—and then predict success or failure.

Your best bet is to diversify among as many programs as possible that fit with your site concept. But there are a number of important qualifiers to this policy:

1. If you represent 15 programs, don't put them all on the same key-word-focused content page. Work in only the *few* that are tightly relevant to the content of each page.

2. Pick the best of breed from each category of merchant.

If you plan unusually heavy support for a given category of product, you might want to represent the best *two* merchants. For example, suppose you foresee hundreds of book links on your site. It might be a good idea to choose the best two online bookstores. If bookstore A and bookstore B fit with your concept, and both seem to be stable companies, then use these two—no more, though.

3. Don't *over*diversify. Tracking each program takes time, so 10 to 15 programs is probably a good balance. If any one of them dies, you don't lose too much.

4. Your best results will come from focusing on a smaller group of quality programs (from within your longer list).

The products you choose must:

- Be excellent
- Be complementary with, even enhance, each other
- Fit your concept
- Be from a rock-solid company

Since you will give your affiliate companies more attention than the others, you must feel very comfortable with their business prospects.

Here's the bottom line: Don't place too much emphasis on any single program unless you have some special reason to feel unusually comfortable with it. Things happen. Protect yourself by diversifying.

Here is how you can prune out the dogs before they cause problems: Find the good programs and eliminate the dogs by considering the following plus signs (+), minus signs (–), and red flags. Let's start with the plus signs to look for, in the approximate order of their importance:

+ *High quality product or service.* Remember, it's your *reputation* that is on the line (and online!). Don't recommend products that under-deliver.

+ *Merchant has a good site that sells effectively.*

+ *Ability for affiliate to link straight* to individual products rather than just to the home page. (If the visitor has to *find* the product that you recommend, your conversion rate plummets.)

+ *Type of payment model.* Pay-per-sale and pay-per-lead models are good.

+ *Affiliate Support*

  - Accurate, reliable, real-time online accounting, preferably with some kind of ability to audit by spot-checking
  - Detailed traffic and linking stats
  - Notification by e-mail when a sale is made
  - Useful marketing assistance, providing traffic building and sales-getting tools
  - High-quality newsletter that educates, trains, and accounts for amounts earned
  - Professional marketing materials available
  - Affiliate discount on products

+ *Pays good commission.* Hard goods have lower margins than digital ones, so their commissions will be lower. Still, you should earn a commission of at least 10 percent (hard good) or 20 percent (digital good) on any product that you recommend. Don't be scared off by low-priced products if they offer a high-percentage commission—the lower dollar value per sale is offset by the higher sales volume.

+ *Must be free* (no charge) to join, no need to buy the product.

+ *Lifetime commission.* If the program pays a commission on future sales of other products to customers that you refer, this is a huge plus.

+ *Two-tier commission.* If the program pays a commission on affiliates who join because of you, this is also great.

+ *Lifetime cookie.* Do you receive a commission if the person you referred returns and buys within one month? Three months? The cookie that tracks this should not expire.

+ *Restriction on number of affiliates.* You won't find many of these. But if you do, grab it.

+ *Monthly payment,* with reasonable minimum.

Do all those plus signs have to be present? No. But the more, the merrier.

Minus signs (−) are definite detractors. Red flags are warning signs. Watch out for the following minus signs and red flags.

The Dark Side of Affiliate Programs

Make certain the program isn't really just a way to legally bribe folks to recommend overpriced, low-value products in order to collect excessive commissions. Don't allow yourself to be bribed into recommending such products. In the long run, your reputation will be ruined. And so will your business. On the contrary, when your visitors are rewarded repeatedly by your rich recommendations, their increasing appreciation and respect for your judgment will keep them coming back!

Red flag: The absence of any plus sign in the previous section is tantamount to a minus sign!

− *Pay-per-click method of payment.* In this method, you are paid whenever a visitor clicks on your link. No purchase or lead generation necessary. Unfortunately, it's wide open for abuse—very sophisticated folks create incentives to induce thousands of people to click on their links. But the visitors couldn't care less about the products being promoted. It's virtually unstoppable. And merchants end up paying for nothing.

Don't worry about identifying all the preceding criteria before you join. Some can only be found after joining. Others become clear only during the following weeks. But keep them all in mind. Don't get hurt. Spend your time on smart, stable, ethical companies with great products.

If you have brainstormed a good site concept, picked your highest-probability topics, and selected excellent merchant-partners who you are proud to represent, then you are ready to roar ahead.

Refine Final Concept and Register Domain Name

Here is how to brainstorm and register your domain. A good domain name is . . .

- Short and sharp
- Meaningful (conveys a clear message)
- Easy to spell
- Easy to remember
- Unique, descriptive, and reflective of you
- Solid, classic, and *not* hokey

In general, if you follow the preceding guidelines, you won't need much help in coming up with a great domain name. But if you really want to make sure that you've left no cyberstone unturned, try these sites. They're good brainstormers.

http://www.NameBoy.com/

http://creator.homepagenames.com/

http://www.domainsurfer.com/

http://www.bestnames.net/cgi-bin/search.cgi

http://secure.kudosnet.com/domain/k2/r.dmc/

http://www.e-gineer.com/domainator/

http://www.startstorm.com/

Note: Don't register your domain at any of these services until you've seen *your very best bet,* which follows shortly.

Here's a site that searches recently expired domains:

http://www.whois.net/searchD.cgi2

If you already have an idea for a great name and just want to check to see if it's been taken, go to the following site:

http://www.betterwhois.com/

Got a great—and available—name? Super! Now use Marksonline or the USPTO to check trademarks:

http://www.marksonline.com/

http://www.nameprotect.com/cgi-bin/FREESearch/search.cgi

Note: It's *not* necessary to trademark your domain. But *do* make sure that you don't violate someone else's mark before you register your domain. It would be a shame to build up a great business and then have someone who owned a prior trademark force you to take it down.

To register your domain name, you need the services of a registrar. There are zillions of them. If you are using one that makes you happy, stick with it. Otherwise, check out the following site that evaluates registrars:

http://www.domainnamebuyersguide.com/

A comprehensive list of registrars can be found here:

http://www.icann.org/registrars/accredited-list.html

Your Very Best Bet

The software I've developed, Site Build It!, automatically takes care of registration for you. The cost is included in the annual fee, so your very best bet is simply to let us take care of it at the time you start building income through content with Site Build It! For more information about Site Build It!, check out the following:

http://buildit.sitesell.com/ken.html

If you already have an online store, building a theme-based content site is *the* single best way to drive traffic to it. In other words, *become your own affiliate!*

If you don't have a store now, keep this in mind. It can be an excellent way to increase the *profitability* of your theme-based content site. In other words, start by marrying the content of your keyword-focused content pages to well-chosen affiliate programs to build your initial income. Then, as you grow, add an online store for extra profitability!

What should you sell in an online store? Here are three ideas:

1. *Products from other merchants via affiliate programs.*

2. *Products that you source from suppliers.* Build a conventional online store that receives traffic from your content site! People who start their stores first simply *die* from a lack of traffic. Not you.

3. *Your own products, especially digital ones like e-books or software.* You don't have to worry about physical inventory, and fulfillment is so easy. Writing an e-book about your area of expertise establishes you as *the* expert and adds another income stream. For more information about creating and selling infoproducts, check out the following:

http://myks.sitesell.com/ken.html

Speaking of additional income streams, once your theme-based content site has built enough traffic, add even more income through banner advertising. While I'm not a great believer in the value of banners for the advertiser, there are certainly thousands of companies willing and able to pay for banner advertising. So don't be shy about taking their money.

For excellent info about ad-selling strategies, read these three articles:

http://www.wilsonweb.com/wmta/adrev-8steps.htm

http://gt.clickz.com/cgi-bin/gt/cz/cz.html?article=850

http://gt.clickz.com/cgi-bin/gt/cz/cz.html?article=1101

The only strategy on this overcongested Net is to target a specific niche with a specific site concept that tells people quickly what *specific* and *high-value* information you are delivering. Take your time on the domain name and the concept—the choices you make will literally make or break your results.

To summarize this entire chapter in just two lines:

Pick something you know and love.

Make certain it has excellent profitability!

More simply: *Do what you love and the money will follow.*

CHAPTER 12

Online Stream #3.
Selling Information:
Turn Your Ideas into Steady
Streams of Cash Flow

"Let's say you want to write an award-winning short story—you just push this key, here . . . "

From zero to $100,000 a year. Yeah, right!

There are plenty of flashy Internet marketing gurus with their fancy e-books, training videos, and home study programs who claim they can show you how to make it big on the Internet. In doing the research for this book, I bought a bunch of information from many of them, and I learned something from every single one.

But do you know where I learned the most? By roaming around the Internet, finding stories of ordinary people who have come out of nowhere to create incredible streams of income. These mom-and-pop operators have found their niche on the Net and are pulling in the cash. If you love the free enterprise system, there is no story more inspiring than that of a person who's started from nothing and become successful.

In this chapter, I share with you the stories of three such pioneers. Their product is information—their own information, packaged and sold over the Internet. At the end of this chapter, I share critical information about how to launch your own e-zine—an essential component of any successful Web site.

How Perseverance Paid Off: The Ruth Townsend Story

Ruth Townsend is a woman earning an income well north of six figures a year. Yet only a few short years ago, she was sitting behind the desk at a dead-end job. There are so many lessons to learn from this true story. I'll let Ruth tell it in her own words.

Hi. My name is Ruth Townsend. No, I'm not going to tell you my age. It's a woman's prerogative to keep it a secret—even if those closest to me are always trying to pry it out of me! You won't find a photo of me, either. I've yet to have a picture taken that I like. Suffice it to say, I won't make the cover of the *Sports Illustrated* swimsuit issue, but I won't be the centerfold in Doggie's World, either.

I live in the Finger Lakes region of upstate New York, where the summers are gorgeous and the winters brutal. Many times during the winter I don't leave my house for several days on end! Isn't it grand to work from home!

I currently have a staff of one full-time and two part-time assistants, plus an office manager—Sara, my cat. As my business keeps growing, off-site office space may become a necessity in the near future. The office manager, however, has already put down her paw about not making the move!

My background is in accounting and asphalt manufacturing and road construction. How's that for coming to the Internet and starting a thriving business from scratch? Just goes to show that you can be successful if you have a positive attitude, determination, commitment, and desire. Isn't that our choice? The choice to be successful?

How did I go from a dead-end job to success on the Internet?

On October 25, 1996, at 11:06 A.M., after 18 years of service to my company, I placed my keys and security card on my desk and simply walked out the door. I have not regretted it or looked back once. I was tired of the politics, the backstabbing, and feeling like a number instead of a player on the team.

For me, it was the right choice and the right timing. (I don't recommend this for you unless you have a plan in place and finances to carry you for at least a year.) I had gotten to a point in my life where I had this feeling of emptiness. Have you ever sat quietly on a summer's eve or in front of a warm crackling fire and asked yourself, "Why am I here on God's earth. What is my purpose in life?"

I've asked myself that question hundreds of times over the years and never came up with a satisfactory answer. A family, a home, a job, financial security, friends, and material things are all fine and dandy, but still I reflected, "Is this all there is? Is this all that there is going to be?"

For several years I stewed over where I was and what my life was about. I wanted more. I wanted to accomplish something worthwhile. I wanted to sit up and be noticed. Maybe not in a big way, but I wanted to leave this world knowing that my life was more than just living, breathing, and taking up space on this earth. I had no idea how or when I would accomplish this, but I knew I was in a rut and my life was not fulfilling.

I had goals and plans for where I wanted to be by the time I was ?? years old (thought you were going to get me, didn't you?). It just was not going to happen working for someone else. And it wasn't going to happen unless I did something about it.

Then the Internet came along. It fascinated me. I still didn't know what it was that I wanted out of life, but I felt that the Internet had something to do with it. I just sensed that the Internet was the wave of the future. I didn't have a clue about what my business would be, but I jumped in with both feet and went for the gusto. And what a ride it has been!

To get some money coming in the door, I started out trying to market one of those typical business opportunities. First I had to find some customers—so I launched my advertising campaign with the free classified ad sites. Needless to say, all that time I spent placing free ads only brought me other business offers. No one gave a hoot about what I had. The wind sure went out of my sails in a hurry.

I think the only people reading the free ad sites are those who want to send you their own offers, which, of course, is not what you're looking for. When was the last time you browsed the ads at the free ad sites because you had nothing better to do?

Then I heard the word *e-zines.* What in the world does *e-zines* mean? I soon found out that an e-zine is simply an *electronic* maga*zine*—hence the word. E-zines are sent only to those people who have voluntarily requested them. Finally I had found a targeted market—unlike the free hit-or-miss ad sites.

Anyone can publish an e-zine. It can be about advertising, marketing, food/wines, multilevel marketing (MLM), parenting, sports, business opportunities, Web development—anything that a person wants to write about. Plus, some of these e-zines accept classified advertising.

I started subscribing to some e-zines and learning about e-zine advertising and marketing methods. Ads displayed in these e-zines are seen by thousands of businesses and opportunity-minded people who voluntarily subscribe to these newsletters!

I decided that this was the market I wanted to pursue—subscribers to e-zines. My first attempt at e-zine advertising brought 18 responses from four e-zines that had free advertising and a total circulation of a little over 3,600. I was in heaven! I finally got some responses from people wanting to know more about my business opportunity, not the other way around, which convinced me that e-zine advertising was the way to go! But I quickly found out I was faced with a new challenge, and again the wind went out of my sails and set my little boat adrift.

With thousands of newsletters out there (I've seen estimates as high as 100,000!), how was I going to find only those that accepted classified ads? Working on a shoestring budget, I wanted to test my advertising with those e-zines that offered free or relatively inexpensive advertising.

I started the routine of subscribing and unsubscribing to many e-zines in an effort to discover those that accepted advertising. Once I started gathering and compiling data on the e-zines, it was easy to see that each had its own rules, regs, and how-tos of advertising with them. Little by little, I began to compile a storehouse of knowledge on each e-zine. There were so many variables!

First I needed to know the subject material of the e-zine. No sense advertising a fishing lure in a food/wine newsletter! Then I needed to find out about the circulation. Paying $20.00 for a three-line ad or $20.00 for up to 10 lines was within my means, but it really didn't mean much without a look at the circulation numbers. If the circulation is 2,000 and the ad costs $20.00, that's $.01 per subscriber. However, if the circulation is 500 and the ad costs $20.00, I'm paying $.04 for each subscriber to see my ad.

Publication and ad deadlines are important if you want to balance the amount of advertising that you have out each week. I didn't want one week of feast followed by one week of famine.

Where do I place my ad? Should I send it by e-mail or place it online? Either way, I'd need the e-mail address or the URL.

What are the payment options—pay online, send a check by mail, fax or e-mail my credit info? Maybe I don't want to give my credit card number online. Maybe I don't have a fax machine. Maybe the publisher accepts only checks by mail. It's important to know which e-zines will accept payment only by snail mail. You need to plan ahead.

It's also nice to know if my ad is going to be posted online for added exposure. If so, maybe the cost of the ad isn't so bad!

Well, you get the picture. Lots of time is spent researching all this information—reading each newsletter to find out how to place your ad. Maybe you need to send an e-mail to get more information. Then you wait for a reply. Maybe it will be a day or two before you get a response. Remember, you are not the only one asking for this information.

I was getting confused and frustrated to say the least! So much wasted time each week trying to place my ads—with so few placed! I was looking for the missing pieces of the puzzle. Remember, I was on a shoestring budget and every penny counted. I was looking for the biggest bang for my buck. I had to spend time researching the best deals. I couldn't place my ads in just any e-zine that happened to come along without knowing all the facts and being able to comparison shop!

After spending considerable time with the search engines trying to find a resource that had *all* of the advertising information concerning e-zines in *one* place, I realized that no such resource existed.

Then the lightbulb came on! I said to myself, *"Why not create that resource yourself?"* I put some feelers out to online acquaintances and found other people who, like myself, wanted to have all of the advertising information at their fingertips and in one place.

E-zine publishers also saw the benefits of having a centralized listing resource. Their newsletters would no longer be lost in a sea of e-zines. Subscriptions would increase and advertisers would be pulling out their credit cards to place ads!

I launched my business, Lifestyles Publishing, with the goal of being the Net's first directory of e-zines, complete with all of the information needed to place classified ads.

It was scary to take on this project and to present it to the world, not knowing if I would fail or succeed. But I would never have known if I hadn't taken a chance on myself. This was what I had been searching for all of these years. Now the emptiness in my life has been filled with a sense of accomplishment and knowing that I am helping other people achieve their dreams and goals.

The road has not always been easy, but I had a passion for what I was doing, and that is what it takes. Yes, there have been ups and downs, challenges of an ever changing technology, mistakes (but they are mistakes only if you don't learn from them), and trends that come and go.

In a nutshell, that's who I am: someone who had a dream and the need to fill the emptiness in my life. I'm no super marketing guru here or someone who has the inside track to success—just someone like you who wants to succeed. I published the first resource tool that contains all of the pertinent advertising info needed to place ads in e-zines. As for the frosting on the cake, I found my niche, and today I have a thriving, successful Internet business.

Why am I telling you all this? First, countless people have asked me how in the world I ever came up with the idea. Now, you know. But, more important, I want you to know that you can find your niche, too. Take a look around you. Think about the problems, frustrations, or aggravations you may be faced with. Is there something you can do about it? Can you possibly come up with a solution? Can you turn that solution into a business that benefits not only yourself but others as well? It certainly can't hurt to take a close look at your situation. Who knows, you might be the next Internet success story! With passion, determination, and commitment, you can be, do, and have anything you want. Go get 'em!

If creating an e-zine or advertising in one interests you, Ruth Townsend is your ultimate resource. You can find more about her at the following locations:

http://lifestylespub.com/msi
     ruth@lifestylespub.com

Ruth is a perfect example of Internet infopreneuring. Her first product was the Directory of E-zines, which she offers as a yearly subscription at a very reasonable price. It truly is a bargain. Her lifetime subscription is an even bigger bargain. She now offers several additional services:

1. *Ruth's Learning Channel:* A resource full of everything you need to know to run successful advertising campaigns in e-zines.
2. *Turnkey advertising campaigns:* Give her a budget from $250 a year to $1,000 a week and she will help you get all the traffic you need.

Her secret weapon is what she calls *emotional marketing.* She's not sure whether she picked up that term or came up with it herself, but it is the cornerstone of her advertising campaigns. She explains that marketing on the Net is changing drastically, and people don't want the in-your-face kind of advertising that is all too prevalent on the Net. She can show substantially better results with a softer approach.

Today, Ruth earns 10 times the income of her former dead-end job—with 100 times the personal fulfillment. Congratulations, Ruth!

An Educator Goes Online: The Pat Wyman Story

Pat Wyman's story is not one of rags to riches. True, she and her husband went from doing okay financially to doing *fantastically.* But, even from the

beginning, it wasn't about the money. For her, it was about passion—doing what you love to do, making a difference, and being pleasantly surprised when the money starts to pour in.

For 20 years before she launched her Web site in 1996, Pat was an educator, a teacher, and an expert in learning styles. Currently, she is an instructor of education at California State University, Hayward, where she is a teacher of teachers—teaching in the continuing education department.

Before she went online, Pat had already created newsletters and videos to help parents and teachers help children learn better. She just felt that an online presence would enable her to share her successful strategies with more people. As she puts it,

> My husband and I created the Web site ourselves. I designed the content and he did the programming. He was in computer software sales. He figured out all the technical aspects. In early days, you had to know HTML [programming language], but today you don't. You can do it yourself with virtually no help.
>
> In the first year, we probably made $2,000 or $3,000. We were just learning. Then, each year, we steadily increased the traffic to our site. The next year we earned about $30,000. The year after that we more than tripled that amount. And it's just gotten better every year.
>
> The breakthrough idea was to offer a free but very valuable learning-styles questionnaire. If you go to my site at www.howtolearn.com, you'll see the free offer right in the center of the page. That one single idea has accounted for a lot of the success of this site because many of my competitors were

charging for this same information. This Learning Style Inventory is currently being used by NASA, Penn State University, Blue Cross, Blue Shield, Motorola University, Bose, hundreds of corporations, and thousands of parents, teachers, and students in schools and universities throughout the world. People use it to help boost their grades in school or perform better at work. From the beginning, so many people asked for the scoring key to the questionnaire (so they could administer the Learning Style Inventory to their corporations, schools, etc.) that we also set up an electronically delivered scoring key for $9.95. This generates thousands of dollars of income and costs us nothing.

Visitors to the site also have an opt-in choice to join my e-mail newsletter, which tells you how to use the proper learning style for each task at hand, raising your grades and improving your learning abilities. Our subscriber base is now up to 70,000 a month. People really enjoy it, and if we're a few days late in sending it out we get e-mails asking where it is.

In our online newsletter, I do a combination of marketing and information. Depending on the month, we do anywhere from $5,000 to $15,000 in sales. We also electronically deliver a paying newsletter called *School Smart Kids* (seven issues via e-mail for $19.95 or in paper for $49.95). The newsletters are set up on an autoresponder for the electronic version. When people enter their credit card numbers and e-mail addresses, the program automatically sends the newsletters to their e-mail, which they then read via Adobe Acrobat Reader. Included in each of these newsletters are specific learning strategies for all subject areas and a page of additional products that people can order. We also send my online book of natural remedies for learning disabilities via a password that allows you to read the book on the Web

© 1993 by Ashleigh Brilliant (www.ashleighbrilliant.com)

site. The cost is the same as the paperback version, and we receive hundreds of ongoing orders.

The secret to building a great site is to think from other people's points of view and give them as much information as possible. Because our site is so content-rich, thousands of other Web sites are linked to our howtolearn.com site. We have even received awards for our site from major companies like Pacific Bell.

Pat's Web site is actually the perfect infopreneuring, multiple-stream model. She markets videos, seminars, paying newsletters, and other people's products, and she is now developing a series of Internet training courses aimed at teachers. The classes will be accredited and count toward teachers' continuing education requirements. She has also authored two books—*Learning vs. Testing* and *What's Food Got to Do With It?*

Pat earns a multiple of six figures a year working about six hours a week with a part-time office manager and farming out work occasionally to subcontractors. She works from a home office that has been built at the back of her property.

As a final comment, she says, "It is so empowering to know that you can begin with little or nothing and create unlimited income streams for yourself and your family."

If you have a child with learning disabilities (attention deficit disorder, dyslexia, etc.) or who just wants to master accelerated learning strategies, check out Pat's site at www.howtolearn.com or call her at 800-How-to-Learn.

From the Funny House to the Money House: The Preston Reuther Story

The year was 1990 and Preston Reuther's manic depression had finally got the best of him. He lost his job, his family, and everything he owned. Financially and emotionally devastated, he was admitted to a psychiatric hospital. His future looked bleak. Here is his story in his own words.

There I was in a mental institution with not much of a future to look forward to. Believe me, there is not much demand in the workforce for someone with mental illness. While in the hospital, I was asked to attend occupational therapy, which consisted of ceramics, art, and jewelry making. I went to the class but refused to do anything. As the hour passed, I began to get a little bored and started making jewelry from some kind of plastic. To my surprise, I found myself enjoying it. It was fun and relaxing, and I really got a kick out of all the crazy designs I could come up with.

As the days turned into weeks, I wanted to go further in the jewelry-making process. I bought tools—a torch and a jeweler's saw—and jumped in with both feet. I was going to be a silversmith or maybe even a goldsmith.

"Oh, yea," I said to myself, "This is it. I've finally found my niche. Something I can do from my home with my illness and make a living—my own home business!"

The very next day I accidentally stuck the jeweler's saw in one side of my hand and out the other. I'm not exaggerating here—it was pretty ugly! Next, my shirt caught on fire from the torch (I forgot that it was turned on—I have short-term memory loss), and while trying to put out the flames, I threw the burning shirt outside, where it landed under the gas tank of my truck and almost blew it up! At that point, I realized I had no skill in using specialized jeweler's tools, torches, and other sophisticated equipment.

It was one of the lowest times in my life. Realizing I needed some training by real jewelers, I sent a resume to 54 regional jewelry stores and offered to work a 40-hour week *for free.* I would sweep, clean toilets—anything—if they would just show me how to use the tools. Not a single shop responded. I know what it means to be *down.* It seemed that I would spend the rest of my life in mental institutions. Maybe they thought I was really crazy. No one would hire me for anything—even without pay!

A few days later I got a two-day pass from the hospital and went to the French Quarter in New Orleans, where I was introduced to a simple way of making jewelry from wire. I watched a street vendor in the flea market making little rings from silver wire. I noticed that he used only a few pairs of pliers to make his jewelry. No torch. No saw. No expensive machinery. I also noticed he had about 10 people waiting in line with money in hand. I said to myself, *"I can do this!"*

I then bought every book and video I could get my hands on and started to practice, practice, practice. I went back to the psychiatric unit and started making jewelry from brass and German silver wire. Actually, my new designs weren't bad. One day a nurse came to me and said, "How much do you want for that pair of earrings you just made?"

I said, "Gee, I don't know. How about $5?"

She bought the earrings and wore them to the cafeteria. Ten minutes later another nurse came in and bought a pendant. Then another nurse and another. By the end of the day, every nurse in that hospital was wearing a pair of my handcrafted earrings or a little wire pendant! *I made over $200 right from my hospital bed by charging only $5 and $7 each!*

It was then that I decided this is what I wanted to do when I got out of the hospital. Nothing was going to stop me. I was tired of the big-business life and all the stress that came with it. I was fed up with 9 to 5, coats and ties, and bosses from hell! I just wanted my own little home business with enough money coming in to pay the bills and feed my family. This began to be my dream.

But I soon found out it wasn't going to be that easy! No one was going to teach me *anything* about making wire jewelry, and that was that! I began to look for information about this unusual art form that few people knew anything about.

Ten years ago, there were not that many wire artists around, and only a handful of people were actually making any money at it. I bought every book and video I could get my hands on and even studied the blacksmiths who made beautiful wrought iron in the French Quarter of New Orleans.

With this information, I started my career in handcrafted jewelry. Every weekend I set up my little card table at flea markets and festivals—anywhere I could create and sell my jewelry. Many times I did not even have the money ($14) to get a booth, so I waited until it was over at 6 P.M. and set up from 6 to 10 P.M. just to make a few dollars for food and next week's booth money.

I was really struggling to make it, but I loved what I was doing for the first time in my life and wouldn't give up. I probably worked every flea market and festival within a 100-mile radius of New Orleans. I pulled the backseat out of my old Datsun and put all my jewelry, tools, and displays in there. Then I bought a steel rack and bolted it to the roof of my car to carry my handmade table, made from a piece of plywood and four aluminum fence posts so it could fold up.

But I never missed a weekend. Not one. My small jewelry business began to grow, and the money kept getting better. I learned lots of tricks on the road: what to sell, how to sell, how to display, how to negotiate, when to discount, and never to have a bad show!

But I really wanted something a little more interesting than the typical wire-wrapping techniques that have been around for 100 years. I wanted to create some really great high-fashion gemstone jewelry using just my hands and a few small tools. What I wanted to do was *sculpture*—the way Michelangelo did—only with wire!

It took time, and believe me, I was no Michelangelo, but I was improving continually. Slowly, I started to develop my own particular style of wire sculpture. It was rough at first, but as I worked all the little fairs and festivals around the state my designs kept getting better. I wasn't using a torch and still don't to this day!

After about two and a half years, over 100 flea markets and festivals, and a large spare room *full* of bent and twisted wire, my jewelry began to take on a totally different look. I called this new look my *gold-wire-sculpting-system*. It was mostly formed by hand—I use very few tools in my method, and because of this each piece comes out differently.

The human hand is the greatest tool in the world, capable of over 1,200 movements! People really liked this new method. I would set up at a fair with some wire, one card table, and five tools. People couldn't believe I could make all that jewelry with just a few pairs of pliers and a wire cutter. Each piece of jewelry I created looked like a small sculpture, and my new method was *fast*. I could make a little birthstone ring in less than three minutes, a cameo in about five minutes! People couldn't believe it. My work really began selling! Customers loved the new look. Especially the ladies. They went wild over the one-of-a-kind pieces. I couldn't believe the reaction. I could not keep up with the demand. People wanted me to teach them how to do it, but I wasn't ready. I was not about to show anyone what took me years to learn. Tiny markets with revenues of about $300 a weekend led to small craft shows with revenues of about $1,000, then larger craft shows with revenues of over $2,000 a weekend, and finally gem and jewelry shows with revenues from $5,000 to $10,000 for a four-day show. If my health permitted me to work 35 shows a year the way I used to, I could easily earn $100,000 a year.

You might be asking why I'm no longer doing these shows. As I told you, I am manic depressive and take a lot of medication. Because of this I can't get around as much as I would like to. I'm not totally disabled, but I just can't travel and do the work I did years ago. I had to continue to make money without traveling so much. Enter the Internet. Even though I knew nothing about computers, I felt that the Internet might be a solution to my situation.

I hired three different Webmasters to get me online, and each one messed it up. It was a nightmare. I had spent thousands of thousands of dollars (a grand or two with each guy), and I couldn't even turn on a computer. I realized that I was just going to have to learn how to do it myself. I attacked the Internet the same way I attacked the jewelry business. I bought all the books and videos and marketing courses I could get my hands on. And I started to apply what I was learning to my site. After many months of trying to figure this thing out, I was finally able to get my Web site to show up on search engines in the top 10 spots. I targeted semiprofessional jewelry makers who want to make some extra money and hobbyists who want to make stuff for their grandkids. Now I started to get some traffic.

About this time, I realized that I was going to have to create my own newsletter. It was intimidating. I barely got out of high school and was in no way a journalist! I stumbled through the first few letters. Eventually, I hired an editor to edit my newsletters for about $100 a week.

I got rave reviews about the newsletter. Everyone loved it, but after seven months I still hadn't made a single dime from my e-zine. I was getting discouraged and thought that I might give it up. Then I remembered that I had purchased a marketing course from Internet guru Corey Rudl, which included a 15-minute live consultation with him on the phone. I called him and explained my situation. He asked, "Do you ask for the order in your newsletter?" No, I didn't. "Well, you've got to ask for the order. Put three offers in your very next e-zine. One at the beginning. One in the middle. And one at the end. Link these orders directly to your Web page so people can immediately see what you're selling."

That was the turning point for me. I earned $3,500 from that very next issue. Then I figured out that a monthly newsletter was not enough. I took a 10-page e-zine, broke it up into four small ones, and published it weekly. It was much more effective. And much more profitable. Today, we're doing between $15,000 and $20,000 per month in revenues, most of it due to the e-zine.

I remember the days when $50 a day made me a very happy guy. Now business is growing so fast it's hard to keep up with it. It's incredible.

Don't let anyone tell you that people aren't willing to spend big money on the Internet. My home study course, Gold Wire Sculpting Business, shows people how to start their own business. The price is $1,597. Sometimes I get orders at 2:00 or 3:00 in the morning. Customers send me $1,600 in cash and don't even call to see if I'm a real person. It boggles my manic depressive mind!

It has been a real learning process to figure this out. I don't want you to think that it has been easy. I've spent hours figuring things out. For example, let me take you through the process of building my e-zine list. We now have over 5,000 subscribers and are adding 300 to 500 new ones a week.

When I first offered to send people the free e-zine, the notice was hidden on my Web site. I was getting three sign-ups a day. Then I added a special sign-up page and my sign-ups jumped to seven or eight a day. Then I put it on the front page in a prominent spot and sign-ups went to 12 to 14 a day. Then I put it on every page on my site and sign-ups again doubled. Then I offered a bonus for people to subscribe to the newsletter (four free special reports on how to start your own jewelry business plus the chance to win one of my videos) and sign-ups doubled yet again! Finally, three months ago, we added one of those irritating pop-up windows and sign-ups increased by a good 40 percent. You should go to my site and see it (www.wire-sculpture.com). And while you're there, check out my jewelry. I promise that you'll be impressed, and if you're looking for that something special, well . . .

Lately, to build my e-zine list, I've been buying subscribers. I list my e-zine with sites like funEzines.com and myfree.com. When someone subscribes to my e-zine through either of these sites I pay about 10 cents per new subscriber. Right now I'm signing up about 200 new subscribers a week. Since these are not highly qualified leads, about 25 percent of them eventually unsubscribe. But of those who remain, about 10 percent end up buying something from me. If I can buy subscribers for only 10 cents, I'll do that deal all day long.

These days, I don't even write the e-zine myself. I found a ghostwriter at ubarter.com and the ghostwriter trades the writing for jewelry. It costs only about $22 in cash to get my newsletter written.

Here is a sample of my newsletter so you can see how I do it.

$$\$$$
"THE WIREWORKER"
A newsletter dedicated to setting up and running your own
home-based business making wire jewelry.

$$\$$$

Issue #32 March 18
IN THIS ISSUE
1. Wire Sculptor's Boot Camp—July
2. Did Ya Know?
3. What's Larry Gillett up to with his new digital camera?
4. WHAT'S THE TOP TWO BEST-SELLERS FOR WIRE ARTISTS?
5. Announcements
6. How Big Is Your Portfolio?

****

This publication is sent by e-mail only to people who have subscribed to or requested it. It is never sent unsolicited. To unsubscribe, click on the link at the end of this document.

America's #1 home jewelry business!
http://www.wire-sculpture.com
Yes, it's still free!

****

Wire Sculptor's Boot Camp!—to be held in the mosquito-infested swamps of Louisiana. One-day seminar and two-day wire-sculpting classes.
July 14, 15 and 16—SOLD OUT
July 22 and 23—ONLY THREE SEATS LEFT!

If you are interested in our Wire Sculptor's Boot Camp, just e-mail me at mailto:preston@wire-sculpture.com and I will send you an e-mail packet with prices and details. The July 14 seminar and classes on the 15th and 16th are sold out.

We have three seats available for the July 22 and 23 Boot Camp. To view the major projects in the workshop, go to http://wire-sculpture.com/workshop.htm.

****

DID YA KNOW . . .

Michelangelo used powdered lapis lazuli to paint some of the ceiling of the Sistine Chapel?

DID YA KNOW . . .

that ancient bead makers of China who made carved wooden beads and colored them with cinnabar (red) had a very short life span? Why? Because cinnabar is the principal ore of mercury and mercury is poisonous!!! Important deposits of cinnabar have been found in California, Nevada, Oregon, and Texas.

DID YA KNOW . . .

the word *marcasite* is believed to come from the Arabic word for pyrite?

DID YA KNOW . . .

the word *opal* comes from the Sanskrit *upala* and means precious stone?

****

What's Larry Gillett up to with his new camera?

The other day I was hanging out at the bulletin board and Larry started talking about this new digital camera that he got. Well, he went on and on till finally I says, "Enough with the talk—let's see some pictures." Well, he called my bluff. And not only did he send us a great picture taken with his new digital camera, but we got a little glimpse at what he is up to in his studio. Check out the attachment at the end of the newsletter. By the way, the pendant is made from pink coral—some pretty rare stuff.

****

WHAT'S THE TOP TWO BEST-SELLERS FOR WIRE ARTISTS???

If you guessed cameos and mabe pearls, you're right! Wire artists from across the country continuously report high sales on both items. It all comes down to this simple formula:

Example

Average cost of cameo/pearl	$10.00
Average cost of wire	5.00
Time it takes to make a sculpted setting	30 minutes
Average retail price of finished product—some sold high and some sold lower	$75.00

Add a 500% profit margin and you've got a WINNER!

Five years ago we realized what the top two sellers were and continually tried to get the best product at the best price. Unfortunately, at that time the product may have been good, but I feel prices were just so-so. BUT with the continuing support of wire artists around the country, we have finally been able to contract with a very large cameo and pearl distributor and have got some incredibly low prices. With these new low prices it will be difficult NOT to make 500% to 1,000% profit. Take a look at these two new additions to our online catalog:

http://www.wire-sculpture.com/supplies.htm

****

ANNOUNCEMENTS

****

Wire Sculpting with Beads part 1 and part 2 for Wire Sculptors and Beaders

http://www.wire-sculpture.com/video16.htm

http://www.wire-sculpture.com/video17.htm

Two Video Specials:

* Wire-Sculpted Beads, Part 1 (Item #1B1)—$49.95

* Wire-Sculpted Beads, Part 2 (Item #2B2)—$49.95

GET 'EM BOTH FOR ONLY—$79 (Item #NS2V79)

FREE shipping—Just type in the item numbers at

http://www.wire-sculpture.com/cobooksvideo.htm

This offer is for a limited time, so take advantage of the price NOW!

****

ARE YOU MAKING BRACELETS?

Bracelets, especially ones with gemstones popping out of them in a rainbow of colors, are TOP SELLERS at any craft or gem show! Here is a starter package to get you going . . .

Bracelet-making special:

* Sculpted Bracelets Part I

This video introduces you to easy-to-make gemstone bracelets using 14kt gold-filled fittings (snap sets) and small-faceted gemstones—easy to use and great sellers.

* Three 8mm synthetic rubies—fire-engine red!

* Three 8mm 14kt gold snap sets—just pop 'em in!

BRACELET PACKAGE (Item #nsbr50)—ONLY $50

Offer expires March 23.

Order here for free shipping with orders $50 or more

http://www.wire-sculpture.com/cobooksvideo.htm

****

A $10,000 OPAL!

Well, I don't think the average jewelry buyer could afford one of these babies, but here is the next best thing! Opal mosaic triplets with lots of blue color and FIRE! A sliver of opal sandwiched between a strong black onyx backing and a well-cut and polished high-dome quartz cap. The result is dynamite!

2—18 × 13—$24.00—Item #nsom18×13

1—25 × 18—$18.00—Item #nsom25×18

GET 'EM ALL—$35.00—Item #nsomall

Offer expires March 23

Order here for free shipping with orders $50 or more

http://www.wire-sculpture.com/cobooksvideo.htm

****

CHAROITE—the purple stone from Russia. This material is difficult to get in AAA quality and very expensive. I would say that this material is about medium grade. Nice, but not top-notch. Frankly top-notch is a little too expensive.

2—18 × 13mm—$10.00—Item #nschar18×13

1—25 × 18mm—$8.00—Item #nschar25×18

1—40 × 30mm—$15.00—Item #nschar40×30

GET 'EM ALL—$28.00—Item #nscharall

Offer expires March 23

Order here for free shipping with orders $50 or more

http://www.wire-sculpture.com/cobooksvideo.htm

```
*************************************************************
```

CHRYSOCOLLA—green to bluish-green mix

Chrysos is Greek for gold, and *kolla* means glue in Greek. It is a minor ore of copper and frequently associated with malachite and azurite. Said to ward off S!T!R!E!S!S!

2—18 × 13—$7.00—Item #nsch18×13

1—25 × 18—$8.00—Item #nsch25×18

1—40 × 30—$15.00—Item #nsch40×30

GET 'EM ALL—$25.00—Item #nschall

```
*************************************************************
```

HOW BIG IS YOUR PORTFOLIO?

What's that—you don't have one?! Well, if you're gonna stay in the home jewelry biz, you're gonna need one, so let's get started!

First, a portfolio is a photo record of your art. It is easy to keep, collect, and maintain. It is for the benefit of your customer when it's time to make a designer set of gemstone jewelry, or maybe pick out a Mother's Day gift, or just a ring to match the pendant you made last year. BUT . . . you will quickly learn that by keeping a photo history of your work you can improve designs, remember designs that you might have forgotten, and match designs for customers with a special need.

A portfolio should be a hardcover photo album. Yes, this book has to be built for durability, because you'll be taking it to craft shows, art shows, and home showings. And travel and packing takes a heavy toll on any kind of paper. So get one that's hardcover and durable.

The inside can be set up any way you like. But make sure you get the glassine envelopes that your photo just slides into because the ones that stick to the back can make the photos impossible to remove and will actually ruin your pictures.

A good idea is to make one page all cameos; another, black onyx; another, blue topaz; and so on. It's easy to look up an item like that, and most customers will look for things according to color. Make sure NOT to place a price on your work, for several reasons. For one thing, your work will usually go up in price as time goes on. The pendant that was $50 last year might be $60 this year. Let the customers ask for the price if they are interested.

Don't keep your portfolio out all the time, because if you do, people will be lined up to see your jewelry and may not be able to decide because there is too much from which to choose. Use your portfolio to help customers match an item, pick out a new one, or if a customer is undecided to help them make a decision. A simple stroll through your portfolio might help make up their mind. Use your portfolio wisely and it will be a great tool.

Hardcover portfolios can be found at most drugstores, dollar stores, or Wal-Mart. When I first got started in wire sculpting, I never bought anything new that I could buy used, and I bought my first hardcover portfolio at the local Goodwill for $1. I still see them there today for about the same price.

REMEMBER—A PICTURE IS WORTH A THOUSAND WORDS!

I can offer a great price on a valuable gemstone, and few people will buy it. I can take the same stone with a great photo for the same price and it will sell out! The same holds true with your portfolio. Pictures are worth their weight in gold! Few people buy expensive elaborate sets of wire-sculpted jewelry without seeing SOMETHING that you have created that is similar to what they want.

COLOR CODING FOR QUICK ACCESS

Most women are attracted by color of gemstones, for one reason or another. Maybe it's a birthstone, maybe it's a dress they are trying to match, or whatever. If you have enough stock completed, you can code your portfolio according to color.

EXAMPLE

Put lapis, blue topaz, and sodalite in one section. In another, you might have smoky topaz, earth-tone stones, and so on. Color coding can help you go to a specific stone quickly when looking for it for an impatient customer. It can also allow the customer to actually see her stone, or one like it, in a setting you will be designing for her.

DON'T FORGET THE ORDER!

Don't get so carried away showing all your wonderful work that you forget to take the order, along with a down payment! Most of these hardcover binders have a sleeve on the inside—if yours does, keep a few order forms in it so that when your customer says "Gee, I just don't know . . . ," you can say, "Well, Mrs. Smith, let me just put the blue lapis together for you and let's see how it looks on you. If for some reason you don't like it, just send it back, no problem. I usually require a 50 percent deposit, which would be $100, but what's comfortable for you?"

BLATANT SELF-PROMOTION

If you have a newspaper clipping or a write-up about you or a ribbon that you have won, or anything else that would add credibility to your work, photocopy it. Make sure you "just happen to have one" slipped into one of the glassine envelopes where a photo would be. There is power in media and third-party referrals, and if you made jewelry for some prominent person, celebrity, or someone well known locally, maybe you can get a testimonial from them about how much they enjoyed your jewelry. Don't be afraid to blow your own horn, 'cause no one else is going to do it for you!

****

Home Jewelers' Special!—With our 90-Day Money-Back Guarantee!

Complete Home Jewelers' Package #1 or our Minipackage #2

Check 'em out here:

http://www.wire-sculpture.com/special.html

****

Happy Twistin'!

Preston J. Reuther, Master Wire Sculptor

http://www.wire-sculpture.com

mailto:preston@wire-sculpture.com

To unsubscribe, write to wireworkerslist-unsubscribe@listbot.com

Preston J. Reuther Master Wire Sculptor

http://www.wire-sculpture.com

preston@wire-sculpture.com

Get THE WIREWORKER, a FREE newsletter on making handcrafted wire jewelry

---

I use a free service, Getresponse.com, to deliver a series of autoresponder messages to those who sign up for my newsletter. Every day, I have 250 people going through this series of automatic messages . . . so the marketing of my program takes place 24 hours a day. Even my newsletter is delivered automatically, by a company called Listbot.com, for only about $65 per year. To think that this one-time computer illiterate could now be making money this way is unbelievable.

I used two specific marketing techniques to dramatically improve the percentage of people who sign up for one of my programs. First, I give an unconditional 90-day money-back guarantee. I worried that this would cause me a lot of refund problems, but exactly the opposite has happened. It increased my sales by 30 to 40 percent, and I've had only two refund requests. It's a no-brainer.

The second idea was to set time limits on customer decision making. I state clearly that my best-price offer is good for only 48 hours—so there isn't time to get a check in the mail. People phone me all the time to ask if the time has expired. Having this fixed deadline really made a dramatic difference—perhaps doubling the number of purchasers.

All in all, it's been a great ride. I really love helping people get into business so they can enjoy the kinds of benefits I enjoy. I make more money than I ever did; do it right from my own home; and I have wonderful customers all over the world.

I hope you are as inspired by Preston's story as I am. As you can see, the process of fine-tuning the marketing machine takes time, but it's well worth the sacrifice and effort.

One of my favorite marketing gurus is Shawn Casey of the *Big Dog Marketing Letter.* I've prevailed on him to share some of his most effective secrets for building a successful marketing-oriented Web site. He agreed to mentor you in this chapter on everything you need to know about starting your own e-zine.

Before I turn the rest of this chapter over to Shawn Casey, I highly encourage you to visit my Web site at www.robertallen.com and download the free report called Infopreneuring: How to Be an Information Multimillionaire. It contains principles vital to becoming successful in the information business—both online and offline. This material is also found in my previous best-selling book, *Multiple Streams of Income.*

Now let's turn to one of the most innovative ways to create massive amounts of Web traffic, recently explained to me by Shawn Casey, publisher of the Big Dog Marketing E-zine. I'll let him mentor you on how he does it.

Shawn Casey on E-Marketing

How to Launch Your Own Successful E-Zine

If you would like to start you own newsletter (and you should), let me give you some good ideas to get you started.

Direct marketing experts have long recognized the importance of building a mailing list of customers and prospects. For many businesses, this list is the key to great success and profitability when they have learned to unlock its value.

For your Internet business, the value of such a list is greatly increased. In the bricks-and-mortar world, you have to pay the costs of printing and postage to deliver a sales message to your list. On the Internet, you can deliver the same message at very little or no cost. Instead of paying $6,000 to send snail mail to 10,000 people, you can send the same message online for nothing. Anything you sell to those people as a result of that online advertisement is profitable from the first sale onward.

Any reference I make to sending e-mail to people refers to an *opt-in list,* which is made up of people who *agree* to be on a particular list. Opt-in is the opposite of spam. *Spam* is the colloquial term for *unsolicited commercial e-mail* (UCE). Spam, while not illegal, is completely unacceptable on the Internet. Don't do it.

No matter what business you're in, you have to build a mailing list. You are virtually guaranteed success if you diligently build a mailing list. You'll be able to continually send sales messages to those on the list, and you should make money every time you send a mailing.

You should send a periodic newsletter (also known as an *e-zine*) to your list for the following reasons:

1. It gives people a good reason to sign up for your list.

2. You can build your newsletter list from other sites, even if those people never visit your site.

3. Businesses will pay to advertise in your newsletter.

4. You can swap ads with other e-zine publishers.

5. You will be perceived as an expert because you publish a newsletter.

6. You can offer your products and services in each newsletter.

7. You can offer products and services from affiliate programs in each newsletter.

How much money can you make with an e-zine? Depending on the size of the list and its composition, you can make a ton of money. If you have an e-zine subscriber count of 10,000 people who are interested in specific information, you can publish one e-zine per week that includes at least $400 in advertising from several advertisers. You can also offer solo mailings to your list for $100 and mail a minimum of one per week. That's $500 a week, or $26,000 per year in advertising alone. On top of that, you have a vehicle to sell your products and services and to make targeted offers for affiliate programs, which should generate another $200 per week.

With this minimal effort, you're now making $700 per week, or $36,400 per year. I am being very conservative with these numbers. Some list owners claim to make hundreds of thousands of dollars from lists as small as 10,000 people.

You're probably worried about where you're going to get information to put into your newsletter. In most cases, this isn't a problem. You can find a lot of people who are trying to get their articles published and will give them to you for free. In fact, I receive two or three articles every week whether I need them or not. Because I have listed my e-zine in all the directories, I've been approached by people who want their articles published. When I let them know that I occasionally publish articles by other people, they keep me constantly supplied.

You must build a mailing list. Otherwise, you're just throwing away money. Your list doesn't have to be big. You just have to use it effectively. When you start researching e-zines for your advertising purposes, you'll find that most have only a few thousand subscribers.

You'll use three different methods to build your mailing list:

1. Getting subscribers from your traffic

2. Getting subscribers from free e-zine directories

3. Buying subscribers

Getting Subscribers from Your Traffic

The first place to find people to join your mailing list is the traffic passing through your Web site everyday. Invite those people to join your newsletter list. You should consider having a link to your newsletter subscription form on every page of your Web site.

One of the best ways to drive subscriptions is to offer the subscription through a pop-up window on your entry page. When someone visits the page, a second, smaller, window will open with a short offer to subscribe to your newsletter. The visitor may subscribe using the pop-up window. After completing the process, he or she can close the window and remain at your site.

You have to give people a reason to join your newsletter list. Very few people will just randomly type in their e-mail address unless you give them a good reason to expend the time and effort. I know, your e-zine is free, but you still have to sell the people on joining the list.

Briefly explain the many benefits of joining your newsletter list and tell people what type of information to expect and when. If you're already a recognized expert in your field, this might be enough to get people to subscribe. The rest of us need to offer something extra.

If you want people to take action *now,* you must give them an incentive. Since this is a free newsletter, you want to give them something that costs you nothing. Often, this is a free report with information they feel is valuable enough to warrant joining your list now. Some people provide access to members-only Web pages after visitors subscribe.

One aggressive technique is to offer new subscribers a free three-line classified ad in your newsletter. You can't do this for too long or it could get messy, but you can use it to get started building your list.

The best incentive I've ever used to get people to take action is a program I created in partnership with a large travel agency. I offer a free three-day, two-night vacation certificate to every new subscriber. I've shared this idea with other people who have also used it with great success. Joseph Mestres of TNTCO International reports that the vacation give-away has increased his business 40 percent. If you want information about using this incentive yourself, please go to www.marketingpromo.com.

After people join your list, you should send them a welcome message. This message should give them information about what they have joined, how to remove themselves from the list, and, by all means, something they might consider buying from you.

The best way to induce people to subscribe while visiting your Web site is to give them a form to fill out and submit. If you aren't comfortable creating such a form, use www.Freedback.com to automatically create it for you.

Getting Subscribers from Free E-Zine Directories

Many people have set up free directories of newsletters. Anyone can list a newsletter in these directories. Anyone can search these directories. If you take a little bit of time to list your e-zine in these directories, you'll receive a few new subscribers every week. As with subscribers from your Web site traffic, these cost you nothing. Here is a list of the largest newsletter directories:

www.lifestylespub.com/

www.freezineweb.com

www.e-zinez.com

www.bestezines.com

www.ezineseek.com

www.ezinesearch.com

www.site-city.com/members/e-zine-master

www.inkpot.com/zines/index.html

www.disobey.com/low/addere.shtml

www.oblivion.net/zineworld

www.newsletteraccess.com/database/reg.html

www.inkpot.com/submit/

www.catalog.com/vivian/intsubform2.html

www.perfecthomebusiness.com/ezines/directory.htm

www.aepublishing.com

www.liszt.com/submit.html

www.newsletter-library.com/ven.htm

www.newsletteraccess.com/database/reg.html

http://gort.ucsd.edu/newjour/submit.html

http://magazines.yotta.com/

When you first launch your e-zine, you'll want to get a few hundred subscribers right away so you'll feel this is worth the time and effort. And of course you'll want to get them free. You can post the announcement about your new e-zine to a few lists that exist solely for the purpose of announcing new e-zines and lists. People who subscribe to these lists are interested in joining other lists. If you write a good announcement, you could get a few hundred new subscribers instantly. You can find announcement lists on the following sites. You usually have to join the list before posting to it.

www.list-business.com

www.onelist.com

Buying Subscribers

If you know that a new subscriber is worth money to you right away, you can afford to buy subscribers and build your list even faster. You can buy subscribers for amounts ranging from $0.10 to $1.25 each. If you can afford to pay more, you can buy subscribers in larger volume.

How do you know how much you can afford to pay? As you add subscribers, you have to track how much profit you make from each subscriber in the first 10 to 15 days. This is the time period when you have your best chance of making the initial sale. If you sell something to 1 out of 20 new subscribers and your profit on each sale is $5, then each subscriber is worth $0.25 to you. If you can buy subscribers for $0.25 or less, you can build your list as fast you can buy them. Of course, now that you have these new subscribers, every additional sale and all advertising revenue is very profitable for you.

As of this writing, you can expect to buy 200 to 300 subscribers per week from the following sources for $0.16 cents or less per subscriber:

www.NewslettersForFree.com

www.BestNewsletters.com

For more information on higher-volume programs, check with companies that run sites for multiple affiliate programs.

I like my marketing efforts to pay off as soon as possible, so I design my marketing plans accordingly. One of my best plans ever delivers thousands of free leads and newsletter subscribers each month.

Here's how it works. I operate a popular (last time I looked at PC Data Online, this site was in the top 1,300 U.S. sites) sweepstakes site at www.MillionDollarDrawing.com. I initially created the site to generate traffic and increase the number of subscribers for my three online newsletters. I consider newsletter subscribers to be very valuable, but they don't generate immediate income. As a result, I didn't want to invest a lot of money per new subscriber and have to wait several months to recoup my investment.

I registered in The Million Dollar Drawing as a merchant with Commission Junction (cost was $795). Commission Junction provides a great affiliate program service for over 1,000 merchants. They provide all the tracking software and reporting as well as handling the payments to the affiliates. Commission Junction also has more than 125,000 affiliates in its database, so I had immediate access to thousands of Webmasters who could market my Web site.

The Million Dollar Drawing offers to pay 25 cents for each new entrant into the sweepstakes. My actual cost was 30 cents per entrant because Commission Junction charges a 20 percent fee on each transaction to cover the cost of the services they provide. When people enter the sweepstakes, I offer them the opportunity to subscribe to one of my three newsletters. The average person joins 1.4 newsletters, so my cost per new subscriber is about 22 cents. Since that's much less expensive than I could purchase subscribers in volume, I'm very happy with those results.

Even better, however, is the fact these subscribers actually cost me nothing! The Million Dollar Drawing is also an affiliate for many of Commission Junction's merchants. With all the traffic received by the site, much of it coming from Commission Junction's affiliates, I'm able to refer those people to these merchants and earn payments for leads and commissions. I actually earn more from Commission Junction each month than I invest in payments to Commission Junction. The net result is that I receive thousands of new leads and subscribers each month at no cost to me.

Hosting Your Mail List

You have several ways to host your mailing list:

1. Most Web-hosting companies provide mailing list programs that will handle up to 1,000 subscribers. You can have people automatically added to the list, but you will have to manually remove them when they want to unsubscribe.

2. When your list becomes unmanageable on your Web site, you can use a mailing program like Aureate Group Mail to send out your mailings. Aureate provides a free basic program, which you can upgrade to a sophisticated program if necessary. (See Aureate's link at www.group-mail.com.)

3. You can develop your own mailing list management program using readily available free CGI scripts. With these programs and the others that follow, subscribers can subscribe and unsubscribe with no effort on your part. This will take some time and effort, but you will retain control if that's important to you.

www.cgi-resources.com

www.list-business.com/list-software/

www.webmaster-resources.com

http://cgi.elitehost.com

www.freescripts.com

www.aspin.com

www.aspemail.com

4. You can hire a company such as SPARKList to provide list manage-ment services for a small fee.

www.sparklist.com/index.shtml

5. You can use free online services such as Egroups, Topica, or ListBot. Some of the following services will provide free hosting and mailing of your newsletter.

www.egroups.com

www.topica.com

www.listbot.com

www.onelist.com

www.listtool.com

www.coollist.com

www.mail-list.com

www.listhost.net

www.list-universe.com

Getting Articles for Your Newsletter

To get articles for your newsletter, you can use several methods. The first is to list your newsletter in all the e-zine directories in the appropriate cat-egories. A lot of people who want to have articles published will be look-ing in these directories for e-zines that accept articles. They will write and e-mail completed articles that are formatted to your requirements. All you have to do is include a four- to six-line ad, sometimes called a *resource box,* immediately following the article when you publish it.

Another way to obtain material is to visit sites that post articles for newsletter editors to use. Here are some good places to start:

www.mediapeak.com

www.ideamarketers.com

www.ezineseek.com/resources/articles/index.shtml

www.homebusinessmag.com

www.web-source.net

www.ezinearticles.com

In addition, you can post your articles at some of these sites for use by other newsletter editors. When they use your article, they'll include your resource box so you get some traffic. Another good site for learning how to create an e-zine is www.ezineuniversity.com.

I hope this information has been useful to you. I wish you well. If you'd like to contact me, you can always find me at www.shawncasey.com.

CHAPTER 13

Online Stream #4.
Eyeballs for Sale:
Making Advertising Pay

"On the Internet, nobody knows you're a dog."

Kevin Nunley is an Internet marketing guru. Yet in 1996 he knew almost nothing about the Internet. He had been working for many years as a morning radio talk show host when he began to dabble on the Internet. Then, in 1997, his part-time, online activities hit critical mass. As he describes it,

One day, I just got more business than I could handle, and it's been that way ever since. I left broadcasting to do this full-time. Every once in a while someone asks me why I'd leave the glamorous world of entertainment. I tell them that I now reach more people in a week—perhaps 1 million people—than I ever did in broadcasting. Articles I have written appear all over AOL, on dozens of major Web sites and e-zines—over 700 articles in all, floating freely around the Internet.

Writing and publishing short, pithy, content-rich articles is Nunley's (he has a Ph.D. in communications, by the way) main way of promoting himself. He submits articles on marketing, advertising, and copywriting to various e-zines and content publishers. He receives no payment for his writing but e-zines include his byline and Web site address at the end of his articles—giving readers a chance to communicate with him.

In fact, that is how I learned about him. I was reading one of the many e-zines I receive weekly when I ran across Nunley's article about earning advertising revenues from your Web site. It impressed me, so I contacted him and asked permission to reprint his article in this chapter. Once again, another of his free articles will bear some fruit, as no doubt some of my readers will check out his Web site to ask about his services.

In the course of building his business at www.drnunley.com, Nunley has acquired 6,000 subscribers to his own free weekly e-zine, DRNUN-LEYS MARKETING TIPS. Because this chapter focuses on building advertising revenues at your site, let's go behind the scenes and see how Kevin Nunley generates advertising revenue from his operations. But first, I'd like you to read the article he wrote about Internet advertising.

How to Sell Ads on Your Site
Kevin Nunley

Just about every Web site owner has thought of a day when they will be able to harvest huge profits simply by putting other people's ads on their site. Put up your site, insert ads, and wait for the checks to arrive.

And why not?

TV pulls down billions, your local daily newspaper probably gobbles up 80 percent of the ad money spent in your town, and your favorite top five rated radio station practically prints money. Media earns. So why can't your Web site get in on the media money frenzy, too?

While Internet advertising has been a bit slow to get started (banner ad rates aren't any higher than they were in 1996), online advertising is starting to show signs of real promise.

Optimistic predictions peg online ad sales topping $23.5 billion by 2005.

That is even MORE than network TV earns. To make matters even more exciting for the small business owner, there don't seem to be many mammoth corporate sites running away with all the audience. Even Yahoo!, the king of Web traffic, is having problems keeping Wall Street happy.

What to Expect

Most Web site ads are in the form of banners. Banner rates are based on how many visitors your site gets. Just like advertising on TV or print, rates are CPM (cost per thousand visitors). The CPM rate for banners has been at $35 for years.

I would be sloppy if I didn't also mention that a great many sites discount their rates if you ask. In reality, the average CPM rate (when you ask) is well below $35. This sort of thing isn't at all unusual in the media world. I once worked for a radio station that had a published rate of $75 per commercial. Most clients got their spots for just $30. One major supermarket that had a knack for negotiation was getting the same commercials for just $12.

One way to tell if a site isn't getting any advertisers is to note how many of their banners advertise their own site. Either they aren't getting anyone to buy their banner space or the rates are so low it is more profitable to advertise the company's own products.

When you publish your ad rates, try to keep them high. It's much easier to negotiate a lower rate than to raise low rates later on. Most media profits come from higher rates. When your unique visitor count goes up, raise your rates. When an important writer regularly sends you content, raise your rates.

Here's Who Can Place Ads on Your Site

Fortunately, there are some very large and growing ad networks that bring thousands of everyday Web sites together. These well-organized packages of sites are very attractive to advertisers. Even for big companies, they are the way to go if you want to do an ad campaign on the Net without spending a month going from site to site setting up the deal.

Make your first stop at TheAdStop.com. They include how-to advice and a host of reviewed ad networks that can get you started.

eAds.com pays from a nickel to 20 cents per click and won't accept sites that get less than 100,000 impressions per month (an *impression* is when a visitor sees a banner).

A site that is highly focused on a specific topic of interest to a certain valuable audience will produce better results for banners. eAds will negotiate a special price for sites with banners getting more than 500 clicks per month.

BurstMedia.com has taken the specialized site concept to a lofty level. They believe highly specialized site content provides better results for advertisers. On a recent visit, Burst was featuring LongHairLovers.com, a site for women with long hair.

You may have noticed, as I have, that many women highly value their long hair. They regard that aspect of their person as very dear. You can imagine how personal the articles, products, and ideas featured at LongHairLovers.com can be to that specific audience. It turns out to be an outstanding place to advertise hair care products.

Other ad networks go for hugely impressive numbers. ValueClick delivers ads to a global audience—including over 30 percent of Internet users in the United States. Banners range over 10,200 sites before 14 million people.

In almost all cases, banners are served up on sites according to standard subject areas like Automotive, Business & Finance, Careers, and Consumer Technology.

Mostly I've been referring to small business sites. If you are in charge of advertising for a larger corporation, you may need a more extensive and personalized campaign designed by an ad agency. Most top agencies, especially those hailing from New York City, have either established their own Internet ad departments or acquired smaller firms specializing in developing online ad campaigns.

The big guys don't seem to have any special secrets. The current method is to search the Net for appropriate sites and negotiate a price. A recent report figured an ad agency worker placed dozens of calls and e-mails to get a campaign going. There are now efforts to build a database network that will speed up the process.

How to Measure Your Site's Audience

Most ad networks pay according to cost per click (CPC—how many people click on a banner) and cost per impression (how many people see a banner, usually sold on the classic CPM model I mentioned earlier).

Before you get into the game, you need a good way to measure the number of visitors you get on each of your pages. Your numbers of unique visitors is most important.

Your Web host may already have a hits measuring feature in place for your site. There are also software packages you can buy off the shelf and online services you can connect to. Perhaps the most popular and full featured is the free service at WebTrendsLive.com. The basic service requires you put their button on every page of your site. You can pay more to go buttonless. You get real-time traffic analysis and a gaggle of reports on visitors, page views, ad campaigns, and revenues.

One trick used by radio and TV is to take advantage of all those reports.

When you can view your audience from every which way, you can bet there is at least one perspective that makes your site look extremely attractive to advertisers.

Maybe you don't get a whole ton of visitors, but those who come spend an hour clicking through every page on your site. That shows visitors value your content and don't mind giving up a considerable helping of their valuable time. That is a quality that would mean sales for many advertisers.

In the end, you may find it's the MEASURING and not the ads that make you the most money. Keeping a constant eye on your site's stats lets you make better decisions on where you place content, what kinds of content you use, what products and services you sell, and how you run your own ad campaigns. This invariably helps your site make more money from the sale of products, services, subscription fees, and through more efficient spending.

The preceding article is an example of one submitted to various e-zine publishers for the sole purpose of driving traffic to Nunley's Web site. Once there, many people sign up for his free weekly e-zine. Using this method, he has built his subscriber base to over 6,000 individuals. Each week Nunley sends out another e-zine and permits three to six paid classified ads. A 50-word classified ad costs $39. He estimates that his monthly revenue is between $1,000 and $1,200.

It's a small stream of income, but Nunley says, "While we make money from the ads, the REAL purpose of the newsletter is to advertise our services . . . and you'll see those ads at the end of each article."

As an example of how advertising works in his free e-zine, I've reprinted another of Nunley's sample e-zines, complete with ads. If you were a subscriber to Nunley's e-zine, this is what you would receive. Image it is your e-zine. Count up the dollars from the various classified ad placements.

All new articles! Forward this issue to a friend.

DRNUNLEY'S MARKETING TIPS!

Sent free only to subscribers from Dr. Kevin Nunley

FREE weekly wisdom to fatten your profits!

****

We provide the articles, YOU take the credit! Get DrNunley's FREE Article Service. Each week we e-mail you Kevin's newest articles. Use them on your site, in your e-zine, or with your sales materials.

http://DrNunley.com/article_service.htm

****

DR. NUNLEY'S MARKETING TIP

TV Channels Are Exploding!

This week I saw a cable TV installer working across the street and took a moment to check on the state of his industry.

"Fiber is coming!" he said.

"Huh?" I replied.

"Fiber-optic cable is being laid five miles from here. We'll have it in this neighborhood in another three months."

"What's that got to do with me?" I asked.

"Instead of 50 channels, you will have more than 100. And that's just the start. Fiber-optic cable lets us send you a lot more channels once they are available," he said, as if his firm had just beaten the Internet at its own game.

The other big development is a very large and growing number of people now have digital satellite dishes on their roofs. They, too, can receive up to hundreds of channels.

This is good news for small and medium-sized businesses who may not have been able to afford TV advertising in the past. The more channels that are available, the better you will be able to specifically target your best customers without wasting money on viewers who wouldn't be interested in what you sell.

The law of supply and demand also steps in. More channels mean more ad slots available and falling ad rates. Cable TV ads are already going for $40, $20, even $2 in some smaller towns. You can also get your ad on national cable networks for no more than you would pay for a spot on your local broadcast TV station.

Promote your business with Kevin's Super PRESS RELEASE Deal. He writes your release AND sends it to 5,000 media for just $345 (everyone else charges $500 for this combination). Ask about our special limited-time offer to send your release to 20,000 opt-in subscribers at no additional charge.

Write me for details at kevin@drnunley.com or see my site at http://www.DrNunley.com.

****

MARKETING ON-LINE

Four Ways to Get a Great Headline

Doesn't matter whether you are writing an ad for a free ad site, a press release, a Web page, or a sales letter—you need to top it off with a powerful headline.

Here are four tried-and-true ways to get a headline that pulls.

1. Write your headline in newspaper style. This works particularly well if your product or service relates to something that is in the news.

NEW FIRM HELPS FAILING DOT-COMs RETOOL FOR SUCCESS.

2. If your price is good, include it in the headline.

WOULD YOU PAY $20.00 TO WORK LESS?

3. Announce your free product or service. Trite as it may seem, "free" (as well as no-cost and complimentary) gets attention and results.

FREE! GET A SECOND PACKAGE WHEN YOU BUY THE FIRST.

4. Talk about the reader, one person at a time.

IS YOUR SITE NOT GETTING HITS?
WE PUT YOU ON SEARCH ENGINES.

Yes! Kevin and his crew write sales letters and Web site copy fast and at low cost. See http://DrNunley.com/copywriting.htm for sales letters, Web copy, and autoresponder letters. Reach Kevin at kevin@drnunley.com.

****

Note from a reader:

Q. Would it be a good idea for my business to have a booth at our industry trade show?
A. Use the trade show to network within your industry. The best experts, manufacturer's representatives, and salespeople will be there for you to talk with. Look for new products, ideas, and alliances with other companies that can give you a breakthrough advantage.

****

NEW AT DRNUNLEY.COM

Kevin's 49-LESSON E-BUSINESS COURSE gives you simple instructions on every aspect of making money online. Read the entire course online, or download the e-book. Get it now for just $39 along with FREE shopping cart, web site hosting, promotion tools, and more!

CLICK http://DrNunley.NET

DrNunley's THREE new FREE e-mail courses: Power Email, Internet Biz Start-up, Get Free Media. Get them all at http://DrNunley.com.

Subscribe to Kevin's DAILY MARKETING TIPS at http://www.memail.com. Look under the Business section.

****

DRNUNLEY'S FREE ENTERPRISE MARKETPLACE:

Your 50-word ad included for $39 per weekly issue reaches out 6,500 smart subscribers. Order at http://drnunley.com/drnad.htm.

GOVERNMENT SPENDING TO REACH ALL-TIME HIGH OF $1.06 TRILLION BY THE END OF THE YEAR 2000. Get your piece of the pie with BIDNET, the nation's largest source of state and local government bids. Try our Internet service, FREE!

http://www.bidnet.com/resources.htm

WORK FROM HOME business just $29! Work independently with an INC 500 company. Web site and free online marketing center for you to use. Enjoy the thrill of no boss, no commuting, and plenty of time to be with family. Earn good part-time money or full-time income. No selling or multilevel marketing.

http://BizGuru.com/mela/

Save up to 70 percent on Inkjet Cartridges & Refill Kits! Our quality printer ink and excellent service make All-Ink-com one of the Net's most popular stops for printer supplies—110 percent satisfaction guaranteed! We also give you Free Priority Delivery, so your order arrives fast. Click NOW!

http://www.all-ink.com

HERE'S HOW TO DO MAIL ORDER. Must have software with all 42,000+ USA zip codes, area codes, cities, states, and counties. Don't do mail order without it!

http://www.quikthinking.com

IDA International. The Easiest way to have YOUR Internet Business. Have your secure Web site with hundreds of 100 percent guaranteed products. No sales, meetings or inventory required. Just promote your Web site. Support from NFLI (15 years experience). Click http://home.coqui.net/idelgado now!

Host4Profit—a host that pays you back, $10 per month for referrals plus four instant sites that make you money. Visit us now:

http://www.slife.com/host4profitred.html

Or e-mail boldwyn@accessus.net and type "host4profit_nunley" in the subject line.

****

> This newsletter is sent weekly ONLY to those who have asked for it (readers, friends, clients, and a few competitors<g>).
>
> We're at:
>
> 9699 S. 2810 W.
> South Jordan, UT 84095 USA
> See you next week!
> Kevin

If you stand back and view Nunley's marketing efforts, you can see that it forms one great cycle. He writes articles to publish in e-zines. This effort gleans customers for his own e-zine. Then he narrowcasts his own e-zine to his 6,000+ subscribers, which generates paying customers for the services he offers on his own Web site. As gravy, he gets the spin-off advertising revenue from selling ad space in his own e-zine. At this time, he does not sell banner ads on his site, but that may be only a few clicks away, as the traffic to his site increases and the number of his e-zine subscribers mushrooms.

This is a perfect model for you to follow. Here is my advice to you: "Go thou and do likewise."

To round out this chapter on earning advertising revenues from your site, here's a great story about someone who made a killing by creating a Web site specifically designed to generate advertising revenues. The story is submitted by Corey Rudl, one of the Internet's leading marketing

gurus. You can visit Corey at his famous Web site at http://www.market-ingtips.com/freebook. I strongly encourage you to sign up for his free newsletter. It's full of fabulous information.

Take it away, Corey.

There are two basic approaches to making money from your Web site. The first is what I call a *portal Web site,* and the second I refer to as a *sales Web site.* A portal Web site is specifically designed to generate the bulk of its profits from the sale of advertising. A sales Web site is designed to generate most of its profits from the sale of products and services.

If you have a portal Web site, your goal is to get as many visitors to your site as possible by enticing them with something special that you offer. You might provide them with valuable information, help, free software, entertainment, or something similar. There are countless possibilities!

If you are giving away something of value, you will attract traffic. Hotmail offered free e-mail accounts, Yahoo! gave away search information, financial portals give you instantaneous financial news, and so on.) Offer something unavailable anywhere else and give it away free—that's how to generate traffic.

You may be asking, "How do I make money if I give it all away for free?" Once you are established and attracting high-volume traffic, you can make money by selling advertising space on your site or by offering products or services.

This is a great way to profit from traffic, even if you have nothing to sell. The *traffic itself* becomes your *asset!* This is particularly true when the traffic that you are generating has very specific interests or needs. Advertisers are willing to pay good money when their ads are being directed at large numbers of their target market.

Let me give you an example of how developing your own portal Web site could be your key to success in online marketing. Although the general details are true, the names are fictitious. I think you'll agree that it's an amazing story!

A friend of mine (let's call him "Michael") had a new-car-invoice dealer-cost-pricing business. What's that? Well, say you want to know the price that a local car dealership paid the manufacturer for a certain vehicle. You just go to his site, pay Michael $15, and he'll send you an e-mail with a breakdown of exactly what that dealer paid for that car. Sound like a great service? It is!

With this kind of knowledge, you can go back and haggle with the dealer for a really good price and probably save yourself hundreds (maybe even thousands) of dollars (all because you know what the dealer paid for that car). Pretty powerful! Is it worth $15? Absolutely.

Michael was selling this service like hotcakes. People were coming to him and buying three and four reports at a time (one for a Subaru, one for a Honda, one for a Toyota). He was making $100,000 a year doing this, and it was taking him only one or two hours a day. Pretty easy income.

I have a second friend we'll call "Chris," who came to me one day and said, "You know what? I can do better than that! I'm going to give it all away *for free!*" He rented (for $2,000 a month) the actual database that provides these car dealer cost invoices. Then guess what he did? He started giving away for free the same information for which Michael had been charging $15. Chris set it up so that you can go to his Web site, punch in any car you want, any year you want, and you get the price. How much does it cost you? *Nothing*—not a dime!

Next, Chris approached all of the big car sites saying, "Why link to places that make you pay for car-pricing information? They charge $15 and I'm giving it away for free! Link to me!" The logic proved irresistible: They all started linking to him.

These links generated hundreds of thousands of visitors to Chris's site every month! Big sites like *Road & Track* and *Motor Trend* began funneling traffic into his site because he offers such a great service. Instead of linking to Michael, they link to Chris. Now they can say to their customers, "Look! We're great because we're telling all of our clients where they can get this great free information!" They even published editorials about his site in their magazines.

After six months, Michael just couldn't compete. His income dropped from $100,000 a year to barely $15,000, and he lost his business.

However, Chris wasn't making any money, either! He still had to find a way earn a living. The database was costing him $2,000 a month in rental fees, and basic necessities such as rent and food cost another $1,500, for total monthly expenses of about $3,500. Chris had only about six months' worth of cash in the bank! Now what?

Imagine what a powerful site this could be! The traffic Chris generates is very specific: people in the market to buy a vehicle. Even better, after six months his site was generating high-volume traffic—300,000 people every month! Guess what Chris did?

He called companies like Toyota and Honda and said, "Hey guys, would you like to advertise on my site? I'll only charge you $35,000 a month each."

Honda said, "We pay $30,000 a month to put a one-page ad in *Car and Driver*. You're going to let 300,000 people that have a direct interest in buying a car see our ad? That's a *great* deal! Of course we'll advertise with you!"

Talk about a target market! And $35,000 *is* a bargain! In his first month

Chris made *over $100,000* in revenue. Why? Because he was willing to lose money in the beginning to offer a valuable service (the portal model) so he could make the money on the back end. Chris created a portal Web site: He drove traffic to his site and then converted it to a profit model after six months.

But Chris wasn't done yet! He called me up and said, "Hey Corey! Can I sell your book, *Car Secrets Revealed,* at my site?" I said, "Sure. I'll give 10 bucks for every one you sell." Now he sells my car book at his site, and every month I send him a check for thousands of dollars in sales! Even better, he started selling extended warranties and insurance quotes at his site, generating even more income for himself through referral fees. It was incredible!

Within a few months, Chris was approached by someone who said, "I'll give you $1 million for 20 percent of your business, and I'll kick in all the venture capital you need to develop it." Wow! What do you think Chris's answer was? How long did it take him to build a successful company? Less than a year! He now has a million dollars cash in the bank plus millions of dollars in venture capital that he can use for whatever he wants!

Today Chris is running a big office with lots of employees and programmers . . . the whole nine yards! The beauty of this is that he started with nothing but an idea. An incredible example showing the potential of Internet marketing.

Portal sites *do not* generate instant cash. They require a good six-month investment (and sometimes years depending on your idea) of time and money. However, once these sites are successful, they pay off *big,* and the time commitment and maintenance from that point on is minimal.

To sum up, the risk is big, but if it works, the payoff is big. Most people are unwilling to risk six months of their lives only to find out that the portal does not work and it was all for nothing. . . . Conversely, a killer idea can make you a fortune.

If this information has been helpful to you and you'd like to sign up for my free newsletter, check out my Web site:

http://www.marketingtips.com

You will be glad you did!

CHAPTER 14

Online Stream #5.
Picks and Shovels:
Making Money from the
Infrastructure of the Net

"THE SYSTEM'S CRASHED! QUICK! GET ME A YOUNG MAN WITH A PONYTAIL AND AN EARRING!"

You've heard it said that the only people who made money in the California gold rush were the people who sold picks and shovels to the miners. While you're laying claims to your Internet fortune, you can always keep money coming in the door by supplying the necessary tools for the millions of Internet miners.

What kinds of tools do they need?

The Technology to Host and Run a Web Site Business

Internet service provider (ISP)

Web hosting

Web design

Autoresponders

Listserves

Shopping carts

Credit card services

Daily troubleshooting

Web site statistics

Product Services

Product design

Manufacturing

Printing

Warehousing

Inventory control

Shipping

Marketing and Advertising Services

Advertising

Copywriting

Marketing strategy

Joint ventures

During the early days of the Net, a lot of money could be made in Web site hosting and site design—because only the geekiest of geeks had the technical expertise to do the work. Now, with free, automated, templated Web design solutions (see, for example, Bigstep.com in Chapter 9), even everyday technophobes can build their own Web sites.

These technical services will become increasingly commoditized. Translation? Too much price competition will cut profit margins to the bone. Don't try to compete in this arena.

Neither will there be easy pickings in product services. The real opportunity is in the area of marketing services. By becoming a marketing expert for hire, you will have a steady supply of new clients while gaining experience to expand your own Internet business. Now more than ever, the fundamental principles of marketing are desperately needed by millions of newly launched Internet businesses.

In other words, I'm going to encourage you to learn the principles of marketing, to become one of the best—a pro. It is the most important business subject you will ever learn. The best products in the world gather dust in the warehouse without good marketing.

Even successful offline businesses need help marketing their products in the confusing new field of the Internet. Since most of these businesses will be desperate for immediate solutions, your services will be in high demand and deeply appreciated.

There follows some excellent marketing advice for offline businesses. The advice sounds almost too simplistic. Yet I'll wager that there is not one business in ten in your city today that is practicing this obvious business strategy to boost sales. This lesson is provided by Corey Rudl, an Internet marketing guru who, as a young man in his late twenties, makes over $5 million a year dishing out practical tips for building business (see www.marketingtips.com/freebook).

How to Make Money with Your Offline Business by Using Online Technology!

I would like to take a moment to speak with those of you who are operating an offline business. Have you stopped to consider how the Internet could improve—even skyrocket—your business profits? Most people do not realize how important it is to give their offline business an online presence. They do not believe that online marketing would work for their particular business.

Guess what? They're wrong! Online marketing can be applied to every business . . . no matter what kind of product or service you sell! You don't believe me? Let me give you some examples. . . .

Let's say you own a hair salon. Obviously, people are not going to search online for a hair salon—they're going to look in the Yellow Pages or get a recommendation from a friend. Your hair salon caters to a local market, not a global market. So why should your salon be online?

If you're a smart entrepreneur, every time patrons come to your salon to have their hair cut or colored, ask for their e-mail address while they are paying. Put it into a simple customer database at your cash counter and make a note of the date and the kind of service that you performed for them. There is a *lot* of power in doing something like this!

Why? Because three weeks later when you realize that business is slow, you can simply sit down and send your customers an e-mail.

Dear [insert customer name here]:

Thank you for your visit on February 10 for the cut and perm. I just wanted to write and thank you for your business. I also wanted to let you know that for the week of March 3, 2000, we're offering a special 20 percent discount on haircuts to all our valued customers.

However, you must book your appointment within the next 48 hours to get this discount. Just call us at (310) 555-1212 right after you read this and we will book an appointment right away.

We look forward to seeing you again soon!

Sincerely,

Your friend at Chop & Frizz Hair Studio

I will explain a little later how you can address this e-mail to all of your customers (whether 100 or 1,000) individually (e.g., "Dear Tracy") and send them all out by pressing *one button.* If you have collected 500 e-mail addresses in the last two months, it will take you about five minutes to write the e-mail and about two minutes to send it to all your customers.

Once you've sent out your e-mail, your phones will start ringing and the seats of your salon will fill very quickly. Will this technique generate more business? *Definitely!* How much time did it take you? *Almost none!* Did it cost you anything? *No!*

Let me give you another example. . . . How could a grocery store profit more by using online technologies? Once again, you can use the Internet to keep in touch with your customers and improve your customer service! Simply get the e-mail addresses of all customers who walk through the cashier line and let them know that you'll be sending them discount coupons every week. By doing this you are going to remind thousands of people, "Come back to our grocery store because we're going to give you 30 cents off yogurt and a dollar off milk." Are they going to come back? You bet! All you need to do is remind them that you're there. And it costs you nothing! *It's all free with e-mail!*

Which grocery store do you think they are going to visit? I won't even bother answering that. . . . You know which one! Do you know how much it costs stores to produce newspaper flyers touting their specials? *Tens of thousands of dollars a week!* Guess what? If you e-mail those specials to your customers . . . it is now *free* . . . and you get to put tens of thousands of dollars directly into your pocket because you don't have those high advertising costs anymore!

This is the beauty of the Internet. Every business—I don't care who you are or what you do—should be online. If you're not online and using the technology to increase your business, you're losing money!

Is this going to make you rich? No, it isn't. But you will surely earn more money than you are making now in your business (sometimes 50 percent more). Think about it, and use the Internet creatively. Don't just do things the standard way. Be unique! Use online technology to create the kind of rapport and loyalty that turns a first-time customer into a life-time customer!

What do you have to lose? If you e-mail your customers and only a few respond with only minor additional sales, *who cares!* You can't fail. Any incremental sales that cost you nothing add to your income. It is "free money," as it cost you only about eight minutes to prepare an e-mail and send it to all your customers.

With technology today, it's so easy to do! For about $100 you can pick up a small database that is fully mail-mergeable. You can use this database to enter your customers' names, their e-mail addresses, the most recent day they were in, the purchases they made, and the services that were per-formed. Later, you can use this information to send out thank-you notes, surveys, and promotion or contest information—all of which will help you build a relationship with your customers and create the loyal clientele base that every business needs!

Even better, with the software that is available today, you can fully auto-mate these tasks. After taking five minutes to write your thank-you notes or promotional letter, you can simply click a button and, voilà, your letter has been sent out to hundreds or even thousands of customers. One excellent piece of software that will do all this for you is Mailloop.

Mailloop is great because it acts as a customer database, a bulk e-mail server, a newsletter server, a Web form processor, and an autoresponder. All the software you need is included in a single application! I personally use this software and highly recommend it! I couldn't imagine doing busi-ness on the Internet without it. For more information on what it does and how it works go to http://www.marketingtips.com/mailloop.

By providing this kind of amazing service, you're going to make your customers feel special. Your business will stand out in their minds because you have taken the time to develop a bond—a feeling of community—that draws them back. It's easy to do, it works, and it takes no time at all when you use the right software.

However, I need to warn you that this is *not* going to last forever. Get in while the getting is good! Soon, more entrepreneurs like yourself are going to smarten up and realize that these kinds of techniques could really improve their business. But guess who will have beaten them to the punch? *You!* Because you knew about it first. Get in there! Get your offline business online. You will see nothing but benefits. Increase your business by developing a relationship with your customers! It takes almost no time and costs practically nothing. . . . How can you lose? The only way you lose is by keeping your business offline. Get online and start using these techniques while they are the most beneficial.

If this information has been helpful to you and you'd like a free subscription to my online marketing newsletter, go to the Corey Rudl Web site:

http://www.marketingtips.com/freebook

Steven H. Kiges: French Horn Player and/or Internet Marketing Consultant

This next story is about an ordinary person who is on the verge of creating extraordinary profits online.

Steven Kiges grew up in Minnesota, trained professionally at The Juilliard School in New York City, and spent the first part of his life playing French horn in various symphony orchestras around North America. He ended up in Regina, Saskatchewan, with a symphony job and a teaching position at the local university. He thought that music would be his life's vocation. Then he took the road less traveled and it's been a wild ride ever since. I'll let him share his story with you in his own words.

In about 1988, I started wondering on a personal level if I was still happy as a musician or if there was something else in life for me. Actually, the question was, "Can I do or am I capable of doing anything else in my life?" While I loved music, and while many of my friends were satisfied with the level they'd achieved, I was not. I started looking at business opportunities—businesses for sale, franchises, starting my own.

Tragedy gave me the push I needed: My wife and I had a premature baby who died. My parents came to visit us from Minnesota and brought an amazing gift basket that was inside a balloon. Although still traumatized and grieving, I later researched the manufacturer of the balloon-making device and purchased the rights to market it in Western Canada. My first sale was to the floral department at Safeway for $40,000. Talk about being naive in business, I told the purchasing agent at Safeway that as soon as I received his check I would send the equipment. He said, "You don't understand. You send us the equipment and in 60 days we will send you a check." Gulp! I went to the bank with our mortgage, borrowed $30,000 to pay the manufacturer, and sent the equipment to Safeway. I didn't sleep much for 60 days but making $10,000 on the deal certainly made it worthwhile.

I spent more and more time researching businesses and talking to business owners, and I finally decided the only way to know if I could make it outside the music world was to take the plunge. After being in music for close to 25 years, I took a leave of absence, and we moved to Vancouver, British Columbia. There I took a job as a commissioned salesperson for a local software company (Mercedes Software) that computerized dental offices. When I started, the company had fewer than 50 clients. By the end of the year we had 150. My first-year commissions were over $80,000. What a change from the music world! About six months later, one of the owners wanted to sell out. I purchased his half of the business and was now 50 percent owner and vice president of sales and marketing for a thriving software company.

Over the next few years the company flourished and totally dominated the market. We did this by offering a simple, easy-to-use program and exceptional customer service. While it was fun making lots of money, and always challenging, the 18-hour days started to take their toll. I became a real workaholic, waking at 4 A.M. and sometimes not getting home until 10 P.M. After our daughter Rachel was born, I would sometimes go days without seeing her. This continued for a few years, and, as you can imagine, I was starting to feel burned out and empty inside.

As a musician, you are your own boss. You do it yourself and people judge your performance. When the microphone is on, broadcasting live across the country, you can't make any excuses. I thought business was done the same way. I'm sorry I never read Michael Gerber's book *eMyth*, in which he explains how to set up systems in business. It would have saved much heartache.

When, in 1997, a large international software company offered to buy us out, I sold my shares. I wanted a life.

Things were pretty good. I spent a lot of time with my family and relaxed. However, not being someone to sit still, by the third week I was off researching new opportunities. I invested in a couple of start-ups that went belly-up, but I was determined to make a living from home. By this time my fax was churning out business opportunities at a rate of about 25 per day. For the next year or so, I tried dozens and dozens of different opportunities—from pay-phone schemes to investments to long-distance shipping to no-money-down computer sales to vitamins. The results were less than stellar: Either I couldn't sell the product or the company would go broke while owing me lots of money. By the end of this period I had spent over $350,000.

Finally, eureka! I found the Internet. Even though I had lost big in all those businesses, I figured that the Internet was the ticket to instant riches. I scoured and researched and found an obvious business that I could tweak and make millions. The business was online coupons, and the site I created was SaveLikeCrazy.com. What a great name! I hired a Web designer and a programmer. I spent a truckload designing, redesigning, and re-redesigning, until finally three months later we were up and open for business.

As a knowledgeable businessman, I had done my market research. I talked to my friends and family and asked them if they would download coupons from the Internet before going to a restaurant. A no-brainer, right? If my friends and family give it a thumbs-up, then it's a winner. Besides, this is the Internet, and everyone's making millions. "Build it and they will come."

On day one I'm off to the local pizza joint for a sure sale. Right? "Internet? What are you talking about? No thanks." Next stop, Subway sandwiches, "Maybe. I'll call the head office." Final results of day one— eight hours of work and one deposit check for $100.

Over the next week I came up with a revised plan charging substantially less for a three-month trial. I also hired a commission salesperson. We actually were doing pretty well, and then my salesperson came in and said, "I think we have a competitor, and they are giving away a six-month free trial." Sure enough, a new Internet company had started: It had issued an IPO and was capitalized at $10 million. Need I say it? SaveLikeCrazy bit the dust!

You know how sometimes things are right under your nose and you can't see them? During this period, while I'm losing money on every scheme under the sun and working on SaveLikeCrazy, I'm also receiving calls from businesspeople looking for Internet marketing advice. I sat on the phone and gave advice, created plans, and suggested how they could use the Internet to bring in more business. I really enjoyed helping these people.

About a year ago, while whining to a good friend about how the business world stinks and how I'm losing all my money, he said, "What do you like doing?" I said, "I enjoy talking to businesspeople about marketing on the Internet." He said, "Are you good at it?" I replied, "Well, I'm not sure, but I seem to know a lot more than most people, and some of my advice has brought in excellent results."

He suggested, "How about starting an Internet marketing company?" My first thoughts were, "I don't know enough." But then I realized that on the Internet *nobody* knows enough. I started my marketing business, charging my clients $75 for an hour for marketing advice. "Want to know the secrets of marketing on the Internet? Give me a call. The Internet is explained to you in plain English."

My first client was the same friend who had suggested that I do what I enjoy doing. Dov Baron (http://www.dovbaron.com) is an international motivational speaker and one of those rare people you can always count on to tell you the truth. He also has a great story: He fell off a mountain while rock climbing and landed on his face. His site has generated lots of publicity. Dov was recently on the *Sally Jessy Raphael Show* as the guest expert in traumatic events.

At first I simply consulted: Do this, try that. Then I formed strategic alliances with the technical people; "Need a person to design your Web site? Let me recommend the best one for you." "Need a logo? I have just the right person." From these referrals I collected a 25 percent fee. Not bad!

One of the ongoing problems that most of my clients experienced was the inability to get an online merchant account to accept credit cards. I negotiated a lead-referral arrangement with a merchant account company. As I knew this was a big issue with most new Netpreneurs, I put up a site to generate leads at http://www.MyMoneyGrows.com, from which I have earned about $3,500 in the past year. Not much money, but I don't *do* anything. People fill out a form on site, e-mail it to me, and I e-mail it to the company. I get 10 to 15 enquiries every week.

How did I design this site? (I don't know how to write one line of HTML code, nor do I plan on ever learning it.) I simply wrote a detailed plan of exactly *what I wanted to happen.* Then I wrote the advertising copy, found some graphics to use, and constructed the layout in Microsoft Word. I called a local community college and hired a top student for $100. Then I hired a programmer for an additional $150 to write an affiliate tracking section. Before long, my site was up and pumping out money.

One thing I learned about the software business and that I stress to all my clients is to *do the planning.* Take your time. If you can't see exactly what your end result is, don't start until you do. Just as great athletes are taught to visualize the outcome and musicians need to hear the phrase before they play it, Netpreneurs need to see the entire system or flow before writing one line of code.

One type of marketing that I like and use in the software business is *joint ventures.* For example, I was contacted by a leader in an MLM company, who sent me a copy of a book produced by the company. Although I was not interested in joining the group, I saw a huge potential for using the book as a lead-generation tool. We did a joint venture, and I created http://www.truthofmlm.com/. The purpose of the site is to create leads by offering a free, limited-time download of the book. We charge each downline member $30 per year for his or her own replicated site. In exchange for access to the free-download site we ask visitors to register. Once they register, we send out nine e-mails, all personalized, from the respective downline member urging them to take action and not to miss out.

I created the following advertising headline for the members to use:

MLM Exposed! Learn the Shocking Truth! Free Booklet Tells All!

One $25 e-zine ad that I ran produced over 1,200 sign-ups for the free book in one week. In less than six months, we had over 60,000 people

wanting to access the free-download site. Our autoresponder system has sent out over 540,000 messages. *Wow!* When I think of the cost in the real world—envelopes, letters, stamps—it's amazing!

While I love working from home and enjoy the flexibility, there can be a few drawbacks. My eight-year-old daughter Rachel asked me why I spend so much time on the phone and don't have a job! I explained that being on the telephone 10 hours a day and helping people on the Internet *was* my job. I also asked her if she remembered how many Dads were in the audience for her afternoon school talent show. She said, "You and one other dad." She thought about it for a moment and then said, "You know, Dad, I think I like your job."

Although I'm a businessperson, I am at heart a musician and artist—I create, whether the medium is a French horn, a business plan, or a Web site. I had a conversation years ago with the famous trumpet player Wynston Marsalis. When we were discussing technique, he said, "Real technique is the ability to draw the audience into having the emotional experience you plan." Is this not what marketing is? We all get hung up thinking we need to figure out the technique—HTML, Java, CGI, flash, whatever. Our true job as marketers is to provide our audience with a planned emotional experience and use the tools best suited to meet that end.

One of my recent clients hired me to create an online hobby site featuring model ships (http://www.northernstarmall.com/). The preplanning for this site is 15 pages long and technically quite complicated. Again, I don't know how to do it, but I know what I want it to do. I know it from the owner's perspective and I know it from the customers' wants. With the potential of 10,000 products, we created a private administration section where the owner adds his own new products and can make the necessary changes all by himself. The owner works with me on marketing and techniques to locate his target market. In the first weeks after launch, he had 100 newsletter subscribers and sold $10,000 worth of product. This is going to be a big moneymaker. I know this because the owner is focused, he has a good-sized market, and we know how to reach them.

Recently, I started a search to find the perfect vehicle for a joint venture. I was looking for someone who might be interested in selling the marketing rights to a product or in forming a joint venture, with me handling the marketing end. I found a wealth of excellent opportunities— actually, too many to choose from. After much research and negotiation, I obtained the exclusive marketing rights to Cathi Graham's Fresh Start Metabolism Program.

Cathi Graham lost 186 pounds 13 years ago and started a business to teach others how to lose weight. She has very successfully promoted her program with seminars, talk radio, and radio infomercials.

You might well ask, "Didn't she already have a Web site?" Yes. Then why does she need me? Because she spent thousands of dollars developing a Web site that was producing no revenue. Cathi had a problem, and I had a solution. Her site had no focus; it was click here, click there. The result was confusion for visitors.

I am very excited about this project. The new site (at http://www .newfreshstart.com/) is laser-focused to sell her main program. A separate site, Cathi Graham's Private Members Only, is where all the goodies are hidden. This is going to be an enormous win-win situation for both of us.

While I may have had difficulty getting my own online business off the ground, I have found enormous profit and satisfaction in helping other people launch their Internet businesses. I have learned so much by consulting with other people that I've now launched another business. Check out my Web site:

http://www.milliondollarsystems.com

I hope my story has been helpful in showing you that failure can eventually lead to success.

CHAPTER 15

Online Stream #6.
Treasure Hunting: Turning Junk into Cash with Auctions

"I got it from eBay."

Let's start with an article in the *Wall Street Journal*. It will blow your mind.

Yard Sales in Cyberspace—

Want Barbie & Ken Salt Shakers? Goat Pictures? Just Click and Bid

by George Anders

After months of trying to run a variety store in this coal-mining town, Wayne and Shanna Bumbaca realized that their shop wasn't going to make it. They put up a "Closed" sign and carted home the vestiges of Rocky

Mountain Discounts, including their most foolish purchase: 144 red Santas with tiny helicopter blades attached to their heads.

The Christmas ornaments lingered in the young couple's garage for weeks. "We couldn't give them away," Mr. Bumbaca recalls. "I put them in my yard one day with a sign saying 'Free,' and no one took them."

Then Mr. Bumbaca tried listing a helicopter Santa for auction on the Internet. His initial asking price: $2.95. Late that evening he got electronic mail from a woman at a U.S. military base in Italy, offering $8. By the way, she asked, were any extras available? "I woke up my wife," Mr. Bumbaca recalls. "I said: 'Honey, I think we're on to something.'"

That was in May 1997. Today, the Bumbacas are selling 800 items a week online, putting them on pace for $600,000 of revenue this year, much of it windfall profits from customers who can't resist making sky-high bids to win an auction. Other people leave the house to work. The Bumbacas simply pile inventory in their garage and then spend most days at a personal computer in their living room, running a giant yard sale in cyberspace.

As Americans become spellbound by the Internet, thousands of ordinary people are recasting themselves as online merchants. It's easy to see why. The Internet's reach is so vast—and its ability to connect buyers and sellers is so quick—that anyone with a modem and a cluttered garage can dream of becoming a high-powered sales machine. Some 2.1 million people use the biggest online auction company, eBay Inc., and thousands more are rushing to join a similar service just launched this week by Amazon.com Inc.

In cyberspace, even the weirdest listings find buyers. Pictures of goats sell. Life-size cardboard cutouts of Xena the Princess Warrior sell. Salt-and-pepper shakers molded to look like Barbie and Ken sell. "At first we worried a lot about what to carry," Mr. Bumbaca says. "Then we realized it didn't matter. We've got two million people looking at our listings. There's always someone who says: 'That's exactly what I want.'"

Whether this boom will last much longer is an open question. Selling online is no refuge from bad checks, angry customers or aggressive competition. And as the number of merchants explodes, there is a growing likelihood that the novelties and outright junk for sale will far exceed anyone's demand.

What's more, many small-time Internet vendors are acutely dependent on steady shipments of cheap merchandise from major manufacturers and distributors. It's no great challenge to open up these suppliers' cartons and then sell items, one at a time, on the Internet at a hefty markup. Distributors might wake up to the juicy profits being made and use the Internet to sell direct to the public themselves. If so, cyberspace could become rough territory overnight for many mom-and-pop merchants.

In the small towns where grass-roots Internet marketing is most alluring, however, no one wants to brood about such problems. "Selling online lets me compete with Wal-Mart and Sears," says Mike Baker, a Springdale, Ark., dealer in posters and celebrity photos. Just a year ago, he was a shift supervisor at a Levi Strauss & Co. factory, about to lose his job in a plant closing. Now he works from home, selling more than 10,000 items a year online.

Fueling this trend is eBay, which each day lists more than 1.8 million items for sale, ranging from antique clocks to car stereos. Users provide all the listings, stock the goods themselves and negotiate prices among one another. EBay simply runs the Web service and collects a token listing fee, plus a commission of 1.25% to 5% any time a sale is completed. The genius of this arrangement is that users' own activity generates organic growth—letting eBay expand rapidly without having to do much of anything.

"A lot of people think we're this quaint, inconsequential trading service where people just buy a Furby or two for Christmas," says Steve Westly, eBay's vice president, marketing. Not so, he declares. He calls eBay the Amway Corp. or Avon Products Inc. of the 21st century: a wide-ranging sales network that draws its energy from an elite group of top sellers who live and breathe their company's way of doing things.

Last autumn, eBay singled out 10,000 people—the top 0.4% of its registered participants—and dubbed them PowerSellers. They get personalized Christmas cards from the company. An in-house newsletter celebrates their accomplishments. Not everyone is thriving. But many retirees, stay-at-home moms and disaffected office workers are making thousands of dollars a month on eBay, letting blue-collar America taste a little bit of Internet riches.

In Wyoming, the Bumbacas typify this new form of commerce. A bumpy dirt road leads to their house, where three preschool children watch cartoon shows most mornings or race outside to play on a swing set. There's no storefront sign, no corporate stationery and no dress code. From the moment they wake, though, the Bumbacas are dead serious about their enterprise.

Mrs. Bumbaca, 27 years old, is the purchasing and marketing expert. Almost every day, she flips through distributors' catalogs, looking for nifty items to sell. Victorian art prints are current favorites, especially pictures of elegant ladies and jolly children. But when a visitor tries to peek at the front cover of a catalog, she quickly pulls it away. "We can't tell you the names of our distributors," she says. "That's precious information."

Once the Bumbacas decide what to carry, Mrs. Bumbaca writes short, joyful descriptions of each item, to be posted on eBay. A Victorian lamp is "beautiful." A koala bear print is "adorable." Such headlines catch people's attention, she says. Then serious shoppers can click the listing to see a digital photo, scanned in by her husband.

Each week, the Bumbacas list about 2,000 items on eBay. Auctions typically last a week, letting people around the globe compete to be high bidder. Only about 40% of the goods sell on the first try, but duds usually can be remarketed at lower prices. When a listing catches fire, the Bumbacas can watch as prices soar, minute by minute.

At times, Mr. Bumbaca winces at how much people will pay. Cardboard cutouts of John Wayne that cost him $14, for example, often attract dozens of bids and sell for more than $40. Economists call this "the winner's curse," and they say eBay is a prime example of the way that competing bidders will work themselves into an irrational frenzy for something they think is scarce. But if customers really want something, the Bumbacas say, it isn't their role to limit the price.

Each evening, after their children go to bed, the Bumbacas dash off 100 or more e-mails to winning bidders, telling them to send payment to Sheridan, while advising that goods won't be shipped until the checks arrive. "I try to be as friendly as I can in two seconds," Mrs. Bumbaca says, "but I don't have the time to do much more."

Mr. Bumbaca is the lucky one who collects the morning mail, jammed with payments from dozens of faraway places. "It's like going fishing!" he says, giggling, on a recent morning as he tugs an enormous clump of letters from his mailbox. Recently the Bumbacas hired two full-time assistants to help process the barrage of orders.

Because eBay's brand of commerce links total strangers, there is always the risk of a transaction going sour. The Bumbacas say that, to their surprise, they have been stuck with only about a dozen bad checks, while handling 40,000 shipments. But they have been briefly misled by pranksters, including a Massachusetts boy who placed a $10,000 order for 100 cow-shaped clocks, with no intention of paying.

Meanwhile, a handful of customers have complained that the Bumbacas can be annoyingly slow in shipping merchandise. "We've got our share of growing pains with this business," Mr. Bumbaca concedes. A bout of flu knocked out his family in February, and it took weeks to get caught up. The basement shipping department, run by Mr. Bumbaca, is an exercise in anarchy.

Every corner is jammed with art prints, clocks, posters and shipping cartons. A tractor is nearly invisible in the garage, buried under hundreds of mailing boxes and tubes. "It used to be even worse," Mr. Bumbaca says. "We lived in a smaller house until a year ago, and we had filled up the baby's room with boxes. There was just a tiny path that let us get to his crib."

Most small businesses lease a postage meter for $30 a month or so. Not the Bumbacas. They hold down expenses by buying stamps once a week. But as their shipping volume soars, their postage needs are overwhelming Sheridan's post office. Each Monday, Mr. Bumbaca buys about $1,300 of stamps. Twice this year, he has emptied out the local inventory of high-denomination stamps. When he asks a clerk: "Do you have an armed guard to walk me to my car?" no one is quite sure if he's joking.

For eBay's most intense PowerSellers, the online auction company can be the most real thing in their life. The Bumbacas hardly know their neighbors.

But they swap Christmas presents and family updates with favorite customers in Hawaii and Michigan. Mrs. Bumbaca pores over her feedback rating on eBay every day, cherishing 3,000 positive comments from various customers and wondering what she did wrong to deserve 53 rebukes. And when the Bumbacas' three-year-old daughter, Mallary, was learning to talk, one of her first words was "eBay."

Some day, Mr. Bumbaca says, it won't be nearly so easy to make a good living from an Internet flea market. He got an ominous warning of changing times when a fishing-lure distributor withdrew exclusive rights to sell on eBay. The Bumbacas dropped that product line rather than fight it out with unwelcome new competitors. "We weren't doing that well with it anyway," Mrs. Bumbaca says. But if their top distributors tried something similar, that could hurt business more severely.

For now, the Bumbacas are thriving—to the point that they are becoming local legends. A few weeks ago, a man in Rapid City, S.D., called Mr. Bumbaca to ask for advice about selling Indian handicrafts over the Internet. "I told him: 'This sounds like a consulting situation,' " Mr. Bumbaca recalls. " 'My rates are $40 an hour, if you want to come out here and talk.' "

"I didn't think we'd ever see him," Mr. Bumbaca says. "But the next Saturday, he drove 225 miles to see us. We ended up talking for four hours—and he paid us right away."*

*Copyright *Wall Street Journal* 04/01/1999.

When you read a story like that of the Bumbacas, doesn't it make you believe that you, too, could pull off something like that? The next story I'm going to share with you is not quite as dramatic, but it's a great success story in the making.

Our ordinary-people success story regarding auctions is about Robbin Tungett. You can find her at www.auctionriches.com. Her eBay ID is *robbin*. Up until three years ago, Robbin was the office manager for an industrial supplies company (valves, plumbing supplies, etc.), where she had worked for eight years. She started to dabble in the auction field on eBay and caught the bug. She would work nine hours during the day at her regular job and then come home and spend another nine hours figuring out the auction game. She immediately began to make money, expecting every month that the money would end, but her income from auctions soon exceeded her salary. Within 18 months she quit her job to pursue auctions full-time.

> My first real auction success was a product I created to help people set up their auction businesses. It was called Handy Home Page Helper. It took me two days to put it together—a neat little product, mostly information and links to some free software that people can use to format a nice little auction ad with colors. My husband laughed when I told him what I was planning on doing, but when I sold 194 copies at $10 apiece he stopped laughing. I've probably sold over 20,000 of them in the past three years. On my Web site, I sell it for $14.99. On my auctions, it usually goes for about $9 or $10. My cost is less than a dollar.
>
> I must admit, the auction business has gotten quite a bit more commercial in the past year, so the prices aren't as good as they used to be. But there is still plenty of profit for the person who is willing to stick it out for the long term.
>
> This type of home-based business gives me the freedom to choose whatever hours I want to work. I work best at night, so around midnight I begin work on Web site design for other clients (which is another one of my income streams) and go until about 4 or 5 in the morning. Then I go to bed. I get up around 11 A.M., check my e-mail, and fill a few orders. I spend most of the time answering e-mails. I'm a one-person business.
>
> Recently, I needed to come up with some extra cash quickly, so I created another product to auction. It's a CD-ROM called Auction Riches. It contains five different items (wholesale sources for various products, how to make money with your Web site, accepting checks online, etc.). It took me a day and a half to put it together. I burned in my own CD and immediately put it online. It's selling very well.
>
> After a while, you learn the tricks of this business. I noticed that most people didn't have any pictures on their auction site, so I added my picture and sales increased right away. People don't want to deal with a nameless, faceless entity. If they can see you're a real person, it's easier for them to trust you.

I try to keep my prices under $10. I think it's better to sell cheap because if people feel they got a good deal they might check out my Web site and buy from me again.

In fact, that's one of the major advantages of having an auction site—it gives you the opportunity to advertise your Web site. Every Web site that sells anything online should have an auction going on. It gives you great exposure.

Online auctions offer an excellent opportunity to make money online! There is no other opportunity that allows everyone the ability to play on a level playing ground, whether you're just looking to make a few extra bucks a week to pay the babysitter or hoping to earn a full-time income! Whether you are a work-at-home mom making a modest income or a big company with lots of inventory to sell . . . everyone has the same opportunity to reach literally millions of people! Think about it. With only a little computer knowledge and a good auction ad you can be selling things at a profit in your first week!

Selling on online auctions can be very profitable! Not only that, but it can actually be a lot of fun as well! There is nothing more apt to put a huge grin on your face than going to your mailbox and finding it stuffed with envelopes full of money! Literally tens of thousands of people are making a full-time income with their online auction businesses!

I've asked Robbin to share some more of her "multiple streams of auction income" wisdom with you in the next few pages. She has graciously agreed to share some of the tips that have taken her several years to learn.

What Are Online Auctions?

Online auctions have been around since the mid-1990s, although it wasn't really until the late 1990s that their popularity began to explode. EBay.com is the king of online auctions, and while they are still the most popular, there are now literally thousands of auction sites to choose from. Many, like eBay, are general, person-to-person auction sites with many categories covering just about anything you can think of. New, specialized auction sites pop up every day.

Online auctions provide a forum for anyone to sell just about anything. Most auctions charge a small fee to list your item for sale, plus a small commission once the item is sold. When you list an item for sale, *you* choose the opening price. From that point, those who are interested bid on your item. Most auctions run for a predetermined number of days. At the end of that time, whoever entered the highest bid wins the item.

When you place an item for auction, you are promising that you have the item available. When you bid on an item that is up for auction, you are promising to pay the amount of your bid plus any applicable shipping and handling charges if you submit the highest bid. It works much like a live auction except for the fact that the bids don't continue for as long as people are bidding. Once the auction is over, it's over.

When you win an auction, you remit the money to the sellers. After the sellers receive your money, they send you the item you bid for and won. It takes a lot of trust to send money to a stranger. Of course, mail order has been around for a long time, and many of us have sent money to brick-and-mortar companies trusting that we will receive what we paid for. With online auctions, though, most often you aren't dealing with companies—you are dealing with individuals who may or may not be honest.

This is where feedback comes in. *Feedback* is essentially the online auction user's reputation. It is a type of rating system that allows bidders and sellers to leave comments about each other. It is the only way for other bidders and sellers to find out who is trustworthy. Normally, there are three kinds of feedback: *positive, neutral,* and *negative.* Obviously, if you have a good experience dealing with someone you would post a positive comment. If you've had a really bad experience that couldn't be resolved you would post a negative comment. Neutral feedbacks do not express strong feelings one way or the other. Each positive comment results in a gain of 1 point, each negative one results in a loss of 1 point. Neutral comments neither add nor subtract from the rating.

While viewing people's feedback files can help ease your mind about doing business with them, people who are just starting out have no feedback or perhaps a very low feedback rating. In this case, you have to make a judgment call and trust your instincts. Everyone starts at zero. Just because a person doesn't have a high feedback rating doesn't mean that individual isn't honest.

My Experience

I discovered eBay while it was still in its infancy. I was intrigued by the whole concept of people selling the types of things online that they would normally sell at garage sales and flea markets. I was amazed not only by the fact that people were trying to sell these items, but that people were actually buying them!

This was when I first realized the true potential of online commerce. Here I was given the opportunity to sell anything I wanted, from the comfort of my home, and have it seen by literally thousands of people! Nowhere else would I get that kind of opportunity! I was excited by the concept and wanted to jump right in, only I didn't have a clue about what I was going to sell, nor did I know how to go about getting an account and placing an ad. I began my research.

First I figured out how to register and open an account. Then I had to find out what people wrote in their ads, how they described their items, what they charged for shipping, and how they collected their money. At the time, the majority of users didn't even have photos listed with their items for auction. The ads consisted of a basic text description of the item. Imagine deciding to buy an item based on a written description alone and taking the seller's word for the item's condition. Unbelievably, people were not only buying things from complete strangers, they were buying them sight unseen!

I was eager to jump in and sell something. At this point, I didn't care what it was, I just wanted to sell something and figure out how the auction really worked. After taking a look around my house, I decided to sell a software program that I no longer needed. It was a very specialized program that few people would be familiar with (much less want to buy). Although the item sold for about $350.00 retail, I knew I would never be able to sell it for that price, so it didn't matter to me how much it sold for.

I listed the software for auction with a detailed description of what it was and what it was used for. I started the auction at a very modest starting price of $10 or so. Then I sat back and waited. The auction ran for seven days, and I found myself logging on often to see if it had received any bids. My enthusiasm dwindled a bit after a few days when my auction hadn't received any bids. Finally, however, it received a few bids. Just before the auction closed, someone bid and won my software for $150.00. Now my enthusiasm returned! I had just made $150 on something that would have ended up in the trash. (It was too specialized even to sell at a garage sale.) The bidder who won the auction was ecstatic because he had wanted the software for a long time but couldn't pay full price for it. It ended up being a winning situation for both of us! That is the real beauty of the auctions. Not only does the seller make money, but the bidder often gets a bargain.

At this point, I was very excited! Even though I had made only one sale, my brain was working overtime thinking about how I could make more money. During the week I had been looking at many of the auction ads. I even bid on a couple of inexpensive items so I could see how bidding worked from the bidder's viewpoint. I noticed the auctions that included photos seemed to get more bids than those that did not. I also noticed that auction ads written using the standard format—black text on a white background—didn't receive as many bids as the few that included colored text and graphics using HTML.

My First Product

That's when the lightbulb went off in my head! I had designed a few Web sites and knew things most of these sellers didn't. I could help them increase their sales by teaching them how to make their ads more appealing. I could show them how to add photos, color, and graphics. I now had a product to sell! At least this would give me the opportunity to really test the auction site and see how it all worked. It would give me the opportunity to raise my feedback rating while I came up with yet another idea.

I got busy right away. I wrote instructions that anyone could understand, even those with very little computer knowledge. I created easy-to-use ad templates so they wouldn't have to learn HTML; they would only have to insert their descriptions and information into the template. I found a few freeware programs that I knew would help them edit and upload their photos and customize the templates. I even included a freeware program that would allow them to easily create a Web page.

It didn't take me long to write the instructions and find the programs. What took the most time was learning how to package them all together for distribution as easily installable files that anyone could use without special training. Soon my package was ready! During this process, my husband noticed my frenetic activity and asked me what I was doing. When I explained, he laughed and told me I was wasting my time—no one would buy it. However, I wasn't going to let him spoil my enthusiasm!

I named my product Handy Homepage Helpers, and I spent quite a bit of time putting my auction ad together. Since I was trying to sell a product that was supposed to help people create attractive ads that would sell their products better, my ad had to look great and it had to sell *them*. Next I had to come up with a price. I didn't know what to charge, so I listed my product in a few categories with a low price to see what people would bid. I was also concerned about what people would think of it. Would they think it was as great as I thought it was? Would they feel that their money was well spent?

The bids started coming in pretty quickly. Within a couple of weeks I had sold a modest number and built up my feedback a little. I received great responses from the people who purchased from me. I now knew that people not only wanted my product, but they also thought very highly of it.

Now was the time to make the big move. I decided to put up a Dutch auction, where you list multiple identical items in the same listing. Thus you can have one ad and many winning bidders. EBay offered a "super-featured" auction ad for a fee of $49.95 that would be listed on the front page of the auction site for all to see. It was a lot of money to spend without knowing for sure how well the auction would do, but I decided to give it a shot anyway and listed a quantity of 100 for sale.

I was blown away by the response! Immediately, the bids started coming in! People were bidding so fast I couldn't believe it! Before I knew it, 100 people had bid, and more bids were coming in. By the time the auction ended seven days later, 184 people had bid on my auction. Although there could be only 100 winners (the 100 who bid the highest), the ones who didn't win wrote to ask if they could get copies, too. Through that one auction ad, I sold 184 copies at $10.00 apiece. After my auction fees and the price of diskettes, envelopes, and postage I netted over $1,500.00!

Remember how my husband laughed at me? He laughed again, this time with amazement, as I opened my post office box and found it stuffed with envelopes full of checks, money orders, and cash!

I was hooked, and I immediately relisted the auction. Although my sales for one auction never reached that amount again, they still continued to do very well. I began listing two, three, and four super-featured auctions a week. Each time I listed an auction, I thought it would be the last one that did well, that the demand for my product would die, and that I would have to find something else to sell.

As each month passed, my product continued to sell well. New people were logging on daily and discovering my offering. Those who had purchased from me were telling their friends, and they bought as well. Of course, other people started noticing the success I was having and came out with similar products of their own, hoping to cash in. As competition increased, my sales went down, but they never died.

At the time I started selling on the auctions, I was working as a full-time office manager. I would go to the post office during lunch, pick up my mail, and bring it back to the office. I often sat in the lunchroom opening envelopes, sorting orders, and counting my money. Needless to say, this got everyone's attention. At first they just stared in disbelief at the number of checks I neatly piled on the lunch table. Then they started asking me what I was doing to make all that money. When I tried to explain, no one knew what I was talking about because online auctions weren't well known at the time.

Almost immediately, I was making more money with my auction sales than I was earning at my full-time job. Even so, I didn't expect the success to continue, so I held onto my job for another year and a half. During that time I continued to improve and sell my original product. I also began to create other products. My most popular is a spin-off of my original idea. It's called Virtual Auction Ad Pro, a software program that creates nicely formatted auction ads with photos.

Finally, I realized that between my full-time job and my at-home job, I was putting in way too many hours and wasn't able to do justice to either job. It was time to make a decision. I'll be honest—it wasn't an easy step to take. I was scared, unsure if I was making the right move, and worried that my husband might not want me to give up my job. He stood behind me and let me know that he would support whatever decision I made, which helped greatly. After eight years with my company, I resigned and ventured into my own full-time business.

Today I am selling my own products on the online auctions and operating several successful Web sites as well. I can honestly say that online auctions have changed my life. I saw the opportunity and jumped on it. It has been a wild ride so far! You, too, may find that the opportunity you are looking for is right in front of your eyes.

Tips from a Powerseller

In 1999, eBay created a Powerseller program to recognize the top sellers on their auction site. In order to qualify as a Powerseller, a seller must maintain a monthly sales volume of $2,000 or greater, must have at least 100 positive feedbacks, and must guarantee satisfaction. There are also other qualifications—and perks—to being a Powerseller.

As soon as eBay announced its new program, I was invited to join. With the experience I have gained through my own auctions, I've learned quite a bit over the past few years. I will share with you some of the secrets that have helped my auction sales.

Ready to Get Started?! What Will You Sell?

The first decision you have to make is what to sell. I suggest that you get a feel for how the auctions work by selling something you have in your house that you no longer need. This will give you the opportunity to learn how the system works. It will also allow you to sharpen your ad-design and ad-writing skills. Before listing an item, do a search on the auction and find out how much other people are charging for similar items. This will help you decide on a reasonable opening price.

You can probably keep yourself fairly busy for a while just getting rid of things you no longer need. Take a look around your house, your attic, and your garage for the following items:

- Books
- Knickknacks
- Toys
- Clothing
- Purses
- Shoes
- Jewelry
- Kitchen items
- Albums, cassettes, 8-tracks, CDs
- Videos
- Video games
- Gifts you received but didn't like (these make great auction items!)

You may find you can easily get rid of all that junk that's been cluttering your house!

Look for items at garage sales and flea markets. The key is to buy low and sell high, so pick up any item you feel pretty certain you could sell for more than you pay. After you've sold a few items, you will find yourself doing what I do, and I'm sure many others do as well. Almost everywhere I go, I see things and comment, "I could sell that on eBay." Now my husband says it good-naturedly before I do!

Although he has not sold anything online himself, my husband, too, has been bitten by the bug. He collects phonographs, and he once received a pencil sharpener that looked like a miniature Victrola as a gift. When he saw a similar pencil sharpener for sale on eBay, he brought it to my attention. Knowing that the pencil sharpener had come from the Dollar Store, we decided to purchase more to resell. Choosing from a wide variety of pencil sharpeners in stock, we bought an assortment of about 25.

I listed the phonographs one at a time, starting at $3.99 plus shipping and handling of $1.50. The shipping and handling fee covered nearly our entire cost, so the bid price would be pure profit. Much to our amazement, many people bid on the sharpeners, driving the price as high as $22.00 on a few of them! At this point I was nervous. What if they received their purchase and weren't happy? What if they found out I paid only a dollar for them? What if everyone wanted to return them? We used my husband's account to test these items so that at least my feedback wasn't in jeopardy. I shipped the sharpeners and waited for complaints. Instead of complaints, I received positive feedback. I also received e-mails from the bidders thanking me and saying what a great addition they made to their collection! The most popular sellers seemed to be sharpeners shaped like musical instruments, so we purchased more of these. I targeted my ads not only to pencil sharpener collectors, but also to people who played musical instruments.

The average selling price ended up being between $12 and $15 for a product that cost $1! I can only imagine what the Dollar Store paid for them, since they, too, were making a profit. I sold these until my supply ran out. (I grew tired of selling them, so I didn't bother to reorder.) I have somewhat immortalized this product, though. Anyone who purchases my software, Virtual Auction Ad Pro, and looks at the sample ad will see one of the pencil sharpeners I sold during this time.

The auction market is quite a bit more competitive these days, but it is still a great opportunity for those interested in putting forth the effort. Find a product. Look around and see what your interests are. Remember, it's important to enjoy what you're doing, so sell something that interests you. Of course, if you're anything like me, you are interested in anything that makes a profit!

Do some research in your area. Do you have any wholesalers? Are there any closeout stores or auction houses? Do you have any friends in business who might be able to put you in contact with their suppliers? Have you invented something? Do you know of someone who has?

My dear friend Marilyn, whom I met through eBay, happened to have some friends who were importers. Since they imported truckloads of Oriental items, she was able to get great deals through them. She quickly grew her online auction business selling top-quality Oriental imports at excellent prices. Collectors were able to add to their collections at reasonable prices while she made substantial profits. A former real estate agent, she now devotes all of her time to her online business.

Another online friend I met through the auctions lives in the country but was fortunate enough to find an auction house nearby that dealt in closeout merchandise. She finds great products of all types at excellent prices and sells them online. Her auction sales enabled her to quit her full-time job.

Yet another online friend sells mainly used books. She buys them at garage sales and closeout sales at bookstores and turns a tidy profit. She also made arrangements with an antique store to list its items on the auctions for a percentage of the profits. Many people are finding this a great way to make money since they don't have to buy or ship products. They list the auctions and facilitate the sale between the bidder and the store. With the price of antiques, my friend earns a nice profit from the sale of a single item. Recently she made $2,000 on one item!

You could also consider doing what I have done. Take the knowledge you have on any given subject and profit by sharing that information with others. How-to products are very hot sellers, especially when it comes to helping others make money, lose weight, or otherwise enrich their lives. You can create booklets to mail or electronic books to download. The actual cost of producing this type of product is low compared to the profits it can generate! Your biggest investment is your time. If you offer the product for download, you won't even have duplicating and mailing costs!

Create an Irresistible Auction Ad

Now that you've found something to sell, you must decide what to write as your description. Your description is very important for a couple of reasons. First, you need to accurately and honestly describe the item you are selling. You need think about it as an advertisement because, after all, you want it to sell. If you type in a boring description of your item, it won't sell as well as if you make the description exciting and inviting. Think about what sells you when you see something online. Try using colors and graphics in your ads to make them look more attractive. You want the bidder to see your ad and think, "I've got to have that!"

Many auction software titles are available to help you create attractive auction ads without having any HTML knowledge. My software, Virtual Auction Ad Pro (http://www.auctionriches.com/vadpro.htm), was created to help both beginning and advanced sellers easily create attractive, colorful ads with photos. It is a simple, inexpensive utility that is easy to use and works on most auction sites. There are other excellent software titles available as well, ranging in price from free to over $100.00.

Use Keywords in Your Description

It's very important that you use keywords in your description. Many people use the search function to find products they are looking for. Think about what words people might type in if they were looking for what you are selling. Be creative. Try to use all relevant words somewhere in your description. You want your auction to be found!

Using keywords in your title is most important. The title shows up when people are browsing the categories or doing searches. The title is really the most important aspect of your ad because that is going to entice people to look at your auction ad. If your title doesn't interest them, they won't click. If they don't click, you most certainly won't get their bid. Other tricks to getting your title noticed: Use all capital letters and symbols like ***. Also, using the underscore symbol_between_each_word causes your title to be longer, which will make it stand out from the other titles.

Shipping Methods

Make sure your auction ad states what your shipping policy is, how much the shipping charges will be, and whether there are additional handling charges. For instance, if an item is being shipped Priority Mail and you know it will cost $3.20 to ship but you also want to cover costs of the special packaging materials, you might charge $4.50. Just make sure you clarify this for your purchaser (e.g., "Shipping and handling via Priority Mail will be $4.50 in addition to the bid amount"). That way your bidder knows exactly what the item will cost, including shipping, and won't be surprised by additional charges when the package arrives. State what method of shipping you will use. It helps when a bidder knows whether it's coming UPS, USPS, or by another delivery method. Bidders may prefer to use one address for USPS and another for UPS.

You may also want to state that the item will ship within X number of days after payment is received. Some people ship daily, some twice a week, and some only once a week. Bidders have a tendency to have unrealistic expectations and assume that the moment you receive their payment, their package will be on its way. If bidders know up front that you ship only once a week, they will be more understanding.

Methods of Accepting Payment

The methods of payment you accept will help a bidder determine whether to bid on your item. It's best to offer as many payment methods as possible. I offer payment by Visa, MasterCard, PayPal, and eBay's Billpoint, as well as checks, money orders, and cash by mail. The majority of people will pay by credit card, but many still don't trust using credit cards online (or maybe they don't have a credit card). Therefore, accepting payments by mail is also a good option.

Building Your Feedback

When first starting out, build your feedback by bidding on a few inexpensive auctions. Look for something you could use or perhaps some little something you could give as a gift. Making a few small purchases allows you to learn how the bidding process works, and it will allow you to build your feedback rating. Remember, your feedback will eventually be your reputation and the measure by which people make judgments about whether to do business with you. Always honor the bids you make and pay promptly. Always leave deserved feedback. If you take part in transactions and don't receive feedback, e-mail the other parties, let them know you are trying to build your feedback rating, and ask them nicely if they would leave feedback for you. It's also a good idea to include a note with your shipments reminding your customers to offer online feedback if they are happy with the transaction. Make sure to include your auction user ID so they won't have to go searching for it. Make it easy so they will be more apt to leave positive feedback for you.

The Best Days and Times to Post

You may hear differing opinions on this subject but I will give you what I believe to be the best days and times to post.

The best day to post a 10-day ad is Thursday. You will get exposure over two weekends and your auction will end on a Sunday. Sunday is a great day for auctions to end because many people are online and bidding on Sundays. A lot of people look for items on an auction's ending day because they want to get an item quicker and are hoping to find deals on items that haven't been bid up too high. Thursday is also the best day to post a three-day ad because—again, because it ends on Sunday. A seven-day ad will do best if posted on a Sunday and ending on a Sunday.

The best time of the day to post your ad is in the evening. I live on the East Coast, so I try to post my ads late in the evening for the best results. If you post late at night, you will have exposure in all time zones in the United States. Your auction will end at the same time it started. So if you want it to be seen maximally by both the East and West Coasts, post so that your auction ends around 8 or 9 P.M. on the West Coast. That way, it will close at 11 P.M. or midnight on the East Coast.

Set Up an "About Me" Page

EBay offers an About Me page that you can use for additional advertising. You can set it up like a mini–business page showing the current items you have for auction along with some of your feedback comments if you choose. You can put in a little information about yourself—maybe a photo or some of your hobbies. I have learned through experimentation that sales go up when the bidders know something about you. If they can put a face behind the anonymous identity, they feel more comfortable bidding. There are rules for using an About Me page, so be sure to read them before you create it.

If you'd like to see my About Me page, go to www.ebay.com. At the top of the main page, click on the Search button. At the top of the next page, click on the Find Members button and enter my seller ID, which is the word *robbin*. Click on the Search button and you will find my About Me page. You, too, can create a page like this to tell your auction customers about you.

While you're online, check out my Feedback Profile. Return to the previous page, enter my seller ID (robbin) in the Feedback Profile box, and click the Search button. This will show you a summary of the feedback people have given me about my service on eBay. I'm proud to say that, as of this writing, I have 3,986 positives, 45 neutrals, and only 7 negatives!

If you're new to the auction world and would like to see how it works, go to www.ebay. At the top of the main page, click on the Search button. On the next page, find the Smart Search bar and click on the By Seller button. Enter my seller ID (robbin). This will take you to a current list of my auction items. By clicking on the number of any item available for auction, you can see a photo of it with a link to my Web site at the bottom of the page. This will give you a good example of how you should set up your own auction business.

Sell More with a Web Page

If you want to make even more money through online auctions, consider creating a Web page. It doesn't have to be anything fancy, and you don't have to be a Web designer. Simple sites can be very effective if planned properly!

If you are only a casual auctioneer (selling items you're trying to get rid of or items you've found at garage sales and flea markets), you can still make money with your own Web page. Affiliate programs are an excellent way to start! Create a link from your auctions to your Web page—when people visit your Web page, they just might click on one of your affiliate links. If they do, that's money in your pocket! Obviously, there are many excellent affiliate programs that you could join. Try to join those that would be of interest to your target audience.

Don't underestimate the revenue potential of affiliate programs. I personally have deposited over $1,000.00 in affiliate checks in a single month! Not all months are that good, but wouldn't $50, $100, or $300 a month be a nice income for simply linking to other people's sites? I think so!

If you run a business and sell on the auctions, you most definitely should have a Web page. If you have duplicate items that you sell on the auctions, by listing your item on the auction and also on your Web page, some people may forgo the auction process and buy directly from your site, even at a higher price! But be careful. On eBay, you are allowed to link to your Web page, but you can't have the same item listed there at the same price or lower. It must be listed at a *higher* price, even if just a few pennies higher.

If you sell your own software and information like I do, a Web page is a definite must. People pay full price for items on my Web site, even when the same item is listed for 30 to 40 percent less on the auction! Why? Some people just don't want to wait for the auction to end; some are browsers but have never registered with the auction site and don't want to go through the bother; some just don't understand the whole auction process. Regardless of the reason, my sales go up when I list my items in both places. You can learn from my experience.

Double Your Sales with Back-End Products

Back-end products are items you offer to your customers after you have already made a sale. If you sell something and you have other items for sale, let your customers know! A good time to let them know about your other products is when you send them instructions about how to pay— offer a discount if they purchase another item at the same time. Include a flyer about your other products when you ship items. If customers are happy with your service, they will be more likely to purchase from you again.

Excellent Customer Service Is Top Priority!

I am proud of my feedback record on eBay. One glance at my 3,500+ positive comments shows that one of my main priorities is customer service. Without a doubt, customers are the most important aspect of any business. Treat your customers honestly and give them the best service you can. Above all else, how you handle customer service is going to make or break you. Remember that an angry customer will tell *everyone* they know about how poorly your business is run. A happy customer *might* tell one or two people.

Even if you process your orders quickly and ship on time, things *will* go wrong on occasion. A shipment will get lost. An order will get mixed up or misplaced. Your customer may just decide to contact you with questions. It doesn't necessarily have to be due to a problem.

The best advice is to treat your customers as you expect to be treated when you are a customer. If there is a problem, be honest. Don't tell someone an order has been shipped when you know it hasn't.

Online Auction Sites

The three best-known online auctions sites are as follows:

EBay	http://www.eBay.com
Amazon	http://www.Amazon.com
Yahoo!	http://www.Yahoo.com

For an extensive listing of the many other online auction sites, visit

http://www.internetauctionlist.com

Auction Software and Resources

For a list of software available to help you with your online auctions, as well as a listing of auction management sites, auction counters, photo hosting, and more, visit either one of my Web sites:

http://www.AuctionRiches.com

http://www.VirtualNotions.com

This is your auction mentor, Robbin K. Tungett, wishing you well as you begin to build your own multiple streams of auction income.

CHAPTER 16

Automatic Pilot:
Making Money 24/7/365

I'M STANDING HERE
ON THE EDGE OF
SOMETHING CALLED
"THE REST
OF MY LIFE"~

~ SHALL I
PROCEED?

© 1988 by Ashleigh Brilliant (www.ashleighbrilliant.com)

Well, that is a *lot* of information to digest. If you're not careful, it will overwhelm you into inaction. Here is what I recommend:

1. Go back and reread Chapter 9.

2. Go online and launch one of the free do-it-yourself Web sites at either vstore.com or bigstem.com. What's the cost? Zip. Zero. Zilch.

3. After you've followed instructions, you should be staring at a glowing computer screen at a Web site that you have just designed by yourself, from scratch. It should be complete with an opening greeting, a nice piece of visual art, your address, and even a map to your

office, a survey questionnaire, a tool for collecting names, and a catalog ready to be filled with wonderful things to offer to the world.

4. Then go back to page 75 in Chapter 6 and stare at the Big Picture. This is what your online business will look like when it is fully functioning. You'll have leads flowing in from search engines, online and offline ads, online and offline PR, affiliate programs, and more.

5. Do whatever it takes to start filling up your Maybe Lake. It may take months or years, but eventually this one activity done well will generate income for the rest of your life—24/7/365.

If you'd like to see how a Web site has been designed and constructed to take advantage of all the ideas that you've read in this book, come visit me at www.robertallen.com.

I wish you well on your journey. Godspeed.

Abraham, Jay, 3, 31, 59, 70–71
Advertising:
    banner, 20, 65–67, 87–88, 110, 113, 197, 228–230
    classified, 87, 91, 110, 143, 144, 201, 221, 231
    in e-zines, 88, 109, 110, 141–146, 177, 178, 202–204, 220, 231
    links as, 88, 124
    offline, 91–94
    on online auctions, 253, 256, 259–261, 264–265
    as profit center, 109–110, 113–114
    rates for, 229, 232
    and stickiness, 120
    on Web sites, 86–89, 94, 110, 228–231, 236, 237
    word-of-mouth, 93, 103–104
AffiliateMatch.com, 191
Affiliate programs, 93, 102–103
    benefits of, 172–173, 192
    for bookstore, 107
    commissions in, 174, 193–194
    conversion rate in, 180–184, 193
    domain names in, 195–196
    finding, 173–174, 179, 188, 190–195, 224
    lead generation from, 174–179

    multiple, 173, 194, 223
    through newsletters, 193, 220
    for online auctions, 267–268
    online stores in, 196
    as profit center, 110, 112, 113, 115–116
    with search engines, 116, 125
    tracking for, 171, 193, 224
    Web site in, 172, 173, 180–190
AffiliatesDirectory.com, 191
AffiliateWorld.com, 191
Alexa Web site, 164
Allen, Robert:
    private coaching by, 21, 24, 61, 64
    public speaking by, 22–23
AltaVista, 116, 188, 190
Amazon.com:
    as affiliate program, 102, 115
    auction on, 252, 269
    origins of, 151–152
    viral marketing of, 131
Anatomy of a Buzz (Rosen), 131
Armstrong, Arthur, 128
Associate-it.com, 171, 191
AssociatePrograms.com, 191
Auction Riches CD-ROM, 256
Auctions, online. See Online auctions
Audiocassettes, 23, 35

Aureate Group Mail, 225
Autoresponder, 175–178, 206, 218, 240, 243

Banner ads:
  in affiliate programs, 197
  exchange sites for, 88
  as marketing tool, 65–67, 113
  rates for, 20, 228–230
  response to, 87, 182
  for revenue generation, 110
Barnes & Noble, 115
Barnett, Mike, 10
Baron, Dov, 246
bCentral, 115
Bezos, Jeff, 69, 151–152
Big Dog Marketing Letter, 143, 219
Bigstep.com, 139–140
BizWeb eGazette (e-zine), 145
Bonus offers:
  to first-time customers, 101, 102, 122–123
  with newsletter subscription, 211, 221
  with purchase, 40–42
  for reading e-mail, 126
Bookstore, as profit center, 107–109, 114, 115
Bulletin boards, as marketing tool, 76, 128–129
Bumbaca, Wayne and Shanna, 251–255
Burst Media, 114, 230
Business cards, as marketing tool, 74

Casey, Shawn, 81, 86, 219
CashFlow Kings award, 117
CashPile.com, 191
Cathi Graham's Fresh Start Metabolism Program, 249
CGI scripts, 113, 114, 224
Chat rooms, as marketing tool, 76
The Cheapskate's Guide to Internet Marketing (Gatchel), 172
Cialdini, Robert, 46, 48
Classified advertising:
  in e-zines, 143, 144, 231
  free online, 87, 201
  as subscriber incentive, 221
  testing, 91
  Web site sales of, 110
ClickQuick.com, 191
ClickRewards program, 127–128

clickXchange, 115
CNN, 87, 120
Cold calling, 76
Columbia House, unique selling proposition of, 40
Commission Junction, 115, 224
Computer hardware, as profit center, 110
Computer software:
  for mailing lists, 224, 243
  for marketing letters, 93
  for online auctions, 259–261, 265, 269
  as profit center, 110
  for tracking Web site hits, 230
  vendors of, in joint ventures, 162
  for Web site building, 190, 196
Content:
  and advertising rates, 229
  of newsletters, 220, 225–226
  and stickiness, 120–121
  on Web sites, 123–125, 182–188, 207
Contests, as profit centers, 115, 117
Conversion rate (CR), in affiliate programs, 180–184, 193
Cooper, Stephan, 22, 61
Creating Wealth (Allen), 6
Credibility:
  and affiliate programs, 194
  and banner ads, 182
  building, 49
  via e-zine articles, 90
  in press releases, 97
  via Web site content, 124
Credit card services:
  in online auctions, 266
  as profit center, 110, 240, 247
  from Vstore.com, 136, 138
Customers:
  attracting, 10, 48, 74, 93–94, 100
  complaints by, 130
  database of, 243 (*see also* Mailing lists)
  first-time, rewarding, 101, 102, 122–123
  lifetime value of, 83, 158, 161
  loyalty of, 127, 243
  of online auctions, 255, 266, 268–269
  relationships with, 32, 67–69, 121, 155
  in virtual communities, 128–130

Dating B2B, 111–112
Davis, Jacob, 36–37
Del Dotto, Dave, 35
DEMC newsletter, 145

Differentiate or Die (Trout), 34, 35
Digital divide, 13
Direct mail:
   versus affiliate program, 179
   evaluating, 93
   versus Internet marketing, 7, 59, 219
Directory of E-zines, 142, 143, 203, 204
Domain name, registering, 195–196
DoubleClick, 114
Draper Fisher Jurvetson, 130
DrNunley's Marketing Tips (e-zine), 145,
   228, 231–235
Dutch auction, 260

eAds.com, 229
eBay:
   About Me page, 267
   bidding on, 254
   feedback on, 255, 258
   function of, 253, 257
   and personal Web sites, 268
   popularity of, 131, 252
   Powerseller program, 254, 262
   stickiness on, 120
   Web address for, 269
E-books, as profit generator, 196, 206
E-commerce, service providers for,
   137–138
Egroups online service, 225
E-mail:
   building mailing list for, 15–16, 101,
      121–123, 145–146
   differentiating, 125
   marketing via, 6–8, 16–29, 47, 50–54,
      59–67, 175–179
   opt-in lists for, 8, 147, 220
   pay for reading, 147–150
   for press releases, 96
   rental lists for, 88–89, 109, 141,
      146–147
   signature file for, 75
   unsolicited (*see* Spam)
Emotional marketing, 204
Empower Yourself (audiocassettes), 23
eMyth (Gerber), 245
Endorsed offers, 156–163, 166–169
Engage Media Advertising Network, 113
Enlow, Mike, 153–154
Epinions.com, as marketing tool, 76
Ethical bribe, 101, 122–123
Evoy, Ken, 79, 180

Excite (search engine), 76, 79
E-zines. *See also* Newsletters
   advertising in, 88, 110, 141–146, 177,
      178, 202–204, 221, 231
   archival content of, 107
   directories of, 142, 143, 203, 204,
      222–223, 225–226
   mailing list for, 211–225
   as profit centers, 6, 235
   submitting articles to, 90, 225–226, 228

Falter, Daren, 10, 22, 61, 66
Fields, Debbie, 48
Filter-feeder marketing, 175
5 Pillar Program, 180, 182
Fortunes in Foreclosures (audiocassettes),
   23, 63
Frequently Asked Questions (FAQs), 107,
   108

Galetti, Carl, 64, 66
Gardyne, Allan, 191
Gatchel, Bob, 10, 73, 171, 172
Gatchel, Joyce, 172
Getresponse.com, 218
Gladwell, Malcolm, 131, 132
Godin, Seth, 46, 131, 133
Gold Wire Sculpting Business (home
   course), 211
GoTo.com:
   affiliate program with, 116, 125
   bidding for keywords at, 142, 188
   as search engine, 80–86
Graham, Cathi, 249
Greeting cards, online, 116, 117
Guarantees, 42–43
Guthy/Renker Corporation, 9, 17, 19, 49

Haines, Scott, 10, 65
Halbert, Gary, 14, 162
Handy Homepage Helpers, 256, 260
Hotmail, 130–131, 236
*How to Make a Whole Lot More Than
   $1,000,000 Writing, Commissioning,
   Publishing and Selling "How-To"
   Information* (Lant), 107–108

Influence: The Psychology of Persuasion
   (Cialdini), 46
Infomercials, 9, 249
InfoPop, 128

Infopreneuring, 207
Infopreneuring: How You Can Become an Information Multimillionaire (seminar), 24, 63–64
Infopreneuring: How You Can Become an Information Multimillionaire (special report), 219
Infoproducts, 197, 200
Inner Circle, 64–67
Internet:
  advantages of, 121–122
  advertising on, 86–89, 94
  profit center opportunities on, 110–111, 113–117, 239–240, 245–249
  publicity on, 90, 94
  terminology of, 13–14
InternetCheapskate.com, 171, 179
The Internet Insider (e-zine), 145
Internet marketing:
  benefits of, 58, 238
  boot camp for, 64, 66
  consulting on, 110, 240–241, 246–249
  via e-mail, 6–8, 16–29, 47, 50–54, 59–67, 75, 88–89, 146–150
  gurus of, 66, 199, 211, 227, 235–236, 241
  ineffective, 14
  joint ventures in, 163–169
  mailing list for, 15–16, 174, 211–221
  for offline businesses, 241–244
  and order generation, 9–10, 210
  passive versus active, 140
  preparation for, 10–11
  principles of, 3, 44
  search engines in, 76–86, 140–142
  techniques for, 218–219
  virtual communities as, 128–130
Internet service provider (ISP), 239

Joint ventures, 155–162
  affiliate programs as, 172, 179
  deal maker in, 162–163
  on Internet, 163–169, 247, 249
Jurvetson, Steve, 132

Kanoodle.com, 81, 86
Kerr, Ken, 10, 22, 62
Keywords:
  in auction ads, 265
  bidding for, 82–83, 85, 142, 189
  selecting, 83–86, 188–190

Kiges, Steven H., 244–249
Klein, Saul, 10

Lant, Jeffrey, 107–109
Leads:
  from affiliate programs, 174–179
  contacts with, 105–106
  controlling, 86, 94
  from e-zines, 211–212
  generating, 32, 48, 126, 223–224, 247
Learning Style Inventory, 206
Learning vs. Testing (Wyman), 207
LeDoux, David, 6, 9
Letmeknow.com, 124
Levi Strauss, 37, 110
Levitt, Theodore, 45, 68
Lifestyles Publishing, 142, 203
Links:
  as advertising, 88, 124
  in affiliate programs, 172, 173, 190, 193, 194, 267–268
  to Amazon.com, 102
  in-context, 182, 184
  for newsletter subscriptions, 221
  as profit center, 110, 117, 237
LinkShare, 116
ListBot online service, 218, 225
Listserves, 240
LoveQuote of the Day (e-zine), 145

Magazines, 89, 96. *See also* E-zines
Mailing lists:
  from affiliate programs, 174–179
  building, 15–16, 211–225
  cold, 155
  exchanging, 109
  managing, 224–225
  for offline businesses, 243
  renting, 88–89, 141, 146–150
  Yellow Pages as source for, 93
Mailloop software, 243
Market:
  cultivating, 45–47, 68
  expanding, through affiliate programs, 172
  finding, 14–15, 29, 92–93
  targeting, 19, 94, 179, 210, 237, 263
Marketing. *See also* Internet marketing
  in affiliate programs, 173, 193
  definition of, 16, 126, 248
  emotional, 204

filter-feeder, 175
importance of, 73
inbound versus outbound, 76
key questions in, 14–15
leverage in, 74, 93, 153, 155
mass, 67–68
network, 103–106
principles of, 3, 28, 33–34, 46, 136
process of, 47–54, 70–71, 93
relationship, 104, 129
special reports as, 109
viral, 93, 130–134
word-of-mouse, 93, 94, 129, 130
Marksonline, for trademark check, 195
Marriott hotels, unique selling proposition
of, 42
Mass marketing, 67–68
MeMail.com, 145
Mentors:
as marketing advantage, 38–40
role of, 10–11
Millionaire Mentoring, 21, 61, 62, 65–67
Millionaire Retreat, 21, 61–67
Million Dollar Drawing, 223–224
MintMail.com, 147–150
Money Classifieds, 65
Mrs. Fields cookies, marketing of, 48
Multiple Streams of Income (Allen), 6, 9,
17, 23, 42, 51, 54, 57, 219
Multiple Streams of Income
(audiocassettes), 23

Nelson, Brian, 147, 149
Netcentives, 127
Netflip.com, 142
Net Gain (Armstrong), 128
Netpreneurs, services for, 110–111, 247
Network marketing, 103–106
Newsgroups, as marketing tool, 76
Newsletters. *See also* E-zines
advertising in, 109, 220
in affiliate programs, 193, 220
content of, 220, 225–226, 228
as customer education, 107, 108
via Internet, 6, 8, 16
launching, 220–226
lead generation from, 223–224
opt-in, 206
Newspapers, 89, 96
NOBOSS e-Marketing (e-zine), 145
Nothing Down (Allen), 6, 35, 39

Nothing Down (seminars), 48
Nunley, Kevin, 145, 227, 228, 231

Offline businesses, online marketing for,
241–244
Online agencies, for press releases, 96
Online auctions:
bidding in, 254, 257–258
case histories, 251–257
feedback from, 255, 258, 266–268
merchandise sold on, 262–264
payment in, 266
as profit center, 111, 252, 257, 259
shipping policies for, 254, 265
timing in, 266
Web site for, 267–268
writing ads for, 256, 259–261,
264–265
Online coupons, 245–246
Online stores, 115, 117, 196
OnResponse, 116
Orders:
generating, on Internet, 9–10, 210
handling, in affiliate programs, 172,
173
increasing average size of, 32
through newsletters, 211

Painter, Thomas, 10, 22, 25, 61, 92
Paul, Jeff, 54, 126
Permission Marketing (Godin), 46, 131
Personal information, obtaining, 127
Persuasion, principles of, 46–50
Postmaster Direct, 88–89
Preselling, 180, 182–184
Press releases, 89, 90, 94–97
Product differentiation, 34–40
Products, services, and information (PSI),
68, 240
Profit center(s):
advertising as, 109–110, 113–114
affiliate programs as, 102–103, 110,
180
auctions as, 111, 252, 257, 259
bookstore as, 107–109, 114, 115
contests as, 115, 117
greeting cards as, 116, 117
main product as, 101–102
network marketing as, 103–106
services as, 110–111, 113–117
Public relations (PR), 89–90, 94, 109

Radio, 89
Real Streams of Cash (infomercial), 9, 19, 53
Recommend-it.com, 124
Red Herring magazine, 124
Reeves, Rosser, 34
Refer-It.com, 191
Referrals. *See also* Affiliate programs; Network marketing
    in joint ventures, 156, 191
    to MintMail, 147
    to Web sites, 125
Relationship marketing, 104, 129
Reporting.net, 116
Reuther, Preston, 207–219
Revenews.com, 191
The Road to Wealth (Allen), 23, 51
RocketLinks.com, 81, 86
Rudl, Corey, 211, 235, 241, 244
Ruth's Learning Channel, 204

SaveLikeCrazy.com, 245–246
Scalability, 86
School Smart Kids newsletter, 206
Search Engine Report, 141
Search engines. *See also specific search engines*
    affiliate programs with, 116, 125
    finding, 76–77
    pay-per-click, 80–86
    position on, 78–81, 141, 142, 180–181, 188, 189
Search Engine Watch, 141
Searchhound.com, 142
Seminars, 21, 24, 35, 249
7Search.com, 116, 142, 188, 189
Sheets, Carlton, 35
Shopping cart services, 240
Site Build It! software, 190, 196
SiteSell.com, 180
Small businesses:
    advertising by, 92, 230
    failure of, 91
Solo blast ad, 143
Spam, 8, 16, 109, 147, 148, 220
SPARKList, 225
Special reports:
    as bonus offers, 42, 102, 122, 221
    as profit center, 107–109
SpeedyClick, 117
Sponsorship ad, 143, 144

Standard Rate & Data Service (SRDS), 92
Stickiness, 119–123, 130, 134
Strauss, Levi, 36–37
Streams of Cash E-Letter, 16, 20, 51–53, 60, 65
Sullivan, Danny, 141
Sweepstakes site, in affiliate program, 223–224

Television, 89, 232
TheAdStop.com, 229
Thomas, Ted, 22, 62
The Tipping Point (Gladwell), 131
Topica online service, 225
Townsend, Ruth, 142, 200–204
Trade journals, 96
Trademarks, verifying, 195–196
Training:
    in affiliate programs, 173
    as profit center, 110, 207
Trivia games, 115
Trout, Jack, 34
Trust:
    gaining, through press releases, 95
    importance of, 42, 69
    leverage from, 155–156
    and obtaining personal information, 127
    in online auctions, 256, 258
Tungett, Robbin, 256–257, 267, 269
2-Tier Affiliate Program Directory, 191

Ultimate Bulletin Board, 129
Unique selling proposition (USP), 34–44
Unleasing the IdeaVirus (Godin), 131
Unsolicited commercial e-mail (UCE), 220. *See also* Spam
Uproar.com, 115
USPTO, for trademark check, 195

Vacation giveaways, 221–222
Value Click, 230
Varga, Ken, 10
Viral marketing, 93, 130–134
Virtual Auction Ad Pro, 261, 263, 265
Virtual communities, 128–130
Vstore.com, 136–138

Wealth Training events, 35–36, 62
The Wealth Training Experience (audiocassettes), 23, 63
Web-hosting services, 110, 224, 239–240

Web Marketing Today (e-zine), 145
Web site(s):
  advertising on, 86–89, 94, 110,
    228–231, 236, 237
  in affiliate programs, 172, 173,
    180–190
  attracting customers to, 74, 93–94, 100,
    130–134, 136, 149, 150, 223, 236
  and company name, 96
  content on, 120, 122–124, 182–188,
    207, 231
  domain name for, 195–196
  FAQs on, 107, 108
  for free stuff, 76, 236
  as income portal, 99, 101, 111–117,
    205–207, 236–238
  interactivity of, 128
  links between (see Links)
  members-only, 221
  and online auctions, 257, 267–268
  recommending, 125
  search engines for, 76–86, 94
  statistics service for, 230, 240
  stickiness of, 119–123, 127, 130, 134
Web site design:
  do-it-yourself, 210
  as marketing tool, 249
  as profit center, 110, 240, 256

  service providers for, 136–140
  software for, 190, 196
WebSponsors, 116
WebTrendsLive.com, 230
Weight Loss and Health Newsletter
    (e-zine), 145
What's Food Got to Do With It? (Wyman),
    207
The Wireworker newsletter, 212–218
Word-of-mouse marketing, 93, 94, 129,
    130
Word-of-mouth advertising, 93,
    103–104
World Wide Recipes (e-zine), 145
World Wide Web:
  building presence on, 74–76, 93
  information quantity on, 3
Wyman, Pat, 204–207

Yahoo!:
  auction on, 269
  popularity of, 229
  as search engine, 76, 236
  stickiness on, 120
Yellow Pages:
  mailing lists from, 93
  as marketing tool, 76
Your Life Support System (e-zine), 145